Jesus' Answer to God

Jesus' Answer to God

by
ELIZABETH BOYDEN HOWES

Guild for Psychological Studies
Publishing House
San Francisco

Jesus' Answer to God has no parallel. It is not about Jesus' answer to mankind as has been theologized, catechized, and preached for nearly two millenia.

It is a book about Jesus of Nazareth and his way of wrestling with the ultimate questions that address one who has chosen to express Life fully.

It is about the myth which was at the core of his life and which was lost along with the person of Jesus in the first centuries when a myth grew up around him as the man-God, the dying-rising God.

It is a book about a way—and not a creed—for each of us to uncover and live our own myth and the eternal motifs of wound and healing, of death and resurrection, and of sin and forgiveness. And—particularly refreshing in our threatened age—a realistic way to transform darkness and evil.

The author shares fifty years of personal study and seminar work on the Synoptic gospels based on a critical biblical study of the texts. Respectfully and skillfully she has separated the myth Jesus lived from the myth of Jesus the Christ that stimulated the faith of the early church. This is her far-reaching contribution to New Testament scholarship.

Incorporating the best of Dr. C. G. Jung's understanding of the human psyche, the author uncovers in an original manner how Jesus articulated in word and life the eternal archetypal patterns that structure for better or for worse outer and inner life. Her articulation of how a religiously committed ego can live the path of individuation, and the discussion of the nature of the God of which the Self is the expression, are her unique contributions to analytical psychology.

The questions at the beginning of each chapter open exciting areas for exploration not possible when one remains in the traditional religious and scholarly constructs. The value of this provocative and original work is not in having found the answers nor is it in learning the answers of Jesus. Rather, it is in finding a way to work with the questions put to us by Life and a way to come to one's own answer to God and to Self.

Elizabeth Boyden Howes, Jungian analyst and founder of the Guild for Psychological Studies, has led seminars in religion—especially the Synoptic gospels—together with analytical psychology, for many years. The transformation process in every person is the central focus of her work. She has travelled widely in Europe, studying in Zurich with Dr. and Mrs. Jung. She has lectured in Europe and in the United States, and is coauthor of *Man, the Choicemaker*, coeditor of *And a Time to Die* and *The Choice Is Always Ours*, and author of *Intersection and Beyond*. She has a Ph.D. in Psychology from the University of California.

Published in the United States of America by
The Guild for Psychological Studies Publishing House
2230 Divisadero Street
San Francisco, California 94115

Typesetting by PAN Typesetters, Eugene, Oregon
Printing by Braun-Brumfield, Inc., Ann Arbor, Michigan

Library of Congress Cataloging in Publication Data

Howes, Elizabeth Boyden, 1907 -
    Jesus' Answer to God

    Includes Index
    1. *Jesus* — Psychology. I. title.
BT 590.P9H68 1984   232   83-10743

ISBN 0-917479-00-9
ISBN 0-917479-01-7

CONTENTS

What did Jesus retain of his Jewish heritage? What did he change?
Why did he come to John the Baptist?
What happened to Jesus in the baptism and wilderness experiences?
What was changed for Jesus, for persons, perhaps for God, in the baptism-wilderness experience?

How does Jesus deal with the laws and traditions of his people?
Does he overthrow them, ignore them, transform them, or what?
What is the relation of law and freedom?
What is behind and beyond following the laws for Jesus?

DEDICATION

This book is dedicated to each and every individual in all the seminars I have led for over forty years. My gratitude especially to the Guild Leaders is beyond words for their rich contributions to the clarification and deepening of insight into this material.

I especially include Dorothy B. Phillips, editor of *The Choice Is Always Ours*, who due to long illness has never physically been a member of these seminars. She did attend an early seminar led by Dr. Henry B. Sharman and has been actively involved in the analytic process. She has followed the development of this book through constant dialogue, despite her limitations.

From all these individuals has come immeasurable fruitfulness. I offer this book as a contribution from my life work toward the establishment in a struggling world of a mutuality and a love wider and richer than has ever been envisioned.

ACKNOWLEDGMENTS

In addition to that which is expressed in the dedication, I wish to acknowledge my deep gratitude to four men, each of whom in very different ways has profoundly influenced the understanding and interpretation of this material. They are Dr. Carl G. Jung, Dr. Fritz Kunkel, Dr. C. A. Meier, and Dr. Henry B. Sharman.

I wish to express special thanks to the following, each of whom has given immense support and concrete time and work:

To Florence Little, who supplied much valuable information from research she did for the book, and who worked through all the drafts of the book with careful and exacting editing.

To Dr. Walter Wink, whose constant interest and encouragement to me to write this book was a major factor in that decision. The dozen fountain pens he sent me on a birthday spoke of his hope! Also, he has read the manuscript and offered valuable suggestions.

The following people have also taken time to read the manuscript and have given detailed and helpful criticisms, each from his/her perspective: Joan Gibbons, John Petroni, Peggy Reid, and Barbara Troxell. It is a great sadness to me that Sadie Gregory died before the completion of this book. Much of the background of the Hebrew Scripture material comes from her help.

To Anne Ogonowski, I offer my profound gratitude for her service of love. She has done the typing of all the drafts of the manuscript and its revisions and has made significant editorial suggestions. She has contributed this without pay, out of her conviction of the value of the work of the Guild and this book. I also wish to thank Gretchen Stoeve and John Williams for their help in the final stages of completing the manuscript, Sue Renfrew for the cover design, and Ann Eberle for the index.

No work of mine, much less this one, would be complete without acknowledgment always of my continued intellectual, spiritual interaction with my two friends and colleagues Luella Sibbald and Sheila Moon. The book is mine, but without the community of dialogue with them (along with all the leaders of the Guild) this book would not exist. Our passionate common concerns for the transmission of the values in this book form a central, intrinsic part of my own life.

INTRODUCTION

Part I:
Historic-Mythic Mode of Understanding

"Enthusiasm engendered Christianity, but it was the enthusiasm of the disciples, not that of Jesus."[1] This statement by the biblical scholar Julius Wellhausen forms the nucleus of this book's meaning. It is not a book about the enthusiasm of the disciples around the person of Jesus or about faith in Jesus Christ. It is a book about that enthusiasm of Jesus of Nazareth, which centered on his relation to God, the Kingdom of God, the world of history, and the inner world of the soul. It is not an exploration of the Christian myth formed around him. It is a book which describes the life and person of Jesus shorn of Christian accretions and disidentified from archetypal*[2] identification—Jesus living his life and his personal myth prior to the later Christian myth. When the original figure can be uncovered from the Christian overlay, he can be seen as bringing in a whole new psychological and religious evolution which could be a vitally transforming power. Jesus was pre-Christian and perhaps post-Christian.

1. Charles Guignebert, *Jesus* (London: Kegan Paul, Trench, Trubner and Co. Ltd., 1935), p. 538.
2. All words with an asterisk are defined in the Glossary.

The title of this book, *Jesus' Answer to God*, puts for me the focus where it belongs. It presupposes an involvement, an interaction, a question from God to human. The question is the prior reality. The human response is to this reality. Perhaps in no place is this concern clearer than in the prayer by God to Him/Herself, in the Jewish Midrash: "May it be my will that my mercy may surpass my anger." Here is an insistent and vivid proclamation of the desire of God, knowing His/Her own duality and ambivalence, to affirm that which makes for life, not destruction. Here the Tree of Knowledge of Good and Evil is known at the heart of things.

A statement from the kabbalistic tradition says, "Man was created for the sake of choice." This book may be seen as Jesus' answer to help God and the Self* in the process of that prayer being actualized. Jesus' whole concern for himself and others arose from his sense of responsibility and choice in the face of the nature of the God he served. In Genesis 3:9, the first question in the Bible is found. Yahweh asks Adam, "Where are you?" Not who or what are you, but *where* are you in relation to the asker of the question.

It is out of my passionate concern for persons wanting fulfillment and for the ongoingness of the planet, in spite of all negatives, that I have been searching for the root meaning in and of Jesus, and the value of that meaning for individuals and for society. It is a fact that a truth or law capable of action and experimentation is discoverable, that it does not demand belief but can be acted on and validated as true. This search is intensified at this moment of history because the planet itself is an endangered species. More is at stake than ever before because of the existence of the tools of destruction. Will there be enough consciousness in some of us to help the Yes overcome all the Nos in our world?

We must, in this time of nuclear danger, realize that what has been the Christian myth no longer holds the deep values of the symbols* of death and rebirth it has carried for vast numbers of people during two thousand years of history. For many the traditional is still the main expression and carrier of religious truth. But also for countless others it does not have vital meaning.

This book is an attempt to outline an approach to Jesus' words, and to set forth their significance for contemporary individuals, for society, and for the field of religion in its psychological and theological dimensions. It is concerned with the entanglements of history and myth (to be explained) in the Synoptic gospels, and their subsequent manifestation in Christianity. After untangling the confusion, and after realignment of the mythic and the historical with no sacrifices of either, we may arrive at a very fresh viewpoint, which I call the Historic-Mythic mode of understanding.

In using this, my colleagues and I enter sacred precincts where things accepted as belonging together are to be questioned, examined, differentiated, seen in fresh historical reality and perspective. This can be done only with deep respect for the material at hand, and with a concern that the time has come for new perspectives. Such emerging will make for more conscious reality and greater wholeness for human understanding and for the God presence. This realignment differs from the usual religious and theological approaches. It is in part due to the contribution of the analytical psychology of C.G. Jung, whose work and insights undergird much that is in this book, although some expansions of understanding will be apparent.

This viewpoint is separate from the two central approaches to the interpretation of the material in the gospels which have been held over the centuries. One approach is the Christological position, where Jesus has been completely identified with the Christ image or archetype. This has dominated Catholic and much Protestant thinking. The other position has been a postion of some liberal Protestant thought, where Jesus has been seen as a historical person, not divine, but too radically separated from the depths of his own being, i.e., from his Source of the Thou within.

The problem resides in the fact that Christianity has historicized (or made literal) the inner mythic elements Jesus lived and taught, and therefore there has been a mythologizing of the history of the man. The deep interior truths leading to individual consciousness that Jesus manifested have been turned into seemingly historical events which became dogma that had to be believed. Also the history that Jesus lived was made into a myth, thus depriving his life of its own truth and substance. He has thus been made the carrier of our inner myth, and his history has become mythological. This confusion of myth and history is the very foundation of the Christian religion, with positive and negative aspects.

This book's approach is based on the facts that Jesus lived his own inner myth as the immanent* expression of God transcendent* and incorporated it into his personal history, and taught others how to live their history. He lived it with extraordinary courage. But what he truly achieved as a supranatural law leading to Life which may be the clue to his and our own potential consciousness has remained unknown. There have been gains and losses from this as we shall see. But even to begin to grasp its implications, some fundamental definitions of myth and history must be given. In losing old forms for new, an even deeper insight and experience of mystery may be found.

What is meant by "myth"* or "mythic elements" in each of us? And what is truly meant by "history"? To define myth in its most creative meaning, we turn to the works of C.G. Jung and Mircea Eliade. Myth is not an untrue tale or story, as is often thought. A myth describes the inner, meaningful world of the psyche.* Or, turning it around, psychic truths are an attempt to explain, through myth, their own inner realities. In the psyche of every person active, dynamic, and powerful forces are at work.

This inner world at the collective level is the source of artistic creation, imaginative thinking, philosophical insights, and primarily religious impulses and longings. There is a deeper reservoir beyond the personal unconscious, whose content Jung called the archetypes. They are the "eternal presences" informing our lives with meaning and pattern. They reside in the psyche and reflect the Eternal beyond time. They offer us dimensionality and a breadth of living if we relate to them. Myth and mythic motifs express these inner realities. Dreams, and art in many forms, do the same. Clearly the archetypal world is not of our own conscious making, but what we do in relation to it is central.

If we understand this inner richness of images, metaphors, dreams, artistic creations, religious visions, and insights, we will more fully come to understand what depths of insight belong to us. Where these depths of insight find their way into myths, small and large, and into histories attached to persons (e.g., Jesus of Nazareth), they tell inner realities that get twisted into outer realities and become dogma and creed. As Jung said, archetypes are dynamic:

> They are instinctual images . . . always there and they produce certain processes in the unconscious that one could best compare with myths. That's the origin of mythology . . . . So the statements of every religion . . . are statements about the inner mythological process, which is a necessity because man is not complete if he is not conscious of that inner aspect of things . . . . [T]he church has several thousand saints. . . .And that is Christian mythology.[1]

Christian mythology is not in the teachings of the man Jesus. His symbols come from his own life history, from his Jewish background, from his relation to his inner images, and from his relation to persons and situations in day-by-day encounters. He gave rich teachings on how others also could relate to their own deep religious meanings. He was not held by dogmatic rules or by what others laid upon him. His individual history was overpowered by dogmatized myths, and he became a mythic symbol.

When inner realities are not permitted to live, or are not lived consciously, they tend to be projected outward. Often they are projected onto social structures—e.g., the church, the ruling class, the leading group. Also they are

1. Richard I. Evans, *Conversations with Carl Jung: And Reactions from Ernest Jones* (New York: D. Van Nostrand Co., 1964), p. 48.

More modern version: Richard I. Evans, *Jung on Elementary Psychology: A Discussion between C.G. Jung and Richard I. Evans* (New York: E.P. Dutton & Co., 1976).

often laid upon gifted persons who have wisdom and ambience from inside themselves. Such persons are often burdened by others' expectations, and what is put onto them by projections beclouds their real gifts and character, their true history.

The history of a genuine human being is defined by how the unconscious contents—the mythic levels—are expressed and brought to manifestation at a conscious (ego) level. It is also defined by socioeconomic and historical factors, and our response to them. When we choose to relate to our inner and outer world creatively, then we may be said to be living our myth in our reality. This makes it clear that true individual consciousness is not to be identified with the conscious mind. Consciousness comes for any person seriously working with the unconscious contents. This work is demanding, because there is much to be untangled of symbol and reality in the symbol, and to be creatively integrated.

Jesus of Nazareth lived his own history out of the depths of his soul's myths, and because of that, others were helped to do the same. But the very depths of living which Jesus consciously entered into constellated for others such rich newnesses of existence that they saw him as a singular symbol for their meanings. To find such meanings within themselves was hard to believe—and thus Jesus was made into the carrier of their inner selves.

Two central facts (expanded in the book) are that, with the baptism and the wilderness experiences of Jesus, the religious-psychological dimensions in the Western world expanded into a new step in evolution. The first central fact was the moment in history when the Holy Spirit which had resided in the transcendent God became immanent in the psyche of the man Jesus in the movement of God, or the God-image in the psyche, or the Self becoming actualized. Put in this depth, Jesus could say, "The Kingdom of God is within."[1] The spirit had come to a new home within human substance. For Jesus this enlivened the flow of the inner world of mythic images which he lived and ex-

---

1. Lk. 17:21 §112A.

pressed in his history. The second central fact in the postcrucifixion events is that when Jesus was made into the center of a new religion these motifs which he lived were identified with him. A whole new focus occurred which, in the Hellenic world, took root at the loss of the new evolving thrust of the Jesus-God dialogue, or the human-God dialogue.

The first mythic motif related to by Jesus is that of the spontaneous and virginal flow of the life force, of vitality from within, from the continual interaction of masculine and feminine psychological forces in the human being. In the baptism experience of Jesus, the Spirit came alive in his substance as he plunged into the water and emerged from it. For him, sonship was surely born then. The hero in many ancient myths "discovered within himself something which, although it 'belongs' to him and is as it were part of him, he can only describe as strange, unusual, god-like."[1] Surely it was an inwardly rich "birth" of an inner Self for Jesus the man, giving him a new sense of an indwelling Spirit of God and an undergirding of his own sonship and his relationship to God. This baptismal event was for him an enlarged individual wholeness.

In later religious history the baptismal experience of Jesus the man was incorporated in the doctrine of the Virgin Birth, and Jesus was made into a divine Son born of Mary and the Holy Spirit in the Annunciation myth. Thus the fact of recurring individual incarnation was changed into the doctrine of the Virgin Birth, making Jesus the miraculous and deified Son born to Mary, impregnated by the Holy Spirit. The continuous incarnation was made into a one-time, one-person, one complete incarnation.

The myth of the virgin birth is universal. It is part of Hinduism, Greek mythologies, Mithraism, Navaho Indian cosmic myths, and many other accounts. It was widely known throughout the Mediterranean world at the time of Jesus, and it must have come into the gospel tradition fairly early. What does it describe? It tells of the supernatural

1. Eric Neumann. *The Origins and History of Consciousness* (Princeton, N.J.: Princeton University Press, 1970) p. 136.

birth of a divine infant—born of the union of a Feminine figure (more often than not a goddess) and a Masculine Spirit father. It tells of a process of "magical" or supernatural fertilization and germination, sometimes from sunlight and water, sometimes from a deity.

In Jesus' own teachings, this new "birth" theme enters into life situations over and over again at a reality level. It is supranatural, not supernatural. The palsied man is born into wholeness by forgiveness. New wine cannot be put into old wineskins. The earth bears her fruit "of herself." The "bridegroom" cannot be welcomed except by the virginal parts who have oil for light. When this became mythologized, original birth of new life in all of us was circumscribed and made the sole prerogative of Jesus.

The second mythic motif is that of death and rebirth. It comes often in the teachings of Jesus as the heartbeat of his own living. Over and over again he states that something must be let go if life is to be lived. We are aware that when we move from childhood to puberty, or from puberty to an adult maturity, or from singleness to marriage, or from midlife to old age, we are at each stage dying to one phase and being born into the next. At the same time, we must "die to become" at a supranatural level to achieve Life.

Jesus' teachings on this are numerous. There is the parable of the prodigal son, of whom the father says "for this my son was dead and is alive again."[1] The rich parables on the nature of the Kingdom also speak of the rebirth process in such images as selling all for the pearl, or for the treasure hidden in the field.[2] The most comprehensive is Jesus' statement of the great paradox: "For whosoever shall seek to gain his life shall lose it; but whosoever shall lose his life shall preserve it."[3]

This theme of Jesus' own teachings was later made into tenets and dogma. What was for him spiritually and psychically alive to be lived was—and is—transferred to a belief

1. Lk. 15:11-32 §105D.
2. Mt. 13:44-46 §48N,O.
3. Lk. 17:32 §112J.

in the physical resurrection. The features of the post-crucifixion appearances are the affirmation of Jesus as the Christ, the promise of the Pentecost, all authority given him, preaching to all nations. Behind all these is the report of the presence of Jesus as physical fact, and his talking with the disciples as proof of his substantial reality.

Within the Synoptic text the reference to the physical resurrection is expressed in the following statement: "And he began to teach them that the Son of man must suffer many things and be rejected by the elders and the chief priests and the scribes, and be killed, and after three days rise again."[1] This same kind of statement is made twice again and is copied by Matthew and Luke.[2] But at one point Luke, copying from this source, does not have the reference to the resurrection.[3] This makes all the references suspect. This belief has largely taken the place of the death-rebirth pattern as indwelling in all humans.

The third motif is that of the savior, the saving archetype. Throughout history there has been the tendency to project this archetype onto savior messianic figures, with a hope and longing that somehow someone will appear who will be the agent of our salvation, rather than our own conscious work. This Self archetype is in every individual, a process of transformation leading to constant change and growth. This archetypal process needs consciousness from the human being to become actualized. Jesus' struggle with the issue of identification or nonidentification with this archetype is pivotal. It is unquestionably the most influential point in Christian thought. He never said "yes" or "no." He never identified with the image, but assumed its presence in the human being. He related dynamically to the inner Self archetype behind the Messiah-Christ image. What happened after his death was that he *was* identified with it. Mythic reality, individually lived by Jesus, was made into a singular historical fact, if one was a believer. When the gospels were written, this Christian development of identification with Messiah-Christ permeated

1. Mt. 16:21; Mk. 8:31; Lk. 9:22 §72A.
2. Mt. 17:23; Lk. 9:44 §76B; Mt. 20:19; Lk. 18:33 §119F.
3. Lk. 9:44 §76B.

them. Some of the words that explicitly identified him with the Messiah-Christ image (versus his relationship to it) are such phrases as "because ye are Christ's," "for one is your master, even the Christ," and where Jesus reportedly says, "I am" to the question "Art thou the Christ?"

He is made into the judge, especially in the Son of man apocalyptic passages. In one place the words "I appoint unto you a kingdom" are added in Luke.[1] Another aspect of the saving element was the image of the Son of man. How he related to this and what happened to it later is found in the book itself. Of course the question continually confronts us as to our personal relationship to this saving element within the Self with its transforming power.

Dr. Jung has definitely stressed the inadequacy of the Christ image because it did not on the whole include the dark and feminine elements. A further step now becomes explicit in this approach—namely, that we need not only to find the central archetypal roots behind the Christ image in the Self, but also to be sure that any identification with Jesus is not left unconscious in the psyche; it needs our work at transformation. Jung writes in a letter to a minister friend that "Christ forced people into the impossible conflicts." Also "that he took himself with exemplary seriousness and lived his life to the bitter end. But we? We—hope he will deliver us from our own fate—We place ourselves under his cross, but by golly, not under our own."[2]

The fourth mythic motif is that of the wounded healer.[3] Jesus, in touch with this healing potential within his psyche and with the wisdom to use it, is nonetheless made into the magical one who does the healing. The gospels are

1. Lk. 22:29 ⁸138N.
2. Gerhard Adler, ed., *Letters of C.G. Jung*, 2 vols. (Princeton, N.J.: Princeton University Press, 1953), 2:76.
3. The ancient Asklepion statement is: "The God sends the wound, the God is the wound, the God is wounded, and the God heals the wound." From C. Kerenyi, *Asklepios: Archetypal Images of the Physician's Existence* (New York: Pantheon Books, 1959) p. 112. Also, C.A. Meier, *Ancient Incubation and Modern Psychotherapy* (Evanston, Illinois: Northwestern University Press, 1967) p. 5.

full of examples where the helper, the one who works with healing, is a wounded one. When Jesus told of the Samaritan in the parable, he testified to this. He made it quite clear on many occasions that he was not the agent of healing. In later texts Jesus was made into the miraculous healer rather than remaining a catalytic agent. The healing for Jesus came from evoking the person's response to a symbol constellating wholeness. Many such symbols can be found in many forms. From the rich depths of the human psyche come the age-old images of gods as words, of dreams of sonship, of sacrificial immolations, of lambs offered to deities. It is clear that such images and such dreams of modern humans come with individual healing and growing personhood. The more they are recognized in our inner selves, not as dogma but as genuine growth processes, the richer our Self becomes. The man Jesus walked his inner Self's world.

All of his history must be seen as a relationship to and an expression of the power within Jesus due to the God-process which was so magnificently lived by him. But he, not the God he served, began to be made central by followers even while he was still alive. The disciples couldn't "hear" him, Jesus, because of his incredible consciousness. An irony indeed!

What is the anatomy of belief at the core of Christianity? To "believe" is to be gripped by any symbol that has acquired power and meaning. Such a symbol is effective as long as it holds that meaning. It becomes ineffective when the meaning is lost.

It is conspicuous that neither our ego nor our choices play much of a role in our beliefs. We are "taken" by the power of the symbol involuntarily. This is its positive aspect. It is compelling as long as the power remains. Its negative aspect is that the choice is taken away as the main factor of consciousness. Belief can strengthen but belief can also blind.

It is also helpful to turn the procedure around and look at some of the central Christian creeds and dogma to see how they were developed out of Jesus' genuine living of their meanings. Jesus carried such consciousness that we are deeply aware of the pull to imitate him instead of finding the method for our own achievement. He was cast as being "sinless," a fulfillment of prophecy for the Hebrew scripture, as establishing the church and other roles. In fact the bulk of the later church accretions come under this heading.

Five examples follow: "The Word became flesh"; "the only-begotten Son"; "He died for our sins"; "Lamb of God who taketh away the sins of the world"; all the places where he reportedly said, "for my sake." "The Word became flesh"[1] presents Jesus as Christ or Logos from the beginning of time. As Jung indicated, when John presented his doctrine of Logos, Jesus was seen "as the Nous and the object of human thought."[2] The Greek Gnostic text says literally, "I will be thought, being wholly spirit."[3] Similarly the Acts of Peter say, "Thou are perceived of the spirit only."[4]

These are profound statements of belief where Jesus is made into the Logos that became incarnate. His experiences of the baptism and many others on through his life were personal expressions of the Word—not as himself but as manifestations of God's living reality of being. These expressions were (and are) available to each person who touches the inner value of the Word as meaning—not the word of Jesus but of God, as Jesus knew it.

Consider the phrase "the only-begotten Son" in the Creed. Sonship can become incarnate, as we saw in the baptism experience. It was not exclusive in Jesus' thought. All persons could become sons or daughters through inner awarenesses and changes, but not through belief. There are conditions to be met. There are expansions of universal possibilities quite opposite to the narrowness of creed and belief that characterize much of religious doctrine.

1. Jn. 1:14 §152D.
2. C.G. Jung, *Psychology and Religion: West and East* (New York: Pantheon Books, Bollingen Series XX, 1958) p. 279.
3. Montague Rhodes James, trans., *The Apocryphal New Testament* (Oxford, 1924) p. 335.
4. Richard Adelbert Lipsius and Max Bonnet, *Acta Apostolorum Apocrypha*, 2 parts in 3 vols., Vol I, (Leipzig, 1891-1903), p. 197.

Consider the phrase "he died for our sins." Here Jesus is made into the scapegoat for the sins of all humankind. He is the object of the projection of the redemptive process of sin and forgiveness. Because of his death our sins are abolished. We do not have to pay the price because Jesus on the cross did it for us.

The phrase "the Lamb of God who taketh away the sins of the world" is an even stronger statement of the archetypal redemptive process. The statement goes completely contrary to any of Jesus' words about sin. His whole teaching was on the need for each person to transform individual sin internally by relating to the process. The insertion in many places of the phrase "for my sake" or "in my name" can be understood as not having been said by Jesus, because this was not his self-estimate. These have been but brief comments about how mythology lies behind theological formulations.

We must now evaluate what have been gains and losses during the two thousand years of Christian history.

What has been gained has been the enormous value of the Christian symbols attached to Jesus, carrying the myths which could be projected into by Western persons. These symbols have expressed all the mythic realities, as previously discussed. In spite of all inadequacies and failures, the power of the Christian message cannot be underestimated. At Sinai monotheism (one God—I AM) was a great spiritual mutation. With Jesus, this evolved God found a dwelling place within the individual Self as another spiritual mutation. With Christianity, the withinness became identified with Jesus as Christ. This has kept the archetype alive culturally. The whole field of Christian art richly portrays the myths involved. Now another step is necessary, where each individual carries his or her own religious meaning. Terribly wonderful things and terribly wrong things were done, but all too unconsciously. If these values had not been carried, we would not have available the truths within them. The consciousness of Jesus of Nazareth, however distorted, would not be available to be understood, as a journey possible for each of us.

What has been lost by this process has been an authentic Jesus, a full image of God, and finally the need for consciousness of each person in human relationships. Consider these three points. First, the picture of Jesus has been so overlaid with Christian accretion out of the experience of the early church that much of his reality has been lost. He has become, in the portrayal, what people projected onto him. Jesus as symbol of hope and vision becomes an archetypal conglomerate of mythic motifs. But the price for this has been the loss of Jesus' own human reality, his struggle for the achievement of consciousness through dialogue with his God. He is seen too often as acted upon, not himself acting and taking responsibility for helping God, not being seen or understood in the nature of his total reality serving a commitment to God, transcendent and immanent. He has not been known as the vessel through whom a new evolutionary step of consciousness emerged. This diminishment of his reality is overwhelmingly important, for it deprives us, as we shall see in the book, of any paradigm for the struggle of individual consciousness.

Second, the image of God which Jesus received from his Jewish heritage and which altered into new forms has been partially distorted. Most central, it seems to me, is the fact that the dark opposite in this God, apparent through the Hebrew Scripture, has become mostly lost in the Christian picture. The uniqueness of Jesus' approach to the transformation of evil into reality is obliterated by the emphasis on God as only good. The genius of Judaism in its emphasis on direct relationship to God transcendent, expanded by Jesus into immanence, changes to relation to God through belief in Jesus as Christ, in all its variations. The fundamental I-Thou alters in character.

Third, perhaps the greatest loss we see today has been the challenge to individual consciousness. In Christianity, the greater collective images of the church have held people and have, in part, fostered relationship between people. But the real individual, the true essence of the Self incarnate in a person, has emerged occasionally in the great mystics and prophetic figures, like Gandhi. This is the challenge of the new age of which Jesus, paradoxically, was a forerunner. Much of Christianity has been deeply significant, but the fact that failures have led to world wars, hostility, inquisitions, cruelties, and racism must dampen any too intense praise we might have. This, of course, is true of other religions. Individual consciousness is difficult to come by, and yet only out of deep individual Self-knowledge and consciousness can creative relationship with other people and nations happen.

Christianity has stressed loving God and neighbor, but has often forgotten and set aside the love of Self. Today the love of Self as the dynamic operative center, intentional in the psyche, reflecting God within the psyche, as a prerequisite of loving one's neighbor, must be carried forward. The great contribution of Dr. Jung is the exploration of the levels of the psyche most hidden from consciousness. Those lonely and lost elements are described in the powerful statement of Jeremiah, where Yahweh says, "Before I formed you I knew you."[1]

What is needed for a wider vision and how is it to be brought about? If there were no insight into the "how," it might be futile to deal with the "what." What is most important is an approach by way of the Historic-Mythic mode to Jesus' lifestyle and his teachings. The purpose is a disentangling of the mythic projections into the history of Jesus, an understanding of Jesus' relation to his own mythic elements, and what this confonts us with. This is an essential need for the Western world because the gospels have historical and cultural values that are far-reaching. If this approach of disentanglement could be done, it could lead to more dialogue with people of other religions, especially the Jewish. Universal religious truths, unhampered by limitation, would be available to become specific tools for mutuality of peoples.

Certainly the need for openness is apparent, as is the difficulty of reaching it, and all preconceived and tightly held points of view stretch one immeasurably. No birth is easy and the step necessary for the birth of a new point of view toward the gospels and this figure of Jesus might be

1. Jere. 1:5.

said to require a death and a rebirth. But the fruits of this approach are plentiful.

A special disposition toward depth-search, a kind of thinking that allows itself to serve the phenomenon of archetypal processes and to try not to dominate them, a feeling of joy at new possibilities rather than rigidly held old views, a perspective toward greater wholeness— these are what is required. There needs to be intense, objective curiosity about the workings of the God-process in human beings, and new openness to how the development took the form it did.

The methodology is spelled out in the section that follows. The main text confronts us with the figure of Jesus in all his numinosity, which comes from the stripping away of accretions, and the naked fact of this man living from his own interior depth, as a mutation, leading to an evolutionary step we have not yet taken.

Part II:
Methodology and Background

How has this book come about? What is its historical background and who is involved? It is a result of study of the Synoptic material, based on critical research and amplified by the insights of the religious depth psychology of Dr. C.G. Jung. It must be stressed that the Jungian insights came after my study of the Synoptic gospels, and were exciting because they confirmed what had already been stated by Jesus in his own way. My own work has been as one of the founders and leaders of seminars held under the auspices of the Guild for Psychological Studies, and as an analyst in the Jungian tradition. The work with the gospels began in seminar and personal study with Dr. Henry B. Sharman,[1] supplemented by courses and study in the biblical field. It was this experience which led me to analytical psychology, both for personal reasons and because it seemed the school of psychology adequate to explain the deeper levels, the archetypal dimensions, of the religious experience of Jesus and its personal meaning. This analytical background included the rich opportunity of some conversations with Dr. Jung and analytical work with Mrs. Jung.

1. Dr. Henry Burton Sharman taught New Testament History at the University of Chicago. His Ph.D. thesis, *Teachings of Jesus About the Future*, was published by the University of Chicago Press in 1909. He was the editor of *The Records of the Life of Jesus* published by Harper and Brothers in 1917.

The book moves sequentially from the arrival of Jesus on the historical scene, his baptism and wilderness experiences and events leading to the crucifixion, together with the subsequent events in the resurrection accounts. Each of the twelve chapters begins with a quotation from Jesus, followed by a series of questions. I hope these questions will serve to evoke questions in the reader that will deepen the experience of the book. The questions at the beginning of each chapter are not definitively or sequentially answered in the chapter, but are spoken to throughout the chapter.

Many books in this field are divided into themes and all the passages on one theme are grouped together. This may be due to the fact that most scholars feel it is impossible to know the exact sequence in which Jesus moved or spoke. Much is by inference. I have followed the order of Mark with the material in Matthew and Luke interwoven as it stands. Whether this order of Mark has been provided by the gospel writers or is authentic to Jesus' life one cannot know. One cannot ever be dogmatic or too certain that the sequence being followed is the way it was. Yet it is only by attempting to make some sequence that one sees a person evolving, making choices, living what he is talking about, confronting personal and divine realities. Dr. Norman Perrin, an outstanding New Testament scholar, speaks of finding some of the "attributes" of Jesus.[1] My own interest is in how Jesus regarded God, life, evil, the Holy Spirit, and Satan, and how he related to those realities and their impact on our consciousness. At the same time, by constantly going back and forth, it will be possible to be thematic. Statements on major issues such as forgiveness, prayer, faith, evil, the Kingdom of God, and the Messianic issue will be dealt with where they come in the gospels.

The text used in this book is the English Revised Version of the Synoptics* as presented in *The Records of the*

1. Norman Perrin, *Rediscovering the Teachings of Jesus*, (New York: Harper & Row, 1976).

Life of Jesus by Dr. Henry B. Sharman.[1] However, in some instances, texts from other translations will be mentioned. Readers may find supplementary translations from other texts more meaningful to them.

The Records presents the three gospels in parallel columns in such a way that the order of each gospel is left exactly as it is in the Bible (with one small exception in Matthew). Therefore, one can read the text of any one gospel in roman type and find it in the same order as in the Bible. Cross-references are in italics and facilitate comparison. In this aspect of order the book makes a special contribution to the field of New Testament scholarship. In this present book the Bible chapter and verse and the section number in *The Records* will be given.

The critical basis for the choice of sequence and presentation of material is presented in Appendix I. One may read the book with no reference to this, but those who wish to know the basis, and the principles used in judging historicity are referred to this appendix. Appendix II includes a description of religious and psychological techniques for implementing in everyday life the basic teachings of Jesus.

The Guild's way of studying the material relies on a critical examination of the Synoptic gospels which aims to identify the inferred documents on which these gospels are based and to compare them and study them in an effort to determine what material within them is most probably authentic and historical, and what material consists of later additions derived from the Christian community. The

1. Henry B. Sharman, *The Records of the Life of Jesus* (New York: Harper and Brothers, 1917) utilized the English Revised Version of the King James Bible dating from 1881. Book II of the volume contains the record of John and is presented separately since it is based on sources not available to the other Gospel writers. The many similarities in Matthew, Mark, and Luke make it possible to study them together; John's account, so distinct in style and historical sequence at many points, deserves to be studied separately. This book can be purchased from the Guild for Psychological Studies.

A revision by the Guild for Psychological Studies of *The Records of the Life of Jesus* using the Revised Standard Version translation of the gospels is now in process of completion.

purpose of this examination is to try to get as accurate a picture as possible of the actual life and teachings of Jesus. What he did and said in his lifetime is told in accounts abounding in editors' biases, witnesses' distortions, and later additions or deletions. To recover Jesus from this material is the task. The tools for this are the ones used by biblical scholars: source criticism, form criticism, and redaction criticism. The criteria are dissimilarity, consistency, and multiple attestation.

Once seminar participants have been enabled to explore the passages as a biblical scholar would, we are in a position to ask such questions as

> **What did Jesus really teach?**
> **What do these teachings mean?**
> **What are their implications for us now, socially and personally?**
> **How did he see himself? How did others see him at the time?**
> **What does his self-evaluation have to do—or not—with the Messianic or Christ images current during his lifetime and afterward?**

These questions have meaning once the critical work has been done. Without the critical study, the life and message lose the historical dimension and become blurred with the projections and interpretations of an evolving religion, Christianity, which may at many points part company with the religion Jesus lived by. There is discontinuity as well as continuity between Jesus and early Christianity.

The seminar leaders use a modified Socratic method of questioning, to open all possible understandings of what the text could have meant to Jesus and to us. Each person in the seminar has a copy of *The Records of the Life of Jesus* and attempts to answer the questions with as much integrity as possible. From all the answers to each question, insight and understandings emerge and each person is left to his or her own conclusion. No unanimity is required for the group. Each answer helps amplify and illumine the possible meaning. It is a process of filling out the text with many possibilities, so each person arrives at an individual decision.

It is the assumption that if people approach the Synoptic material suspending their normal preconceptions, they will be able to see new truths emerge. This requires openness and willingness to examine the material freshly. This is extremely difficult to do with material so fraught with meaning, but only with such an attitude can the reality of Jesus, his teachings, and the truth behind them emerge from later additions.

The Synoptic gospels themselves were written approximately thirty-five to sixty-five years after the death of Jesus, but their bringing together was not finalized until 325 C.E.. No one in modern times has seen or had access to the original documentary sources on which they are based. The existence and form of these sources are inferred from a study of the gospels themselves. Scholars find no evidence that they were written by the disciples, but neither can they say which individuals among the early followers of Jesus are responsible for the accounts later collected into these documentary sources. The remarkable fact is that we *do* have a record, accounts that, while not reliable at all points, *do* enable us, if critically examined, to form an accurate picture of a man who lived, taught, and struggled with his vocation and life meaning.

Throughout this book, Hebrew Scripture is the name used instead of Old Testament, as honoring both traditions. Also, B.C.E. (before Common Era) and C.E. (Common Era) are used. Both these changes honor the *two* traditions. All words referring to or related to the Divine Source or Power are consistently capitalized. These words include God, Messiah, Christ, Self, Source, Transcendence, and Immanence.

The word "God" always includes the idea of a Source which is both masculine and feminine. Although in the Judeo-Christian tradition God has been thought of primarily as masculine and patriarchal, the notion of the androgyny of God is found in most creation myths and also in our own, the Genesis creation myth. There it states, "And

God said, Let us create man in our image—male and female he created them."[1] Because of the age in which Jesus lived and spoke, there is no question that most of his illustrations are masculine. There are, however, many aspects of the feminine included in the gospels in reference to figures, symbols, and attitudes. It would be impossible to change every reference in stories and parables to include the feminine. But it can be done individually, where one can insert in one's mind "woman" for "man," "daughter" for "son," and so forth. Some may find this quite unnecessary and some quite helpful.

It must be stressed that although this book is one person's own response, it contains an added core of objectivity due to the fact that the insights have been molded, sifted, shaped, and formed by the responses of hundreds of people to the material. This continued search for possible truths lends, I believe, an integrity of objective meaning quite different from what could be personal bias or subjective fantasy, or even personal critical study. Yet in the last analysis, I assume full responsibility for my conclusions. Readers are free to agree or disagree, but even more it will stimulate them, hopefully, not to an intellectual response, but to a personal, involved, confronting response to the never-ending mystery of this figure, Jesus of Nazareth, and of his challenge to us and our world.

1. Gen. 1:26-27.

I

"For Man Shall Live by Every Word That Proceedeth from the Mouth of God"

What did Jesus retain of his Jewish heritage? What did he change?

Why did he come to John the Baptist?

What happened to Jesus in the baptism-wilderness experience?

What was changed for Jesus, for persons, perhaps for God, in the baptism-wilderness experience?

Jesus of Nazareth came to the river Jordan to be baptized by John the Baptist. This was Jesus' entrance into written history, unless we include the account where he is depicted as a precocious boy of twelve with deep religious yearning.[1] Because Jesus came to John and baptism as a Jew, what issued from his coming, where it led him, and

1. Lk. 2:41-50; §15.

what it did to him, for him, for God, and for the evolutionary process and development of consciousness then and now can only be understood if we first consider his religious heritage and the existential situation in which he lived.

Jesus must be divorced from the later Christian myth, which began even before his death. His roots were not Christian, but Jewish, so he must be seen, understood, and felt into at a point between the Jewish roots from which he emerged and the Christian myth which later developed. He is not to be identified with either.

Jesus came to the river Jordan wanting baptism from the prophet John and seeking a new turning and direction in his life. What are some of the dynamic, religious realities of the genius of Judaism of which he is an inheritor?

The God that brought him to the Jordan was a transcendent, purposive God, a God of will and intentionality, a restless, wandering God continually entering into human history. Thomas Mann, in his novel *Young Joseph*, says:

> Thus it must be because one served a God whose nature was not repose and abiding comfort, but a God of designs for the future, in whose will, inscrutable, great far-reaching things were in process of becoming and thus was a God of unrest, a God of cares who must be sought for, for whom one must at all times keep oneself free, mobile and in readiness.[1]

This wandering God was and still is a central concept of Jewish existence. The Covenant between Him/Her and the people is the outstanding characteristic of this concept. What is the Covenant and how did it develop?

The Mosaic Covenant, the most highly developed and central one, was between Yahweh and the people, conditioned by the people's choice of, and obedience to, the Law:

> The Lord will establish you as a people holy to himself, as he has sworn to you, if you keep the commandments of the Lord your God and walk in his ways.[2]

1. Thomas Mann, *Joseph and His Brothers* (New York: Alfred A. Knopf, 1945).
2. Deut. 28:9.

This God of the Mosaic Covenant was both a loving and wrathful God whose anger was easily aroused if the Covenant was broken, and whose rewards were equally great when the Covenant was followed by the human.

Prior to Moses, the Genesis covenants made with the patriarchs were unconditional and were offered to the individual and his descendants:

> When the sun had gone down, behold a smoking fire pot and a flaming torch passed between the pieces of the sacrificial animals. On that day the Lord made a covenant with Abram saying, "To your descendants I give this Land, from the river of Egypt to the great river, the river Euphrates."[1]

These covenants are gifts of Yahweh and are dependent on His/Her grace.

The first covenant appearing in the biblical text (one which probably was added later) is that with Noah in Genesis 9:8-17:

> Then God said to Noah and to his sons with him, "Behold I establish my covenant with you and with your descendants after you and with every living creature that is with you, the birds, the cattle and every beast of the earth as many as come out of the ark. I establish my covenant with you that never again shall all flesh be cut off by the waters of a flood to destroy the earth." And God said, "This is the sign of the covenant which I make between me and you and every living creature that is with you, for all future generations: When the bow is in the clouds I will look upon it and remember the everlasting covenant between God and every living creature of all flesh that is upon the earth."

This acknowledgment by Yahweh that He/She has unconscious regressive qualities—forgetfulness—counterbalances the richly purposive thrust forward. Other covenants after Moses include the one with David—a covenant at the heart of prophetic Messianism: "And your house and your kingdoms shall be made sure forever before me; your throne shall be established forever."[2]

---

1. Gen. 15:17-18.
2. 2 Sam. 7:16.

Later, with the words "I will be your God and you shall be my people,"[1] Jeremiah stated a new covenant for a new age:

> Behold the days are coming when I will make a new covenant with the houses of Israel and the house of Judah not like the covenant I made with their fathers . . . but . . . I will put my law within them and I will write it upon their hearts.[2]

(Here is the greatest step toward inwardness in the Covenant, later taken farther by Jesus.) Other covenants are renewed in Joshua (24:1-27) and in many of the prophets, from Amos (3:1-2) to Ezekiel (11:16-20).

The Covenant was sometimes interpreted as a marriage contract between Yahweh and Israel (e.g., Hosea 2, Jeremiah 3). Often at the heart of prophetic teaching is covenental reality. And whether the word "covenant" was ever used by Jesus is not as significant as the ways in which he viewed his life and teachings as an expansion of this reality—, in such statements as "our father" prayer; in the "not everyone who says 'Lord, Lord,' but those who do the will"; in sell all for the pearl of great price. These are individual covenants—a step forward from tribal covenants.

The God of Jesus' inheritance not only made covenants. That God also contained opposites (especially the masculine and feminine aspects). In the Garden of Eden story (the Judeo-Christian myth), the Lord God created humans "in our image," "male and female created he them."[3] As in very many creation myths, this God is androgynous, the masculine and feminine equally present. In the myth of the Garden, the Lord God planted the Tree of Knowledge of Good and Evil and the Tree of Life. The fact of Substance created by Spirit sets forth this good-evil pair of opposites as the desire of God for obedience. And the urging of the serpent to disobedience is a second example of the ambivalent opposites. There are dark and light opposites throughout the Hebrew Scripture. This Judaic

1. Jer. 7:23.
2. Jer. 31:31-33.
3. Gen. 1:27.

stress on, and deeply held conviction about, the concept of opposites conditioned the whole development and thought of Jesus. In Isaiah 45:7, God says, "I wound and I heal." Job says, "If I receive good from God, how shall I not receive evil?" (Job 2:10). The Kabbala states, Man was created for the sake of choice. Why is the human needed? What will this human, Jesus, contribute? The opposites are in the Godhead, but can consciousness be available without such a human? With the capacity of choice, the human may bring self-reflection and self-knowing to a God not intrinsically conscious without the human.

An understanding of these opposites in the Godhead gives background for the whole development of God concepts and Messianic concepts in the Hebrew Scripture and the gospels. The Kingdom of God, the reign of God on earth, would be established for the Jews by the coming of a Messiah in one form or another. ("Messiah" and "Christ" are essentially the same word, one being Hebrew and one Greek.) The Messiah, the anointed one of God, the instrument, the Redeemer, the Savior, would come to establish a society of political freedom, moral perfection, abundance in nature, earthly bliss for the children of Israel and, according to some prophets, for the entire human race. Contained in the Messianic longing and expectation was a vision of a Kingdom variously described, as in Hosea 14:6-8:

> I will be as the dew to Israel;
>   he shall blossom as the lily,
>   he shall strike root as the poplar;
> his shoots shall spread out;
>   his beauty shall be like the olive,
>   and his fragrance like Lebanon.
> They shall return and dwell beneath my shadow,
>   they shall flourish as a garden;
> they shall blossom as the vine,
>   their fragrance shall be like the wine of Lebanon.

This dream of God's working on earth expresses, perhaps, the greatest genius of the Jews. It is the opinion of some scholars, especially Klausner, that this dream first took the form of a Messianic age not ushered in by a

Messiah.[1] Later, this dream took the shape of a hoped-for Messiah, a specific person who would be the deliverer from wretched times to a fulfillment time. (This shift from Messianic to Messiah needs to be kept in mind as we see what Jesus did with the image.)

Many of the prophets also believed that the Day of the Lord, the day for punishment of sin, would occur before the Day of the Messiah that would bring in the new era of fulfillment. This Day of the Lord would include exile, destruction, humiliation, and repentance of sin. Amos describes it thus:

> Woe to you who desire the day of the Lord!
> Why would you have the day of the Lord?
> It is darkness and not light
> . . . .
> Is not the day of the Lord darkness and not
> light, and gloom with no brightness in it?[2]

At the time of Jesus, this hope for the Messiah took mainly two forms, one apocalyptic* and one political. The latter conception was that only political freedom—in this case, freedom from Rome—would bring about spiritual freedom. Rome was relatively tolerant regarding synagogue worship but intolerant politically. The function, therefore, of the Messiah was to free the people from political bondage in order that they might totally and freely worship. This conception, seen in the early, nonhistorical parts of Matthew and Luke in the birth narratives, was attached later to Jesus. "To grant unto us that we, being delivered out of the hands of our enemies, should serve Him without fear in holiness and righteousness, before Him all our days."[3]

1. J. Klausner, *The Messianic Idea in Israel,* (New York: MacMillan, 1955).
2. Amos 5:18-20.
3. Lk. 1:73-75; §7D.

On the other side, in apocalyptic Messianism, there was the hope of a sudden and immediate revelation about to break into history. The new golden age would erupt into the present.

The apocalyptic conception[1] held by John the Baptist needs to be understood in its relation to the eschatological* and prophetic Messianism discussed. The message about the coming of the Kingdom through the intervention of God and the call to righteousness of the people was most intense from 760 to 550 B.C.E., although after this came II Isaiah as a great prophet. Prophets endeavored to make God's will effective in building toward the future new world. Prophecy is dated as ending around 330 B.C.E. John the Baptist stood at the end of this long line as a minor prophet, proclaiming the need to change and to turn to God, whose wrath was visited upon the people in the form of political servitude. Such minor prophets called for righteousness and obedience. They were people for whom God was a very living and dynamic reality to whom they were related. They were special servants of God, fully human, yet called to a vocation. To understand the prophet John and all the archetypal implications of his message is to enhance the understanding of the roots out of which the man Jesus emerged, for Jesus did not just appear out of nowhere. He came out of Something into Something new. In order fully and freshly to understand the archetypal roots of Messiah, of the Messiah-Christ reality and its specific formulation in Jewish thought and what Jesus did with it, several ideas must be clear.

The longing for a Messiah, for one who would save and redeem the people and act as intermediary between God and human, is a longing universally expressed. From where does this longing come? First, the human being is

1. According to Ringgren, Old Testament apocalyptic writings came late, and were a development from prophetic writings. Daniel is the earliest of the apocalyptic books of the Hebrew Scripture. It was rejected by Rabbinic Judaism and is "based on the view that the entire history of the world takes place according to a plan previously determined by God." Helmer Ringgren, *Israelite Religion*, (Philadelphia: Fortress Press, 1966), p. 334.

split from its potential wholeness through the struggle to exist, and is thus separated from its Source. This is the human wound, inevitable and unavoidable. At the same time, perhaps the Source is also split in itself.

In ancient Greek Asklepion healing centers, it was stated that the God sends the wound, the God is the wound, the God is wounded, and the God heals the wound. If the Source desires to be restored to Its wholeness, such restoration can only come by way of the human's struggles to be whole. (This expression of God's longing for human helpers is expressed time after time in the Hebrew Scripture.) Thus both God and human are wounded, and both God and human desire healing for this wound.

In terms of the psychology of C.G. Jung, the wound is either a split between the deep and central Self and the psyche, or it is within the Self itself. Healing of this split is related to the longing for a savior or a saving element. Jung felt that this wound—this split—and its healing are both resident in the deep central Self itself. Therefore, when we are dealing with Messianic and Christological questions, we are dealing with the ultimate religious nature of the human psyche. In either case, the longing and the potential healing are also there.

Martin Buber, the great Jewish philosopher and mystic, said, in a conversation with this author, that the main difference between Judaism and Christianity is that in the former the Messiah is still to come; in the latter he has come. The central task throughout this book will be to see how Jesus himself answered this. Where was the Messiah-Christ for him? How did he understand and experience it within himself? How did he relate to it? How did it influence him and he it?

In addition to the prevailing Messianic forms at the time of Jesus is the profound influence of the Suffering Servant concept, which comes from the servant poems in the Book of Isaiah (40-55). Most of these poems assume the servant to be Israel itself, e.g., Isaiah 41:8-10a:

> But you, Israel, my servant,
> Jacob, whom I have chosen,
> the offspring of Abraham, my friend;

> you whom I took from the ends of the earth,
> and called from the farthest corners,
> saying to you, "You are my servant
> I have chosen you and not cast you off;"
> fear not, for I am with you. . .

In these poems the servant, though wounded for the trans-
gressions of others, and stricken and suffering, becomes a
radiant, majestic, all-powerful one who will usher in the
new era. This especially appears in Isaiah 53. Christianity
has assumed that Jesus has fulfilled this suffering servant
function, and has given him this title among others. Our
question is how much the moving and transformative
features inherent in the Isaiah suffering servant moved
and touched Jesus—in the Son of man as suffering, and in "I
am in the midst of you as one who serves."

This cursory look at the Hebrew Scripture background
gives some sense of the religious culture into which Jesus
came. John the Baptist was a carrier of this tradition as a
minor prophet. The account of John's activity and preaching is found in all three Synoptics, and it is striking that the
two oldest sources, Mark and Q,[1] begin with the presence of
John. The brief but basic account in Mark puts John in the
wilderness, "clothed with camel's hair," having "a leather
girdle around his loins," and eating "locusts and wild
honey." His message was a call to repentance and deep
moral purgation, symbolized by baptism in the river Jordan. People came to him from all Judea, and for them the
river Jordan became penitential waters. Going into them,
emerging from them, was an act which signified repentance and turning—a metanoia. No motivation for this act is
given in Mark except the general call to repentance. John
spoke of one to come after him, and in the Mark account
said, "I baptized you with water, but he shall baptize you
with the Holy Spirit."[2] The reference to the one to come is
here, in the text, in no way to be identified with Jesus, but
is an articulation of the Messianic hope.

---

1.   Mk. 1:1-8; Mt. 3:1-12; Lk. 3:1-20 §17. For an explanation of documentary sources, see Appendix I.
2.   Mk. 1:8; §17P.

10

The account in Matthew and Luke (from Document Q) is much fuller. This rugged, ascetic man poured out his longing for his people to take a new, more individual step toward righteousness:

> You offspring of vipers, who warned you to flee from the wrath to come? Bring forth therefore fruit worthy of repentance: and think not to say within yourselves, We have Abraham to our father: for I say unto you that God is able of these stones to raise up children unto Abraham. And even now is the axe laid unto the root of the trees: every tree therefore that bringeth not forth good fruit is hewn down, and cast into the fire.[1]

"To have Abraham to our father" was no longer enough to guarantee personal salvation. To bring forth fruit worthy of repentance was a radical change in the nature of the Covenant. It altered the root and origin of Covenant from being chosen to choosing. There was an imminently cataclysmic day of judgment at hand: "Even now is the axe laid unto the root of the trees."[2] Yahweh's decision whether a person was to be destroyed or saved rested, in John's message, on the individual acting by a choice to repent, to change. For John the Baptist the waters were thus not just a generalized symbol of cleansing. Very specifically, they were penitential waters. They were the outer symbol of the possibility of and need for individual repentance, for turning, for changing so that one would be saved on the day of destruction. John addressed the crowd as "offspring of vipers," and warned them of this day of wrath, this judgment day to come when all those who had not repented would be destroyed.

Psychologically speaking, John's apocalypticism is based on a split in the Self between positive and negative, where the negative takes the form of a fiery judgment. This split is later integrated by Jesus, and becomes the internal basis of ethical choice.

The end was at hand; the new age was to come. At this time of ferment many people were preaching, "Lo, here; lo, there." The Kingdom was about to come. The prophets

1. Mt. 3:8-10; Lk. 3:8-9; §17M.
2. Mt. 3:10; Lk. 3:9; §17M.

had always stressed righteousness in the people and in individuals. Individual responsibility and action were ·now called for, and the new emphasis for John was baptism for repentance. This was a strong, dynamic, passionate man, preaching these things to his people and emphasizing choice. John was, of course, outside the established religious structure of his time.

The Q account continues to preach the function of the Messiah in an apocalyptic form. In contrast to the Mark account, John says of himself in the Document Q account, "I indeed baptize you with water . . . but he that comes after me . . . shall baptize you with the Holy Ghost and with fire: whose fan is in his hand, and he will thoroughly cleanse his threshing floor; and he will gather his wheat into the garner, but the chaff he will burn up with unquenchable fire."[1] In Mark, it is clear that the one to come will baptize with the Holy Ghost, whereas in Document Q it is Holy Ghost *and* fire. It seems logical to conclude that the original Q had fire, the later Mark had Holy Spirit, and they were put together by Matthew and Luke. This would probably have been done because "fire" continued the Hebrew Scripture tradition, and "Holy Ghost" was a later Christian term. The Messiah to come (and there was no indication of who this would be) would fulfill the desire of God for complete separation between good and evil and for the establishment of the Kingdom of Righteousness. He would be the instrument through which God's will would come about, and the Kingdom of Righteousness—with the elimination of all evil—would be actualized. This concept of apocalyptic Messianism was—as we have seen—extensive at the time of Jesus. The opposites within God, dark and light, wrath and love, were to be torn asunder and the Kingdom established as only good. What did Jesus do with these opposites? What has later Christianity done?

It was to this movement that Jesus of Nazareth came. Why did Jesus come to this unorthodox, prophetic John? What was his motivation? What kind of thinking, feeling, moral concern, were going on inside him? We will never know what occupied him in the carpenter shop at Nazareth

1. Mt. 3:11-12; §17P-Q.

that led to this step, nor will we know what he anticipated out of his baptismal experience, or whether he expected to return to everyday life. We can only speculate.

Could he have come out of a deep personal need for repentance, out of facing his own darkness and need for change? A person who later included as much realism as he did about the dark and evil forces in the world knew something of their reality. In addition to deep personal need, he must have seen the need for his people's repentance so God could be rightly worshipped. He responded to John's insistence on individual responsibility. He may have come because his life in Nazareth no longer fulfilled him and he was restless, so that the religious stirrings in him took him out, away from Nazareth. He may have come because he was truly gripped by the apocalyptic vision and believed that this was the way God would function. John's message, probably the most challenging, vital, and authentic one current at that time, appealed to him. What may have been his visions and dreams we can never know. This is not to say he saw a Messianic role for himself, but that he believed in this Messianic vision. It may have been a combination of all these elements. Ultimately, it will always be a mystery, one of many still existing despite speculation and research. But he came, and something happened which led him to a life away from the known and familiar into "a Kingdom different than any had supposed."[1] Wherever the emphasis belongs, something was deeply moved in him concerning the way God functions, the nature of the divine and the Holy Spirit, and the function of the Messiah. A change in the God-image was coming into being. A new I-Thou Process was born.

The task of entering into the experience of this man rather than seeing him as *object* of experience, and the task of seeing behind what has been projected onto him for two thousand years, will not be easy. Such an attempt must be made, however, for his baptism was the pivotal moment which conditioned everything that came into his life. Whether the description we have in all three books

1.   Sheila Moon, *Joseph's Son*, (Francestown, N.H.: Golden Quill Press, 1972), p. 16.

comes from Jesus' sharing this experience with friends, or whether it is in part a description by later writers, we can never know. Perhaps its authenticity is enhanced by the fact that all that came later in Jesus' life and teaching seems to have derived from the baptismal experience. Thus how it is here expressed cannot be too far from reality. The experience has about it a quality of depth, decisiveness, authenticity. Surely it was a dynamic situation full of opposite movements, opposing forces, God action and human action. Everything we have seen about John's message and the possible reasons for Jesus' coming to John must be kept in focus as background, for this experience did not just occur. It happened within the history and the religious and psychological realities of Jesus' Jewish homeland.

There were causes of this experience—whether human, divine, or both—and there were outcomes. And between the causes and the outcomes is a man, a person, a human instrument *on* whom, *in* whom, *to* whom the reality of sonship in God was subsequently taken in a new direction. After asking why Jesus came to John for baptism, it must be asked, With what attitude did he come? Regardless of all the possible mixture of reasons, is it too much to say that he came with a whole-hearted, intense giving of himself to the experience? Is it possible that nothing was held back, and that this could be the first clue to all we may learn about his religious experience from this central incident?

> And it came to pass in those days, that Jesus came from Nazareth of Galilee, and was baptized of John in the Jordan. And straightway coming up out of the water, he saw the heavens rent asunder, and the Spirit as a dove descending upon him; and a voice came out of the heavens, Thou art my beloved Son, in thee I am well pleased.[1]

The first movement in this crucial experience was downward into the broad river, into John's waters of repentance for sins. It was not just any river's water, but water in the central river of Israel, cleaving the land from

1. Mk. 1:9-11; §18.

the northern mountains to the Dead Sea. And it was a dissi-
dent Jew, John, who drew him there. To this, he came
with all he knew of himself. It meant a confrontation with
his own dark reality and the willingness to risk change by
responding to the powerful cleansing meaning of water,
producing opposing movements: the descent and the ascent. In a tradition that has tended to see the experience of
God as outward in history, it is significant to see that
Jesus' experience here was inward, a sense of indwelling
sonship. This descent is not to be equated with going into
the unconscious, although possibly some of the same elements are operative.

"Straightway coming up out of the water" Jesus had
three highly dramatic experiences, leading him to
withdraw to the wilderness: "the heavens were rent
asunder," the "Spirit as a dove descended," and "a voice
came out of the heavens." What, for a Jew, could this have
meant? The heavens were the abode of God, the celestial
heights of the throne of the transcendent deity. Here they
were torn apart. As in a birth, there was a tearing so the
new life could emerge. Some fresh emergence was happening within the cosmos. As with Moses on Sinai, God was
manifesting in a new way. It would have been like an earthquake, but it was a "heavenquake." What was happening
on the side of God? What had been heretofore held within
the Transcendent now moved. A mutational shift was occurring—perhaps on both sides of the God-human dialogue.
What was the God-presence needing? What was the
human bringing to God and human evolvement? Was a new
dimension of Covenant added by Jesus' response? A new
radical alteration of consciousness had occurred.

"The Spirit as a dove descended upon him." The
Spirit, known throughout the Hebrew Scripture as breath,
wind, *ruach*, first appeared in Genesis as the "Spirit of God
that moved over the waters." The Spirit of God spoke
through the Hebrew prophets to the people. The prophets
were God's voice. And now that Spirit was moving down
into a human, Jesus. As Jesus ascended from the water,
the Spirit descended and took up a new abode in the inner
person of Jesus. This was a radical movement not only for
humans, but for God. A new archetypal shift was occurring

that had been intimated in the accounts in later Hebrew Scripture—in Job and Jeremiah.

In his challengingly radical book *Answer to Job*, Dr. Jung pointed out how Yahweh wanted to become more human, or longed for more consciousness through human-kind.[1] Here, then, at this river, was this event which was destined to be a turning point of history. For Jesus, that which had always been transcendent now lodged in him. The impact of this for him as experient was almost over-whelming. Did the indwelling of the Spirit produce a new organ in the psyche, or did it awaken something already there which had been known only in a projected form? Was it the purpose of the Spirit as part of God to come into, to incarnate in, the human or to find its counterpart in the human? The text says, "the Spirit as a dove." The dove is the bird of Astarte, of Venus. It suggests the feminine God qualities of gentleness and flexibility in contrast to the God that John the Baptist had been talking about, a God more violent and more aggressive.

What had happened? As Jesus had gone into the waters of penitence and ascended out of them, in his ex-perience of heavens torn apart a new step had been taken, not just in Jesus individually but in Jesus as instrument and vehicle for humankind. There is a statement by one of the early church fathers, Justin, that when Jesus came out of the waters, the waters were aflame. The God of opposites that John the Baptist talked of had moved, through this descent and ascent, into the human dimension in the per-son of Jesus, where a new integration could take place. Because the Godhead was now confronted within and without by human choice, its power became available in the psyche for a confrontation. Yahweh, or the image of Yahweh, was now changed. The Transcendent, which had been manifesting itself in human choices and in situations in history, now also manifested itself in the person. It could be said that there was a new marriage of God and Israel at an intensely personal level. The wandering God had found a new residence. It remains to be seen whether this was a

1.   Jung, *Psychology and Religion*, p. 397.

one-time revelation in Jesus only, or whether it became a continuing incarnation in humankind.

Out of the heavens opening and the Spirit descending, a voice came which said, "Thou art my beloved Son, in thee I am well pleased." There are similar words from Psalm 2:7: "Thou art my beloved Son. This day have I begotten Thee." The first words, however, are found in the Hebrew Scripture (Isaiah 42:1) and refer not to an individual but to the nation as servant of God. (They are also in Matthew 12:18, used in an eschatological way.) The second statement is to an individual. The historical movement is from nation to person. What could this have meant to the hearer of these words? In this experience of the Holy Spirit indwelling there must have been, for Jesus, a question as to the meaning of "Son." Of all the possibilities that could have been entertained, the possibility of Messiah could have been included. Was Jesus to be the expected savior of his people? If so, in what form? Did "this day" indicate the immediacy of the moment, the here and now? Such questions must have gone with him into the wilderness.

Why did this experience come as a voice? What does it add? Is it not the same voice that we find addressing kings, prophets, and judges throughout the Hebrew Scripture?

Here, perhaps, it is more internalized. Whatever its source, it announces a new birth. It differentiates the hearer, Jesus, from God and it articulates an I and a Thou.

How might Jesus have been most different after the experience than before it? With what questions did he go to the wilderness? Why did he go to the wilderness at all? Out of this overwhelming experience what clarity was needed by him? What needed to be served and how? What changes in him had come?

Before moving to the next step, into the wilderness, let us look at what Luke and Matthew, following Mark, have done with the baptism experience. One difference between Mark and Luke is that in Luke there is a reference (found throughout Luke) to Jesus praying. But the most striking difference is that Luke has, "The Holy Ghost descended in a bodily form as a dove." "Holy Ghost" is a term known later to be an English Christian word. What in Mark was symbolic became literal and concrete in Luke. What is

behind the urge to make a symbol concrete? Is it the longing to make visible what needs to be left invisible yet real?
To let the symbol stay symbol forces one to face the
mystery behind it. To make it literal is to force it into
substance at the loss of the symbolic meaning. (The implications of this for later so-called miracle stories will be
examined in Chapter V.)

In Matthew, the baptism story is quite different. Most
strikingly, Matthew changes the "Thou art" of the address
of Yahweh to Jesus to "This is my beloved Son," making it
a public announcement rather than a personal experience.
By this change, Matthew does away with a dialogic relation
between God and Jesus. (Matthew prepares the way for
this by an insertion of a discussion between John and
Jesus.)[1]

What happened to Jesus at his baptism was a result of
his personhood. Committed to what John was saying, he
entered the water in utmost obedience and expectancy. He
brought himself as a container for what might come. On
the side of the Other, God was ready and prepared for a
new manifestation. The meeting of the two became a quantum leap*, a new mutation.*

The possible questions with which Jesus moved into
the wilderness have been suggested. What was he to do
with a new power, a new reality? How was he to live it?
Was it Messianic in content, or not? What did the totality of
this God whom he had found in the baptism now ask of
him? It is enriching to observe all the opposites contained
in the baptism, some of which have been suggested. There
was Spirit-Substance, up-down, heaven-earth, masculine-
feminine. (The feminine was expressed not only by the
dove but by water as a mother symbol, and by the inclusion of Substance.) And because these were penitential
waters, the descent into them included acknowledgment of
sin and imperfection.

And there was Silence and the Voice.

What is the wilderness? Whether he went to a literal
place, or to an inner place, or both, wilderness is unknown,
uncharted, uninhabited territory, open to exploration. He

1. Mt. 3:14-15; §See Appendix I.

was "driven" in Mark, or "led" in Matthew and Luke, by the Holy Spirit to be there forty days (or a long time).[1] Whether he was "driven" or "led," it is conspicuous that the Spirit was responsible for a new confrontation with the tempter (devil, or Satan). What does this say about the Spirit now lodged in a human person in a totally new way? Jesus was completely obedient to the Spirit. But what did the Spirit, whose indwelling in this man was an evolutionary step, want now? Jesus neither rested on the religious experience he had had, nor allowed the numinosity* of it to overwhelm him. The Spirit seemed concerned that Jesus should confront the meaning of his experience and see where it would lead. It seems as if the Spirit of God was involved in producing consciousness in Jesus, through choices presented to him by Satan as God's alter ago.

In a world where the Holy Spirit was, as it had been many times throughout history, an active religious force, its moving of Jesus toward the unknown wilderness adds a significant aspect. Too often the numinosity from the archetypal depths of the Spirit is experienced and then left as an autonomous factor, unrelated to the ego-consciousness* and, therefore, not truly integrated. That the Spirit has about it the quality of desire not only for incarnation, but also for transformation within the person is an exciting thought. The Spirit in Jesus was concerned that the religious experience lead to facing issues involving conflict, choice, and even temptation. None of these can occur in unconsciousness. Rather, they demand consciousness such as emerged from the baptism. The Holy Spirit as Comforter and Paraclete in the Gospel of John is quite different from the Holy Spirit who initiated a new phase of history through Jesus of Nazareth at the baptism. Also, the experience of Pentecost described later in Acts is qualitatively different, because it is a group experience and occurred in very different circumstances.

Mark's postbaptism account is limited to a statement that Jesus "was in the wilderness forty days tempted of Satan; and he was with the wild beasts; and the angels ministered unto him."[2] What experience for Jesus may

1. Mk. 1:12-13; Mt. 4:1-11; Lk. 4:1-13; §20.
2. Mk. 1:12-13; §20A, G.

have been behind the words about "wild beasts and angels?" Surely they represent a pair of opposites confronting Jesus from within and without. Wild beasts could be deep, instinctual, unconscious forces—powers not necessarily negative but overwhelming, dark realities that had been unleashed in the baptism experience as part of God's reality. At the same moment that he was with these "wild beasts," "angels" were also present as potential integrative forces, as presences and powers that need to be known. Both wild beasts and angels, then, may be manifestations of God. Perhaps we know all too little about the healing presence of angels because we do not face the dark world of wild beasts. The recognition of this at the beginning of the public life of Jesus may help us better to understand all he will soon have to say about ambivalence and dualities and singleness.

Matthew and Luke include the three so-called temptations and confrontations with the devil or Satan. These three issues are placed in slightly different order, and the Matthew order will be followed here.[1] As it is written, the tempter or devil came three times with a proposal, and each time Jesus rejected that proposal. Who or what came to Jesus and at what point he called the temptations Satanic we will understand better after we examine their content. All three issues have about them not so much a purely personal sense as that of vocation or leadership.

One of the burning questions with which he left the baptism was whether being a beloved son had Messianic content for his vocation. Jesus had, in the Jordan, entered into the heart of God and perhaps, equally, it could be said that God had entered newly and wholly into his heart. Did this mean he might become the "savior" who would bring economic well-being and bread for all, or become the miracle worker defying natural law by jumping off the pinnacle of the Temple and being saved, or become the political Messiah for the kingdoms of the world? Each of these possibilities was, in fact, a facet of the Messianic hope. Whether it meant the rejection of the reality behind the form of Messianic expectation remains to be seen. Where did he get the consciousness to turn down these

1. Mt. 4:1-11; §20B-D.

sacred hopes of his people, at least these forms of them? These were deep values, visions of how the Messianic age should come about, but Jesus knew that these were not the way that the Kingdom could come about.

By whom were these issues presented to Jesus according to the text? The figure is described as tempter, devil, or Satan, in that order. But to what does this refer? At what point during the time in the wilderness did Jesus designate these experiences as satanic? It is hard to imagine that Jesus started with the destructive or truly negative reality we as Christians have put into the word "Satan." For the Hebrew people, Satan presented suggestions which had much positive content for them. They were not negative concepts, but collective positive images and hopes. It seems more likely that Jesus entertained these three issues as genuine possibilities, forms of what it might mean to be a beloved son. With each of these he struggled. He rejected each one. But he listened to the satanic voice before rejecting it. Only after he had considered the issues, had found them less than adequate as content for his new vocation, did he label them as from the tempter, devil, or Satan. They were not seen by him as evil when presented, but as less than the best in God's will.

Already the reality of how Jesus would work with the will of God becomes apparent. The Holy Spirit brought about this confrontation in Jesus, who would be the new abode for the Spirit's concern.

Under no other circumstances than that of the struggle for full consciousness in the human being can the two sides of God become unified. Jesus was not meeting Satan as separate or distinct from God, but as part of God. He was searching for God's will and meaning as alternatives arose. This is the first insight in the gospels where the coming together of the opposites is the expression of the will of God. To choose is always the function of consciousness. Satan, then, becomes God's freedom in us. He is the "prodder," the "pursuer," the "adversary," the "accuser," the putter of questions that keep God the One, not split off but with alternatives for the human respondent.

What did Jesus reject and what were the implications of the rejections for his future? He would not put the major emphasis on feeding the people in order to restore the meaning of the Kingdom as a time and place of plenty, a land of milk and honey. He would not use supernatural miracles or powers to bring in the Kingdom, because God would function within the wonders of the natural. These refusals must be remembered as we consider the so-called miraculous element in the gospels. Jesus would not conform to expectations of a political Messiah. What he would do, or how he might live his life, is suggested by two positive statements: "Man shall not live by bread alone, but by every word that proceedeth out of the mouth of God"[1] and "It is written, Thou shalt worship the Lord thy God, and him only shalt thou serve."[2] These are the center of what is to be the motivating force in his life and of the message he will express out of it. How the Word will express itself through Jesus' words, how it will take form and substance in him, will be central. How the fulfillment of the Word will compare to or be different from the Word used by Hebrew prophets must be seen.

Another central question for Jesus was—as it is for us today—What is the relation between the coming in of the Holy Spirit and the sense of being the Son with a possible Messianic content? What happened to the archetype of the Self, the *imago dei** (image of God), which had been projected onto Israel by the Jews in relation to Yahweh and the Covenant? Was the Self then behind the Messiah-Christ-Son image, or was it the Holy Spirit, or both? The experience of Jesus never led him to identify with the Self as imaged in the Messiah-Christ image, yet he did not rule it out. Joachim de Flora, a mystic of the eleventh century, characterized the Christian era as that of the Son, the era of the Hebrew Scripture as that of the Father, and the new era to come as that of the Holy Spirit.[3] The few significant statements by Jesus on the Holy Spirit must be carefully considered. In the wilderness, the Holy Spirit revealed itself to him as the core resource and manifestation of God

1. Mt. 4:4; §20B.
2. Mt. 4:10; §20D.
3. C.G. Jung, *Aion: Researches into the Phenomenology of the Self,* Bolligen Series XX (New York: Pantheon Books, 1959), p. 82.

within his humanity. Perhaps today is characterized as the era of the Holy Spirit because the reality of God in the Self cannot and should not be limited to a projection into one person. The true Messianic process behind the hoped-for Messiah might be described as the Holy Spirit working within. Christianity has confined the Self to a Messianic-Christ function in one person. Psychologically the Self can express itself through the Holy Spirit as guide and teacher, as a divine element in the human.

With what conviction, knowledge, answered and unanswered questions, did Jesus leave the wilderness? What can we know about what was moving in him? We can only know by the possibility of his own reports to those closest, or by inference from the later teaching, or by assuming the editors' writing was accurate. What kind of a man was he, what would he teach, how attractive or potent a figure would he be? How had he answered the questions put to him? What did he know? What did he not know? Both sides of the question are of equal significance for consciousness. He knew that he would serve God and God only in some unspecified way (which could be called the resurrected life). He knew that he was not going to identify himself with any current Messianic hope. He did not know whether any Messianic content would be attached to him after his baptism experience. He knew that he would confront powerful issues, and that he would have to take an individual stand against them. He knew much about the power and *tremendum* of God. He knew the descent of God into himself in the form of the Holy Spirit and its subsequent manifestations in him. He did not know exactly what God's will for him would be.

He knew that he must be open to newness; he knew that he must live by every word that came from the mouth of God. He left the wilderness as one poet has said with "a sure, fierce love."[1] This love was his love for God—rooted in his tradition from the Hebrew Scripture and newly manifested as the Holy Spirit within—and was also the sense of being a beloved son with some mysterious, undefined content. "Him only shalt thou serve" was his response in

1. Moon, *Joseph's Son*, p. 20.

the wilderness. Whatever the content of his inner myth was to be, it would surely be played out in the world of persons, where the Kingdom of God could be established, and also within himself. He moved directly into the world, his world, into synagogues, into everyday contact, meeting all classes of people, discovering what his way would be and what his message would be. How much would it be rooted in the already established patterns of Judaism? How much would it be a new creation? Where would the balance be? How could he maintain his integrity as he had to deal with projections and images that would arise and be put on him? Would he perhaps find and establish his identity by the way he related to such images?

In his first movements out of his wilderness interiority into society, he encountered ordinary people—fishermen, some of whom would choose to follow him, and persons with various degrees of unwholeness whose encounter with him produced healing. From these persons more often than not he received approval, commendation, praise, and deep acceptance. Following these first incidents he moved into a series of encounters with the strong criticism of the religious authorities of the society.

Thus, the story of his active life after emergence from the wilderness came under three headings: acceptance, rejection, and affirmation. Each of these crucial meetings of beginning must be examined for what it reveals of Jesus' attitudes, his relations and communications with people, his own self-estimate, and his relation to and perception of the workings of God. These beginnings determined the future course of his personal history, and previsioned the vital and transforming effect of his life on the history of the Western world.

The first period, one of acceptance and positive reception, begins with "preaching the gospel of God, and saying, The time is fulfilled, and the kingdom of God is at hand: repent ye, and believe in the gospel."[1] Here the message of Jesus is summarized by the editor. The repentance is reminiscent of the words of John the Baptist. Is this truly what Jesus would have begun with after his experience in

1. Mk. 1:14-15; §21C.

the baptism and wilderness? Matthew does not have the reference to "the gospel," "the good news," and this fact, plus the fact that the word itself reflects a Christian development, may eliminate it as originating with Jesus. Inasmuch as Mark and Luke always have "Kingdom of God," in contrast to "Kingdom of Heaven," it is considered probable that Jesus said "Kingdom of God." This will be used throughout this book.

Would Jesus repeat the message of John, or would he have preached something about his new insight into the immediacy of the Kingdom of God? At this point Luke has nothing like Mark, but includes a brief account, presumably from Q, which simply speaks of Jesus' fame, his teaching in synagogue, and his being glorified by all.[1] We are free to follow Luke, and to consider Mark and Matthew as reflecting early Christian thinking. Ultimately, the attitude toward the historicity of the beginning summary can be checked by comparing it to Jesus' teaching in the whole Gospel, as to whether it is cohesive and consistent. Another reason in favor of Luke is that he continues immediately with Jesus' first appearance in Nazareth,[2] while Matthew and Mark place it much later.[3] Luke's account offers a coherent possibility of beginning, even though it may be a condensation of two incidents.

In Luke, we may have the first authentic record of Jesus' entrance into public activity and affirmation. He entered the synagogue in Nazareth, his home town, having returned from the Jordan. As was the custom of the day, he was handed the Book of Isaiah and read the text:

> The Spirit of the Lord is upon me, because he anointed me to preach good tidings to the poor: He hath sent me to proclaim release to the captives, And recovering of sight to the blind, to set at liberty them that are bruised, to proclaim the acceptable year of the Lord.[4]

1. Lk. 4:14-15; §21C.
2. Lk. 4:16-30; §22.
3. Mk. 6:1-6a; Mt. 13:54-58; §54.
4. Lk. 4:18-19; §22.

At the end of the reading, he stated, "Today hath this scripture been fulfilled in your ears."[1]

Careful attention must be given to this passage because throughout the centuries it has been misinterpreted as Messianic. Taking the passage as it stands in Isaiah, it is clearly a declaration of prophetic vocation made by Isaiah at the time of the exile. By reading this text, which was handed to him as a continuation of the reading from the Sabbath before, Jesus placed himself squarely in the prophetic tradition. This tradition, so beautifully portrayed in the Hebrew Scripture through the prophets Isaiah, Jeremiah, and Amos, has been distinguished from the Messianic tradition. What is the essence of the pro phetic mission? The prophet spoke for God, spoke the truth as he perceived it, from God to the people. In the original passage in Isaiah one line, "and recovering of sight to the blind," is not there. If that is omitted (assuming that it was added in a later redaction), then the prophetic vocation is described as being initiated by the Spirit of God for the purpose of preaching, proclaiming release to captives, and setting at liberty the bruised. In the critical times of exile, and in other desperate moments in their people's history, great Hebrew prophets arose to give hope and to speak with passion and authority. Jesus' reading of this text, on the first Sabbath after his return from the wilderness, was not a prediction of the future or of outer Messiah. Typical of his subsequent teachings, it was a here-and-now description. Nor was Jesus predicting any Messianic hope. He was saying, "Today, once again this is fulfilled." "And the people wondered, is not this Joseph's son?"[2] Familiar surroundings tend to dampen people's ability to hear the new.

Jesus then passed along by the Sea of Galilee and for the first time encountered the fishermen who would become his disciples. In Mark and Matthew the command or invitation "Come ye after me and I will make you fishers

1. Lk. 4:21; §22B.
2. Lk. 4:21-22; §22B, C.

of men"[1] is given. Simon and Andrew and James and John came—two sets of brothers. Had we no other account it would be difficult to explain this amazing response to a man who wandered past them as they cleaned their nets. However, Luke has another account which gives much more motivation for the first movements of the disciples. In this account,[2] two incidents occurred that enlarge the picture. In one incident Jesus spent time teaching the multitude from the boat. These men who had followed had a chance to hear whatever might be new, different, challenging, which it must have been. What did Jesus say when outside the synagogue and on his own?

The second incident is the description of a large catch of fishes after a period of long waiting, so large that their nets were broken. This is the first account in the gospels of the so-called miraculous element. Because other miracles are reported and must be dealt with in any understanding of Jesus, some definitions and possibilities are in order.

The word "miracle" presents a semantic problem which must be clarified. In one sense all of life is a miracle, a reality that makes one breathless and awestruck. But the more particular meaning of "miracle" in the fishing incident is that which is seen as the expression of supernatural power coming from Jesus. Super-natural, as distinguished from supra-natural, power is seen as a special power exhibited by a human (here it is Jesus) in performing acts against natural laws. Supranatural power is the power *within* nature, beyond most human knowledge but not including a special power. It allows for all the discoveries today in the fields of nuclear physics and depth-psychology, of heretofore unheard-of things but things within natural law. That Jesus related to this second category, as others have and can, seems evident.

What, then, are the possible explanations for the catch of fishes? It could have been a supernatural event. It could have no actual basis in fact but be a legend developed to give motivation for the disciples' following of Jesus. It could have been a quite natural phenomenon where a

1. Mk. 1:17; Mt. 4:19; §23B.
2. Lk. 5:1-11; §23.

school of fishes passed by. It could have been an exag-
erated account of a natural event. It could have been
supranatural, a synchronous* event, wherein an inner attitude and outer event parallelled one another. Not all
supranatural events are synchronous, but all synchronous
events may be considered supranatural.

Simon Peter, having heard Jesus preach and having
seen the catch of fishes, knelt before Jesus and said,
"Depart from me, for I am a sinful man." "And all were
amazed . . . and Jesus said, 'Simon, fear not. From hence-
forth thou shalt catch men.' "[1] What lay behind Simon
Peter's reaction? Even if he interpreted the catch of fish as
a completely supernatural event, is that all that is behind
it? Did Peter, perhaps, realize that he was in the presence
of a man whose stature he could not comprehend? Suddenly, Something or Someone numinous confronted him,
and, as is often the case in the unwhole person, this may
have produced fear, alarm, and a sense of guilt. Whatever
consciousness Jesus had brought from the baptism-wilderness experience, it now began to manifest itself in his being. A larger Being to which he was related was reflected
through him and this produced Peter's reaction. Peter did
not leave, run away, or ever turn back from Jesus, not even
later in the courtyard scene after the trials.

This is our first meeting with the figure of Peter, so
prominent later, whose first reaction to Jesus may be
diagnostic and prognostic of his later reactions. Simon
Peter did many things, but he never ran away! His ambiguity and ambivalence are consistently shown, but he
stayed with the central value. His initial reaction was a
testimony to what was inside him, and can be inside us—
his ability to perceive those qualities in Jesus against
which he saw himself as simple and partial. The fact that
he could see the contrast was because he had both things
in himself—partialness and potential wholeness.

Jesus moved for the first time into Capernaum by the
Sea of Galilee, and for the second time we see him in a
synagogue. There was great astonishment that he taught
with such authority. Continually the question presents

1. Lk. 5:1-11; §27.

itself: Where did his authority come from? How did he so trust himself? What can we as seeking persons learn from this?

A man with an unclean spirit—in those days called a demoniac or one possessed by a devil—called out and addressed him: "Jesus of Nazareth, art thou come to destroy us? I know thee who thou art: the Holy One of God."[1] Jesus rebuked the spirit, saying, "Hold thy peace, and come out of him." "And the unclean spirit, convulsing him, and crying with a loud voice, came out of him."[2]

What was Jesus reacting to in what the man said to him? Why did he reject and cast out the spirit? Was he only concerned with the healing, or was he reacting to the *content* of what the man said? A rebuke to the possessed man could hardly have been the appropriate response for healing. It seems more likely that Jesus did not like what the man's demonic side called him because it placed Jesus in the apocalyptic Messianic tradition. The man, feeling sinful and unable or unwilling to repent, saw Jesus as the threat that could destroy him. Jesus had known in the wilderness that he was not going to be the apocalyptic Messiah, and that he was not going to accept any identification with that Messianic function. Did the unclean spirit say things because the man projected the apocalyptic Messiah on Jesus? Or was the man frightened, as Peter was, by the perception of Jesus' wholeness?

It is important to note that, whereas Luke follows Mark here, Matthew, who has also been following Mark, omits the incident of the demoniac addressing Jesus by these titles. Matthew also omits two similar situations where this happens[3] and twice insets quotations from Isaiah instead. Something is behind this in Matthew's mind, and the reason will be discussed in Chapter VI.

When Jesus left the synagogue "straightway"—a characteristic adverb of the book of Mark—he went to the house of Simon's ill mother-in-law. Here we find the first record of a healing incident separate from the exorcism of

1. Mk. 1:24; §24C.
2. Mk. 1:26; §24D.
3. Mt. omits Mk. 1:21-28 (§24), Mk. 1:34 (§25F), and Mk. 3:11 (§34E).

an unclean spirit.[1] Jesus took the woman's hand, raised her up, and the fever left her. The essence of this account is copied by Matthew, but in Luke it is changed to "He stood over her and rebuked the fever, and it immediately left her."[2] Obviously, Luke changes a natural event related to Jesus' presence into one where the healing is seen as closer to supernatural power (as discussed earlier).

That healings occurred in the life of Jesus cannot be doubted, and that healings occur in many other situations cannot be questioned, but it is necessary to see each healing in its own context and to try to account for the *source* of the healing. Did Jesus observe the fact of the healing? Did he take himself to be the healer, the major cause of healing? What did he contribute to the healing? In addition to looking at most of the healings, we shall later deal with the one unique place where Jesus spoke of and summarized the problem of healing.[3]

When his fame as a healer spread, many people—Mark says "all the city"—came to him. What follows immediately in Mark indicates Jesus' strong reaction against this reputation. Simon came to him, when he had gone into a desert place to pray, and said, "All are seeking thee." To this, Jesus responded, "Let us move so that I may preach, for to this end came I forth."[4] This statement decisively adds to the content of how he saw himself and his function after the wilderness. Teaching and preaching, rather than healing or any miraculous activity, were his dominant concerns. Interestingly enough, Luke at that point has, "For therefore was I sent."[5] This Lukan phrase changes the "for this end came I forth" into a statement where Jesus is a chosen instrument, a more passive vessel of the divine, rather than a chooser having a role to play in his own destiny. This Lukan shift deprives us of the sense of the emergent ego of Jesus at the time of his baptism and wilderness experiences. The Lukan account resembles

---

1. Mk. 1:29-33; §25A-D.
2. Lk. 4:39; §26B-C.
3. Mk. 6:5; §54J.
4. Mk. 1:36-38; §26B-C.
5. Lk. 4:43; §26C.

what is developed so fully in the Gospel of John. Jesus' emphasis on his preaching and teaching functions decisively confirms that the core of his life was to be devoted to fulfilling the Word of God in the exercise of the prophetic mission.

When he started his ministry, Jesus was accepted by those seeking healing and the authenticity of his teaching, as we have seen, but when he later met the authorities of the religious status quo, he was rejected.

II

"I Came not to Destroy the Law, but to Fulfill It"

How does Jesus deal with the laws and traditions of his people?

Does he overthrow them, ignore them, transform them, or what?

What is the relation of law and freedom?

What is behind and beyond following the laws for Jesus?

In the encounters that follow, Jesus' stand is so radical that at the end of them "the Pharisees and Herodians took counsel how they might destroy him."[1]

Why did opposition to him and rejection of his work begin so early? What did he do to bring this about? What boldness, conviction, and courage issued from his baptism and wilderness experiences? What consciousness enabled him to cut through those traditions that had become rigidified and unconnected to their original meaning?

1. Mk. 3:6; §33G.

The first incident in Mark[1] (copied by both Matthew and Luke) occurred in Capernaum, in a house crowded with people, so much so that there was no room for more. Jesus was there, obviously drawing many. Among them came four friends bearing a man "sick of the palsy." Because they could not enter the house due to its crowdedness, they uncovered the roof and let down their comrade on a pallet. They apparently were aware of Jesus' presence and its value for helping others, or they would not have acted as they did, so boldly and urgently.

These four friends could be actual persons or they could represent inner helpers. They did not do the healing but knew where to go for healing. They knew something of Jesus and his value. As inner figures they could be anyone or anything that helps move the sick, neurotic part of ourselves to a healing place. They are in this situation mediators between wound and healing. They are intrinsic elements of the whole process of healing, representing concern and compassion and knowledge of healing sources. As outer figures they are those who, in any of our lives, care enough and act on their caring enough to help us to have the courage to risk new and not usual ways to find wholeness.

The hole in the roof was a threshold not unlike the "narrow gate" in Jesus' parables. And Jesus helped this crippled man through the gate by saying, "Son, thy sins are forgiven." With no previous knowledge of this man except that he had been brought for healing, Jesus spoke not to the physical condition but to some deep inner anxiety or self-negation which must for the person have been the cause of his illness. The Jewish view of illness at that time was that it was caused by guilt for sins committed and could only be forgiven by God through specific sacrificial ritual acts. The wrath of God aroused through wrongdoing was customarily appeased by an act of animal sacrifice.

Jesus did not say, "I forgive you your sins," nor did he say, "God forgives you your sins." He did not say that the man had not sinned, nor did he say there was no need for forgiveness. He did not say, "Heal yourself." What could be

1. Mk. 2:1-12; §29A-H.

behind the shockingly simple statement "Thy sins are forgiven"? Forgiven by whom? By what action? How? Why? What was Jesus' insight and how did he come to know this truth? (In Christianity, the sacrifice of atonement has been put upon Jesus, the Christ. In Judaism, Israel was the suffering servant.) What is the position of Jesus relative to these? Certainly he did not see himself as savior or as the sacrificial lamb of Judaism. The sacrificial element was an inner change in the person and the saving element was what one did with that change.

Surely Jesus' baptism experience (which echoed with the sonship as stated in the Hebrew Scripture) gave him a rich and enduring sense of how human frailties can hold eternal meaning. It is possible that out of it he could know that a person could be fallible and sinful and in need of forgiveness, but that healing comes not from an outer sacrifice such as the sacrifice of an animal, or from belief that one group of people or one person became the sacrifice, but from the alteration or turning of a person coming to repentance. Jesus had come to John the Baptist seeking greater wholeness, sensing that this act of change of direction was what God wanted. By it the person and God came into rapport and relationship again. The personal action helped God to express His/Her overcoming of wrath by a new sense, in the human, of belonging. To be sure, the wrathful side might still be there and even produce alienation, but the other side of God, the living side, was available in a new way. In the Jewish Midrash, as we have seen, God prays, "May it be My will that My mercy may suppress My anger, and that My compassion may prevail over My other attributes." Through the descent of the Holy Spirit at Jesus' baptism, it was possible in a totally new way for him and other humans to help God to ensure that His/Her Love overcome Wrath. This is what happened in the episode of the paralyzed man.

Jesus' genius lay not in a totally new concept of God, but in a new concept of the human-God dialogue and its role in personal consciousness. This difference in Jesus' concept led to a new possibility of human freedom and rebirth. And this is borne out in a story of the paralytic. After his statement to the man, the scribes thought Jesus was blaspheming, was putting himself in the place of God, was saying that he had taken on the prerogative of God. To this accusation Jesus replied, "Is it easier to say to the sick of the palsy, Thy sins are forgiven; or to say, Arise, and take up thy bed, and walk?"[1] Forgiveness was redefined by him not as belief, or even as attitude, but as action.

This is not a sequential or causal matter. Two things are equal, of the same content and meaning. To be able to arise, to actually arise and to walk—this is forgiveness. The imperative command is to the Substance and to the Spirit* within it which enables movement. The wrathful side of God is not holding back or judging or forgiving. The person is free to act, to move, to change direction. There is something new now, not only about God, but about the human. The sacrifice of the person sick of the palsy had been the giving up of his defenses, pride, and self-will in seeking and acknowledging the value in Jesus. To let go of these attitudes was for the man to experience the death-rebirth archetype in himself. A resource within the person had become available to Jesus and he believed it to be available to others. His function was not in what he did in this situation, but in pronouncing the word "Arise"—the Word which was not identified with his ego and which was not derived from a sense of personal power. It was a word that arose from his depths, from the interior place where something new had been born in him and informed and brought to consciousness a new possibility, an impossible possibility!

To this is added the statement "That you may know that the Son of man has power on earth to forgive sins, I say unto you, Arise, take up thy bed, and go to thy house."[2] If this is a statement by Jesus, it is the first time we see the phrase "Son of man" used. I have serious critical questions about it here. If it was not said by Jesus, then we can see it as a Christian addition. It appears very soon again in connection with working on the Sabbath, where I would take it as an authentic statement.

It is an enigmatic phrase of great significance from the

1. Mk. 2:8-9; §29F.
2. Mk. 2:10-11; §29G.

Hebrew Scripture (appearing in Daniel, Ezekiel, and Enoch), and it also appears in the gospels in many forms, both apocalyptic and nonapocalyptic.[1] It appears very little after the time of Jesus and then finally dies out. The history of this archetype is fascinating, and Jesus' use of it and relation to it help in our understanding of his own self-identification.

In the Hebrew Scripture, it is used relative to kingship: "You are the fairest of the sons of men. . ." (Psalms 45:2), and relative to the individual person: "What is man that thou art mindful of him, or the son of man that thou dost care for him? Yet thou hast made him little less than God." (Psalms 8:4-5). Ringgren states that the king *could* have played the role of first man in such a passage.[2] In the first century B.C.E. the phrase was used in several ways. In Ezekiel, Ezekiel is addressed by God as Son of man. He is urged to listen to God and then to go and say God's words to the exiles regarding what they should do to keep God's covenants. Here the Son of man is a human being expressing God's desire and will, personally addressed by God. Whoever or whatever it refers to, it initiates a dialogue between God and a concerned man trying to help his people. Ezekiel uses the Hebrew *ben adam*, which is an idiom for an individual member of the human race, or human being. Ezekiel is probably closest to the use of the words by Jesus as we shall see.

The book of Daniel, in the second century B.C.E., describes the Son of man as a heavenly being who will break into history at the end of time eschatologically. This Son of man is not of the earthly sphere and is not an earthly king. The words in Daniel 7:13 are "I saw in the night visions, and behold, with the clouds of heaven there came one like a son of man . . . and to him was given dominion and glory and kingdom. . . ."

Son of man in 1 Enoch (130-64 B.C.E.) is an instrument of God who will intervene in history as an apocalyptic judge. This Son of man will separate the elect from the

---

1. Elizabeth B. Howes, *Intersection,* (San Francisco: Guild for Psychological Studies, 1971), pp. 171-97.
2. Ringgren, *Israelite Religion,* p. 231.

damned for all time.[1] In 1 Enoch (also called the Ethiopic Enoch), the Son of man is described as preexistent and as "chosen and hidden before God," but is also described as the judge at the end of time seated upon a throne of glory to choose and to separate the chosen from the rest of the people.[2] 2 Esdras describes a similar Son of man who rises from the sea, breathing fire, and who separates the elect from the others.[3] (The Messianic, apocalyptic Son of man in these later books was probably related, in part, to the Persian concept of primordial man.)

In the gospels, on the one hand, it appears in an apocalyptic form, describing one who was to break into history and separate the saved from the lost. However, it is also used in a nonapocalyptic way with three possible meanings. It is used in reference to a Messiah who will come to save humankind in history. It is used to refer to humankind in general. It is used to describe a special indwelling quality of judgment for actions. This last category puts the Son of man into the areas of existential living and universality.

It will be an essential part of our picture of Jesus to see how he used it. Here in the incident of the palsied person it would not be consistent to see this image as centering on Jesus, in the light of what he already said about forgiveness. Rather, it would seem to suggest that there is a deeper center within the human being out of which this profound movement of forgiveness issues.

The implication throughout this passage is that the dark, hurt, resistant, unacceptable sides of ourselves must find inner friends and be open to a new way of finding the Source of Love as Center. The symbol[4] of the healing reality here is found in Jesus. It is the reality he embodies and his clear words that constellate the healing. And countless symbols exist in our own tradition, as well, if we can discover and relate to them.

1.   1 Enoch XLVI:3-8.
2.   1 Enoch XLVIII:1-10.
3.   Esdras 2:13-15.
4.   See Appendix II on the role of symbols.

Following this incident at the crowded house in Capernaum, Jesus entered the house of Levi the Pharisee, where there were many publicans and sinners.[1] Levi had invited Jesus to his house, an unusual event, since Pharisees usually would have nothing to do with sinners and publicans in fear of ritual defilement, whereas Jesus allowed them to come to eat with him. In fact, one has the impression that he sought them out and thoroughly enjoyed them! He probably felt much closer to them. The Pharisee comments, "He eats and drinks with both publicans and sinners!" in what one may assume was a biting, critical tone of voice. What was the basis of their attitude about this? Out of what came this sharp cleavage, according to their judgment, between righteous and consciously held religious attitudes, and darkness and sinning?

This phenomenon is so common, so much a part of human beings, and so malicious in its result that it must be carefully examined. Jesus clearly did not agree with his critics. He had another criterion for action and judgment. These first encounters seem to give a clue to his whole attitude toward darkness and especially to that form of it which is evil. The mechanism behind the Pharisee's attitude is one where the dark side of personality, understood as both unknown and evil, is repressed into the unconscious and then is projected* out onto the individuals or groups. It is the work of Jung and Erich Neumann[2] that has helped us clarify this devastating mechanism of our human personality. What is unconscious in us is seen outwardly and thus considered by us as not being a part of ourselves. Thus it is not included in our wholeness. Our rigid collective ideas of goodness and righteousness have cut us off from knowing the full dimension of our total personhood. We are both light and dark, as is God, and our wholeness includes both, but we refuse to see it.

The unseeing Pharisees (and the Pharisee parts of ourselves) feel superior. So our outer world of humanity,

---

1. Mk. 2:13-17; §30.
2. See Erich Neumann, *Depth Psychology and the New Ethic* (London: Hodder & Stoughton, 1969).

then and now, is contaminated with the seemingly negative, despised part of us projected out. These rejected parts
of ourselves are the core of social, ethnic, and minority
problems, because our disowned sides are carried by
groups as well as by individuals. Outer social problems
reflect to a large degree the tension that such projections
cause.[1] What made in Jesus this difference in attitude? He
was able to move with the "sinners" as rejected, dark
parts, because he had encompassed his own darkness. His
relationship to these parts in himself enabled him to respond honestly to others.

Jesus answered the Pharisees, "They that are whole
have no need of a physician, but they that are sick; I came
not to call the righteous, but sinners."[2] Out of what in Jesus
did the statement come? Did he really believe the
Pharisees were the righteous ones? Did they think they
were? This was a bit of sarcasm, of irony. Jesus was affirming here that the one judged as sinner by the Pharisee was
far more open, flexible, and able to hear his message.
Those who relate to both sides are able to have ears for the
new, to be receptive and spontaneous. Jesus placed himself, as always, on the side of the poor, the hungry, and the
neglected ones, outer and inner. They had need of a physician and knew that they did. He was saying, in essence, "If
you don't feel the need of healing and wholeness, do not
trouble me. Stay with your egocentric righteousness and
let me go my way and do what for me is God's will!"

The third confrontation in Mark,[3] followed by Matthew
and Luke, began with the disciples of John asking Jesus
why his disciples did not fast. "And John's disciples and
the Pharisees were fasting: and they come and say unto
him, Why do John's disciples and the disciples of the
Pharisees fast, but thy disciples fast not? And Jesus said to
them, Can the sons of the bridechamber fast, while the
bridegroom is with them? As long as they have the
bridegroom with them, they cannot fast. But the days will

1. For techniques on how to deal with projections, see Appendix II.
2. Mk. 2:17; §30E, G.
3. Mk. 2:18-22; §31.

come when the bridegroom shall be taken away from them, and then they will fast in that day."

On what basis did Jesus' disciples break the rigidly held rules about fasting, the times being definitely specified by calendar? The question assumed that the disciples did not fast at all. What is Jesus' answer? He gave a symbolic answer, a symbolic statement which has received a great deal of Christian interpretation. (It may possibly have some actual accretion.) He stated that one did not need to fast at a wedding when the bridegroom is present and it is a joyous occasion, but fasting is for a time when the bridegroom is not present. (The bridegroom is perhaps here understood as a symbol of the Spirit being present, or of the combination of Spirit and Substance* as in a marriage rite.)

There are times for mourning and for joy. The decision comes from within. Jesus did not do away with fasting, but changed the basis for it. Here, as often, he went to the core of the matter, to the genesis of fasting and why it was needed in the first place. That he could decide what was the basis for fasting out of his own integrity and authority reveals the strength and depth of his character. It is not an easy thing to make an individual decision against collective standards. Only a mature individual can do that.

The Christian position has, on the whole, identified the bridegroom with Jesus. Many scholars would say that the words "the days will come when the bridegroom shall be taken away from them" could well be a later Christian addition after Jesus was deified by the Church. Coming close to the beginning of the Synoptic account, it would be important if we saw Jesus referring to himself and his presence as the basis for human action. It would be even more striking psychologically if Jesus was not referring to himself, but to some source of individual judgment within each person.

The Mark account follows with two striking symbolic statements:

> No man seweth a piece of undressed cloth on an old garment: else that which should fill it up taketh from it, the new from the old, and a worse rent is made.

And no man putteth new wine into old wine-skins: else the wine
will burst the skins, and the wine perisheth, and the skins: but they
put new wine into fresh wine-skins.[1]

These statements call for new vessels or garments to hold
newness for persons. The old and new in one sense cannot
be mixed—yet we shall often see Jesus combining old
elements of his tradition with strikingly new ones. The interrelationship of old and new is to be watched in his
teachings. Whether these statements apply only to the
question of fasting or are more general comments on his
own estimate of the radical nature of his teaching can be
left open.

The fourth confrontation with the authorities came
when his disciples plucked ears of grain on the Sabbath,
again a forbidden act in Jewish law.[2] Jesus' answer here
was in two parts, rather characteristic of him. First, he
referred to the tradition of King David eating the
shewbread when he and his followers were hungry and
had need. This was legal only for the priests. Then Jesus
plunged into the depths of the concept of the Sabbath.
"The sabbath was made for man, and not man for the sabbath."[3]

As to the genesis of the meaning of "Sabbath," the
seventh day was God's, to rest and enjoy His/Her creation.
For humans it was a time to remember God and thus implement the God-human dialogue. But at Jesus' time apparently the Sabbath had become hedged about by laws
and minutiae of detail, and had thus lost its original
creative meaning because its sacred significance had been
violated. The Mark account begins with relating the Sabbath to the human, and gives priority to personal need.
This is to say that what is needed for individual development is the basis for choice, rather than some pre-
determined rule. Is this to say all humans can do or have
what they want according to selfish and self-centered
needs? Not at all. Jesus went on to add an enriching, modi-

1. Mk. 2:21-22; §31 C, D.
2. Mk. 2:23-28; §32.
3. Mk. 2:27-28; §32 F-G.

fying statement. "The Son of man is lord even of the sabbath." He did not say that either God or human was lord of
the Sabbath, but that it was the Son of man who must
reflect something of God. The general statement about the
human is followed by the statement on the Son of man.

Is Jesus here identifying the Son of man with himself
and saying that only he can be lord of the Sabbath? If so, it
would be highly inconsistent with what we have seen him
say throughout the first part of his teaching. It seems,
rather, that the Son of man refers to an element of psychic
reality inside the natural human being, an element which
forms a basis for creative decision making. This would
enlarge the previous reference to the Son of man as being
an element within the psyche enabling the action of forgiveness. The Son of man becomes the bearer of choice,
able to go to the genetic point of issues. Such an inner element takes a choice of how to act on any religious law or
custom out of a set pattern and into individual choosing
based on the specificity of the situation. This is dangerous
indeed, because the line between an egocentric, negative,
self-oriented choice and some deeper source is very small.

The Son of man, for and in Jesus, seems to be emerging as a decisive supranatural element. The implications of
this are tremendous for the recreation of human beings,
society, and social institutions. Ultimately it is the question Who or what is to be trusted? Will we get more insight
from Jesus on this? How shall we discern this Son of man
within humans?

A significant and curious thing happens when we turn
to the account of the same occasion in Matthew and Luke[1].
For the first time and one of the few times, both Matthew
and Luke (who have been following Mark) omit the first
part of Jesus' recorded statement "The Sabbath was made
for man, and not man for the Sabbath." Through this
omission they turn the words of Jesus into a totally different answer. Without the premise of the Sabbath belonging to the human, the statement seems now to refer to

---

1. Mt. 12:8; Lk. 6:5; §32G.

Jesus himself as Son of man in a specialized, even Messianic, way. This dramatic shift, especially for Matthew, is to be questioned throughout. Matthew also adds two statements from the Hebrew Scripture where Jesus is affirming himself as above law and Temple.[1]

This concludes the first series of Jesus' encounters with the authorities and the second phase in the acceptance, rejection, and affirmation movement. These encounters reflect the actual situation, where the dynamic confrontations must have been perceived as threatening to the religious authorities and their solid, rigid structure of religious code and law.

After acceptance and rejection there is movement to the third phase, namely, to affirmation. Jesus the man began to stride through his world with courage and conviction born out of his experience of the baptism and wilderness. His own answer to God was being shaped as he moved through these and other situations. His first actions brought him into his world of concern and vitality for possible newness of depths of understanding of his own people. Nothing indicates that he was rejecting his tradition or his people. There is, rather, the sense that his love for his tradition and people would cause him to set his compass toward an ever-deepening grasp of the genius of his Judaic background. To plumb these depths would require his examination, analysis, and understanding of his background, not in a cold or unimpassioned way, but in an agonizing appraisal of the value of the old and a courageous openness to the possible emergence of the new that did, indeed, threaten the status quo and led him ultimately to the cross. And behind all this there is always the question How did Jesus achieve this way? How did he acquire this insight? Where did it come from, both inside himself and in his history?

Out of his boldness, integrity, and revolutionary spirit he moved into his first long discourse, commonly called the Sermon on the Mount (or in Luke, it is a Sermon on the

---

1. Mt. 12:5-7; §32D, E.

Plains). This discourse is found primarily in Matthew.[1] This is his great answer to preceding accusations. He began with "Think not that I came to destroy the law or the prophets: I came not to destroy, but to fulfill. For I say unto you, that except your righteousness shall exceed the righteousness of the scribes and Pharisees, you shall in no way enter into the kingdom of heaven."[2] This showed immediately that his concern was to get behind rigidity and codification to meaning, to the point of genesis of the laws and customs in the Hebrew Scripture. And beyond discovering meaning, he would also add how to fulfill these meanings. This is the third stage of affirmation.

To whom is this discourse addressed? In both Matthew and Luke, it is addressed to the disciples, understood as a much larger group than the twelve apostles. The sequence to be followed here will be that of Matthew 5:1-8. It begins with the Beatitudes, moves to the above statement about the fulfillment of the Law and illustrates five instances of this, speaks of ostentation and three religious practices, moves to three dynamic statements on relationships between people, and concludes with an invitation to enter the narrow gate that leads to life, and the description of the condition for entrance to the Kingdom of God as doing the Will of God. A more dramatic buildup to what evidently will be his central teaching could hardly be imagined.

The introduction in the Beatitudes takes two forms. The simpler one, in Luke, seems the original one. Jesus directly addressed his hearers—the poor, the downtrodden, the oppressed—with a series of blessings: "Blessed are you. . . ."[3] Just because of their outer and inner situations, because they did hunger and weep and were poor, they had an openness to receive what he was talking

---

1. Fritz Kunkel, *Creation Continues* (New York: Charles Scribners Sons, 1947), p. 8. Dr. Kunkel has stated that Matthew was a great architect in the way he built his book. Matthew has six discourses; within the discourses is material from several documents and editorial comment. Out of a variety of possibilities, there is an attempt here to find how it might have been stated by Jesus.
2. Mt. 5:17; 20; §36P, S.
3. Lk. 6:20-23; §36B-F.

about. These were people without defenses, or pride, or arrogance. He added that "you are the salt of the earth" and "the light of the world."[1] What groups actually thought themselves the "salt" and the "light" in those times? (Although these appear in Matthew, they seem to be part of Luke's Beatitudes from Document Q.) Obviously, the Pharisees and religious leaders thought of themselves so. Jesus came reversing this. The lesser, the least, he said, hold the possible value. The personal inner significance of this also forms part of Jesus' paradoxical religious thinking. Values do not necessarily lie where they seem to. The Matthew form of the Beatitude suggests a later Christian idealization, a series of beautiful but more abstract philosophical statements. A stunning contrast to the "blesseds" is to be found in a later discourse on the "woes" (in Matthew) spoken to the scribes and Pharisees as hypocrites. Again all seeming values are reversed.

After the Beatitudes Jesus made the statement on the Law, and his desire to fulfill it in depth. There are five laws, full of richness and depth of insight, dealing with anger, lust, simplicity of speech, relation to evil, and all-inclusiveness. In each of them Jesus started with "You have heard that it was said" (quoting from the Hebrew Scripture), and each time he continued with "But I say unto you." Thus he added his interpretation of the Law, taking it to a psychological depth that has never been surpassed. It is striking that Jesus did not use the prophetic form of the Word coming from Yahweh—i.e., "The Lord said unto me." Rather, the authority resided somehow within Jesus. "I say unto you" does not mean the "I" of the ego, but the "I" as manifesting the indwelling Word of the Lord. To understand the source of this authority and its relevance for the authority within human beings is one of the purposes of this book.

At the end of the examination of the five laws, Jesus still left unanswered the question of how to do these things, of how to act this way.

If we struggle hard enough to conform to the norms Jesus described, will we automatically follow them? This

1. Mt. 5:13-14; §36K-M.

has been a serious Christian problem, for on the whole these norms have been accepted as ethical standards to follow. They have been assumed to be the *way* to enter the narrow gate—which Jesus spoke about later—but the history of Christianity in no sense reveals the fruits that one might expect from following these norms. So we might question whether these are the *way*, or are they the *outcome* of something else to be followed? Are they the *way* of transformation, or a description of how a person who is transformed might act?

The first law, from Hebrew Scripture, states: "Thou shalt not kill." Jesus added that behind killing is anger that must be dealt with:

> Ye have heard that it was said to them of old time, Thou shalt not kill; and whosoever shall kill shall be in danger of the judgement: but I say unto you, that every one who is angry with his brother shall be in danger of the judgement; and whosoever shall say to his brother, Raca, shall be in danger of the council; and whosoever shall say, thou fool, shall be in danger of the hell of fire. If therefore thou art offering thy gift at the altar, and there rememberest that thy brother hath aught against thee, leave there thy gift before the altar, and go thy way, first be reconciled to thy brother, and then come and offer thy gift.[1]

He did not condemn anger; he did not say, "Do not get angry," but he did say, "If you get angry you are in danger of a judgment and, therefore, do something about it." What is the judgment? *Raca* meant "fool" or "scoundrel" in Aramaic. If one allows anger to stay, then one is expressing totally the dark side of oneself, and perhaps of God, and the wrath of God is expressed without any balancing other side. Any integration of the two is delayed. We meet, then, the fact of the problem of the two sides of our own nature, and the possibility that these reflect the nature of God. The previously quoted Midrash prayer comes to mind. In this prayer of God it is the desire and longing of God for the Will toward Love to overcome the ambivalence. For this to happen, consciousness in the human is required. Jesus affirmed that it is possible to deal with anger and pointed the way which leads to reconciliation.

1. Mt. 5:21-24; §37A.

The first step is to go to the altar, or if one is at the altar and discovers anger, to "leave the gift and go to be reconciled to the brother." This step itself involves a seemingly easy, but actually enormously difficult, affirmation, i.e., in the presence of God at the altar to acknowledge the darkness of anger, whether it has been caused by what one has done or by what has been done to one. The clause "if thy brother hath aught against thee" suggests something of provocation. This acknowledgment comes hard to us who have been schooled in perfectionism and being "good,"and our great sins are easier to admit than the pettiness of small anger and irritation. Yet it is the sum of the small sins in us that, if not dealt with, leads to violence and outbreaks of hatred, personally and socially. Infectiousness is the result.

Following the discovery of anger, the gift is to be left when one goes to one's brother. How can this gift be understood? Not, surely, just as an outer sacrifice, but as the offering of oneself to the God whose presence is known at the altar. This offering remains at the altar as the symbol of relatedness of one's conscious side to the Source, while the part caught in anger is dealt with. And who may the "brother" be? It may be an outer person, male or female, with whom alienation has occurred. It may be necessary to go to that person in a spirit of openness and willingness to dialogue toward understanding. It may be the brother or sister inside, an inner component of one's total personality. The problem may have been touched off by an outer situation that has aroused the inner shadow,* understood as that part of ourselves we like least to look at and acknowledge. The fact that one has been to the altar changes greatly what one brings to the confrontation, outer or inner. Without the religious value of the Presence, the anger can be so powerful it overwhelms. Such is the nature of wrath in us. With the religious value at one's center, the situation is seen in a different perspective and becomes capable of transformation.

The best way of confrontation is through written dialogue.[1] The outcome of such a dialogue, such a meeting with the dark other, can lead to a reconciliation with the brother. Does that always mean an outer change, so difficult if the outer other makes no effort? One may hope for that, but not expect it. The reconciliation must first be understood and experienced as two opposing elements within, coming into mutuality. And if this is actualized between persons, a further step is achieved. Some point not in the middle but beyond the opposites—a third new point—is achieved whereby the two opposing elements are transmuted into newness. And one may ask from the place of the third point, what may it be wanting? Is it that God, the *unus mundus*,* the third point, waits in the wings for humans to open themselves to His/Her grace? With reconciliation, one returns to the altar and offers one's gift. How will the gift then be different from what the gift was before the work of confrontation and reconciliation was performed? Now the gift of oneself is more total, more inclusive, because the dark part is not left out but is part of the whole. And the reconciliation becomes a gift received and thus the split is defeated. One stands more naked, whole, simple, humble, and imperfect.

In the second law, Jesus quoted from Hebrew Scripture, "Thou shalt not commit adultery."[2] This was understood then as sexual relationship with another man's wife. But Jesus went on to say that adultery consists not only in the overt sexual act but also in lust, and he issued a radical and difficult injunction that if one lusts the need is to cast out the eye or the hand that does the lusting. What is lust? If one takes it outside the sexual area, it can be seen that lust is an inordinate desire to possess any object, animate or inanimate, to manipulate things as one wants, thus to act from compulsion and not from free choice. If that be true, then lust in the sexual area would also be compulsion and must be differentiated from sexual desire.

Sexual desire becomes lust only when allowed to become inordinate and possessive. Lust is characterized

1. See Appendix II.
2. Mt. 5:27-30; §37C.

by manipulation, desire to control, egocentricity, domination, and insensitivity to the needs of the other as well as to one's own need, perhaps, for real relatedness. Lust does not give space or time to relatedness and growth between persons. It violates one of the main characteristics of God, which is Love. It thwarts the heart's true desire. Lust and love do not go together, for there is no "other" in lust; there is blind, subtle, autoerotic satisfaction. The lusting person becomes an It instead of an I, and the person being lusted after becomes an It.

Because the treatment for lust in the words of Jesus is so strong, one must see how deeply wrong it was in his mind. To know the real value of sexuality is to take lust seriously, so that real desire and love can be accepted creatively. This insight about the nature of lust must have come from a person who knew what lust was and who honored the nature of true sexuality in love in not wanting to see it violated. For egocentricity contaminates true sexuality. The harsh treatment recommended for lust was in proportion to the value to be discovered. What was that treatment? It was to pluck out the right eye or to cut off the right hand if they offended or caused to stumble.

What could this mean symbolically? It has been taken literally by some during the ages, but nothing in Jesus' way of thinking supports this kind of literalness. Rather, the truth behind the symbol needs to be discovered. The eye perceives; the hand is the organ of holding and doing. Each is very active in relation to the person. If either organ is contaminated by the egocentricity of lust, the perception of the eye or the creative doing by the hand is woefully impaired and there is a need to get rid of this attitude of the eye and the hand. It is perplexing to many whether Jesus was here speaking of a one-time event, or of a continuous transforming process. One must see his total teaching to answer this, but the emphasis throughout will probably make us favor the second postion. Egocentricity is not done away with in one dramatic action, but an egocentricity such as this may have to involve a continuous drastic activity of one's conscious life with a part of one's psyche that is self-willed.

The third law from the Hebrew Scripture stated that one must swear only to God, but Jesus went on to say not to swear to anyone or anything "by heaven, by the earth, by Jerusalem, or by the head." Rather, he said, "let your speech be, Yea, yea; Nay nay."[1] Let your speech be of absolute simplicity and integrity. To say what we mean and to mean what we say is an art of great achievement, for the tendency to want to justify, to rationalize, to elaborate, is very strong. The statement of Jesus related to integrity of speech came out of respect for the use of words as expression of the Word. Words are bits of the Word in concrete situations, and the Word as Logos, as meaning at the human level, is God expressed. Therefore, "yea" and "nay" are to be treated as sacred.

It is creative to keep in mind the question raised before as to what was *behind* what Jesus said throughout this discourse. In these first laws dealing with anger, lust, and speech, Jesus called for a way of behavior that involves great consciousness. Is this way of behavior itself the *way* to Life and the fulfillment of God's will, or is this way of behavior an expression and fulfillment of something already achieved? If so, what is to be achieved?

The fourth law Jesus dealt with was "An eye for an eye, and a tooth for a tooth." Here is absolute, equal retaliation: we do back what has been done to us. This is equal justice. It seems right on the surface. But Jesus said, "Resist not evil: and if you are struck on one cheek, turn the other; and if you are required to give a coat, give more; or if compelled to go a mile, go more."[2] The implication behind much of the old law is that evil should be met by evil—in essence, that two wrongs make a right.

As I said before, both the evil and the good are present in the Godhead, as in Deuteronomy where God says, "I create good and I create evil."[3] The Midrash prayer expresses the desire of God to move to a third point of Love beyond both opposites, and it is the human who can help to increase love over evil. That is the superb meaning of

1. Mt. 5:33-38; §37F.
2. Mt. 5:38-41; §37G-I.
3. Isa. 45:7 (King James Version).

Jesus' statement. The abundance of meeting evil with non-resistance becomes clearer. Usually we meet evil by expressing evil, or by repressing it and pretending it is not there, or by projecting it onto another and becoming defensive. But the way Jesus describes is the way of complete acknowledgment of the evil, a direct confrontation with it, and a commitment to work with it and to transform it into love and mercy.

Nothing is harder, Jung says. As Christians we have avoided the deep individual meaning of this by making the injunction not to resist evil primarily social. But this is not its primary meaning. Its deepest original meaning is to look at the evil and the shadow in ourselves, and work with it there. This requires an honesty and faithfulness to self-discovery that is not easily come by. Everything in our Christian culture has told us to be good, perfect, and without blemish. This very struggle blinds us and represses the dark side of ourselves—our own ambivalences, insensitivities, and cruelties.

Out of deep personal struggling with the inner adversary, a social point of view of nonviolence can be achieved. Perhaps the most beautiful instance of this overcoming of the adversary is the story of Jacob's wrestling with the angel, where he says to the adversary, "I will not let you go until you bless me."[1] Within the core of evil resides a blessing. It is clear that most nonviolent movements have failed because deep personal darkness has not been met. When it has been met, as in the case of a Martin Luther King, Jr., or a Gandhi, then the social impact of the movement is strong. Unless darkness is met within the person first, it will come out in subtle, unconscious ways. All our evil must be looked at and transformed personally. How?[2]

The fact that Jesus later says, "Sufficient unto the day is the evil thereof" puts further emphasis on the ever-present reality of evil, outer and inner. There is no escaping that evil is part of things, that it is of the nature of reality. If we keep it split off with the traditional position that "all good is from God, all evil from man" (*omne bonum a*

1. Gen. 32:26.
2. See Appendix II for some concrete suggestions.

Deo, omne malum ab homine), then it is never dealt with as part of the *tremendum*. The injunction in the gospel of John "Behold the Lamb of God which taketh away the sins of the World'"[1] puts the responsibility for eliminating evil on belief in the person of Jesus Christ. For Jesus, sin and evil were not "taken away" even by an inner process, but were to be transformed.

The fifth law follows the fourth in a natural sequence. The old law "Thou shalt love thy neighbor and hate thine enemy" is replaced by "Love your enemies, and pray for them that persecute you."[2] The differentiation between neighbor and enemy is kept by Jesus the realist. There is no pretense that all are our neighbors, for this is not true. But he does advocate love over hate, "that you may be sons of your Father which is in heaven: for he maketh his sun to rise on the evil and the good, and sendeth rain on the just and the unjust." The term "which is in heaven" is a Matthean usage; Mark and Luke have "Kingdom of God," not "of heaven." Therefore it is undoubtedly the more original.

The change, therefore, from hate to love is based on becoming sons of the Father who is all-inclusive in bestowing the good things of nature. And when what Jesus reportedly says as "Ye therefore shall be perfect as your heavenly Father is perfect'"[3] is translated as "You therefore shall be all-inclusive," a whole new meaning is revealed. "Perfect" means to be whole or sound, or "to be turned with the whole will and being, to God, as he is turned to us.'"[4] Few things have done more damage to human nature than the attempt to be perfect in the usual sense. Whether perfection is achieved or not, the goal itself is inhibiting and repressive because it keeps down all the imperfect and growing elements of oneself. To be all-inclusive means including light and dark, and letting go of all the ego images one has of one's self as at least struggling to be good and perfect, even if not achieving it. All-inclusive means giving

1.   Jn. 1:29 §154.
2.   Mt. 5:43-45; §37L, N, P.
3.   Mt. 5:48; §37R.
4.   Alan Richardson, ed., *Theological Word Book of the Bible* (New York: Macmillan Publishing Co., 1950), p. 167.

up a simple way of looking at one's self and others, and admitting we are duplex and complicated beings with mixed emotions, with things in our unconscious not yet known to our conscious side. This means to be compassionate to our own and to other people's dark side in the hope of transformation.

To return to the question put earlier: How is one to achieve these ways of acting as stated by Jesus in these laws? Is it a matter of pure determination and will? Can a person's ego alone achieve reconciliation of outer anger, elimination of lust, simplicity of speech, nonresistance to evil, and all-inclusiveness through commitment to these qualities as good ethical norms? This has been tried and certainly has not eminently succeeded, judging by the world we live in. No, we must search deeper, realizing that this achievement came out of Jesus' experience, and learning where that experience can be ours and can bear such fruits. Are the laws the way of transformation, or the fruits and action of a transformed person? If so, how is the transformation achieved? Where, if anywhere, will we find these fruits? Also, where did insights come from for Jesus? How did he achieve this level of perspective? These questions must continuously be kept in mind.

Following these laws, Jesus warned against the hypocrisy of ostentation: "Do not do your righteousness before men, to be seen of them; else you have no reward with your Father which is in heaven."[1] In the instances of religious customs, almsgiving, praying, and fasting, he contrasted the reward from men in the street and the reward from the Father. It is striking that Jesus did not do away with reward—again the realist—but shifted the reward from the human egocentric ones of praise, flattery, and approbation from others to the reward of being approved and loved by God inwardly. The phrase "in secret" is repeated twice each time. "Do the almsgiving, praying, and fasting in secret and the Father which seeth in secret shall recompense thee."[2] Jesus learned this at the baptism experience. Thus he conveyed his deep knowledge that God sees in

1. Mt. 6:1; §37S.
2. Mt. 6:4, 6, 18; §37T, U, Y.

secret, in the heart of persons, that God is in the interior, immanently working there. The action done within is accessible to that aspect of God which dwells within.

Three statements on human relationships follow.[1] They are statements of profound insight into the complexity of the human personality, discerned by Jesus and today being rediscovered primarily through the tools of depth psychology. The first statement is "Judge not, that you be not judged. For with what judgment you judge, you shall be judged." Is Jesus here condemning judgment, making a flat statement of "Don't judge"? A careful reading of the words does not suggest this. In fact, Jesus seldom says "do" or "don't" without giving reasons. Rather, he states that when we judge, or how we judge, will reflect back on what or how we are judged. Our statements concerning another, the nature of our perception or insight in evaluations, will expose us, will reveal where this judgment comes from in us, and that revelation and exposure will bring back on ourselves the reaction of the other people to it. Beware how we judge, lest the source of our judging bring certain things to us. If we judge from a negative, ego-centered, manipulative source, then the judgment is distorted, and not only is the object of it hurt, but we are hurt. The judgment then will come back to us, not only from the other person's reaction, but from the unconsciousness with which we judged. Something inside us works and wants to be used creatively in the service of the whole, a moral fact of discrimination, judgment, evaluation. When this faculty is misused, there are dire results; when it is used creatively, the judgment comes clear and clean. Judgment not used creatively becomes judgmental.

The next statement follows inevitably as the rationale behind the injunction not to judge:

> And why beholdest thou the mote that is in thy brother's eye, but considerest not the beam that is in thine own eye? Or how wilt thou say to thy brother, Let me cast out the mote out of thine eye: and lo, the beam is in thine own eye? Thou hypocrite, cast out first the

---

1. Mt. 7:1, 3-5, 12; §38F, I, L.

beam out of thine own eye; and then shalt thou see clearly to cast
out the mote out of thy brother's eye.[1]

What is essentially described here? It is that we tend to
worry and be concerned about motes and specks in others,
to criticize them and feel negative, and do not face the bigger beam. The darkest things in ourselves we are quite
blind about become so hidden in the recesses of our depths
that we tend to see them only in others. This is to be differentiated from genuine, objective criticism which comes
from a centered place.

Seeing these negativities only in other individuals and
whole groups of people is the psychological basis of racial
and religious intolerance. Groups different from ourselves—-
ethnic, economic, or religious—tend to carry for us the
qualities we do not know or would not like if they were in
us. As Jung said, "We do not project, projection happens."[2]
It is a totally unconscious phenomenon until some consciousness is brought to it and we slowly begin to face and
integrate these projected elements within ourselves. The
problem of dealing with projection is very subtle. There is a
growing tendency today to assume that a projection is
solved because it is seen or known. That is not the case,
because having intellectual insight into the mechanism of
projection is not the same as dealing with the tremendous
archetypal energy of the projection. Unsolved projection is
certainly a wonderful device to keep us from facing our
own darkness.

As we saw when dealing with evil, the evasion of darkness is very deep. To make someone else a scapegoat is an
unconscious, natural device. Yet at the same time, if faced,
darkness can become a central tool for self-discovery and
wholeness. If the courage is there to work with it for transformation, much value is achieved. We then know more
about ourselves than we did earlier, and that is to know
more of God's working within. Projection, therefore, is
helpful as a tool. Even though Jesus here was referring to
negative things, beams and motes, it must be realized that
we can also project positive things. This may not seem to

1. Mt. 7:3-5; §38I.
2. Jung, *Aion*, p. 9.

be a problem, but it is, because it deprives us of the reality of that which is inside our own psyche. It leaves us partial and too dependent on the other.

A significant area of projection is that of love in man-woman relationships where masculine or feminine gets projected onto the partner. However, projection extends to all relationships, especially those between parent and child. We tend to project authority onto leaders, ministers, doctors, and therapists. This is important and helpful if dealt with and internalized. Most centrally in the religious realm we have projected onto Jesus himself the roles of savior and carrier of the divine, and have failed to actualize these in ourselves. Jesus has carried for people the light Christ as symbol of the Self. This has been the cornerstone of the church. Today we need to know the reality behind this and experience it inside ourselves.[1]

This leads to the last of the three statements on relationship—one of the best known and least understood of Jesus' teachings. It is the golden rule: "All things therefore whatsoever ye would that men should do unto you, even so do ye also unto them: for this is the law and the prophets."[2] Read it as it stands, and seek better understanding, for surely the way it has been interpreted has not been very effective. If I want to know how to treat someone, where do I look? Clearly, it says, "Look at what you yourself want and how *you* want to be treated." It does not say, "Try to see what the other person wants." It says, "Look at how *you* want to be treated."

If we stopped to make a list of how we really want to be treated, it might be quite revealing to us: not how we want to be treated on the surface, but deeper in our core. Our list might include such things as the desire to be treated with respect, consideration, honesty, sensitivity, challenge, and loving kindness. If this is our desire, what is being said? That we need to treat the other this way. This sounds simple, but it is in fact not simple but very difficult because it requires great objectivity. To look intensely at our own deepest subjectivity (how we want to be treated) and then

1. See Appendix II on ways to deal with projections.
2. Mt. 7:12; §38L.

to look into others and treat them that way would be greatly to enhance human relationship.

If we put this statement alongside the second commandment (which appears later)—"Love thy neighbor as thyself"—we have not only the essence of Jesus' social teaching, but great insight into how he saw God at work within the human community. We have here a process of how to treat others, but the specific actions each time must be each individual's decision. This is yet another aspect of the existential dimension of the transcendent God working in the webbing and connective linkages between people.

If we take seriously the three statements on judgment, projection, and the golden rule, questions arise. How do we live them? What kind of person can do these things? Are they process or outcome? Does their achievement depend on something first happening within the person? The same kinds of questions emerge as were asked earlier about the laws as processes and outcomes.

We come to the conclusion of Matthew's first discourse.[1] Within these short verses we find strong statements of opposite ways of living, exhortation to choice of the way to life, and possibly a clue to the underlying question that has appeared over and over, namely, *how* to achieve these attitudes in action. The impact of these fresh interpretations by this young Jew must have been overwhelming to those he reached. We have to get past our familiarity with them and our assumed understanding of them to let them yield meaning and freshness.

The first exhortation is

> Enter ye in by the narrow gate: for wide is the gate, and broad is the way, that leadeth to destruction, and many be they that enter in thereby. For narrow is the gate, and straitened the way, that leadeth into life, and few be they that find it.[2]

Perhaps no statement of Jesus' is more challenging, leaves gray so untouched, and stays with black and white.

1. Mt. 7:13-29; §38M-X.
2. Mt. 7:13-14; §38M.

There are for him two ways, two outcomes, and one choice. Symbolically, the ways are entrance through a narrow or wide gate, the choice is between a broad or straitened way, and the outcome is achieving either life or destruction. Nothing could be clearer. There is no shilly-shallying between. What do these ways describe, psychologically and symbolically, and what do the outcomes of life and destruction refer to? To enhance the richness, let us also consider the outcomes in the two other descriptions which complete the discourse. In these passages Jesus contrasts a good with a corrupt tree, which bring forth good and evil fruit respectively. The tree can only produce the fruit which belongs to it.[1] He also contrasts the building of two houses, one on sand and one on rock, and their outcomes: one stands the buffeting of the storm; the other falls with the storm.[2]

Do destruction, bad fruit, and the downfall of the house all describe symbolically the negative outcome of choosing the wide gate and the broad way, or of letting oneself become a corrupt tree, or of building on the shifting element of sand? And life, good fruit, the house on the rock that stands the storm—do all these describe the positive outcome of choosing the narrow gate and the straitened way, of becoming the good tree, and of building a house on solid rock? These are three vivid descriptions of outcomes. They can be characterized as a life of futility, boredom, sterility, hecticness, meaninglessness, versus a life of meaning, fulfillment, adventure, spontaneity.

The gate leading to destruction suggests plenty of space where many people go together as a collective body in groups, thereby avoiding individual challenge. The narrow gate suggests a gate which is so narrow one must enter alone without much baggage or encumbrance. There may be many others who have entered through it, but not at the same time. It is individual. The contrasting descriptions of the two ways as broad and straitened suggest an easygoing, smooth, collective way versus one of constraint, difficulty, and discipline. A strait way is not straight, a

---

1. Mt. 7:19-20; §38T.
2. Mt. 7:24-27; §38W.

distinction that is often overlooked. It may be very circuitous and labyrinthine, thereby demanding more consciousness. There will inevitably be much difficulty. Indeed, there will be on the straitened way much falling by the wayside into the gutter, but not a retreat back through the gate. It is conspicuous that the *way* to enter is not stated here, just the exhortation to enter. Entering the narrow gate and embarking on the strait way need to be done, but how? An answer is suggested in the statement where Jesus contrasts the building of the two houses. The person who builds on rock is likened to "everyone which heareth these words of mine, and doeth them," while the person who builds on sand is likened to "everyone that heareth these words of mine, and doeth them not."[1]

These words come at the end of the discourse, after the one central statement, not yet examined here, which may hold the key to the "how," the method behind everything in this discourse. It is so well known that we must try to forget that we have ever known it. Jesus says, "Not every one that saith unto me, Lord, Lord, shall enter into the kingdom of heaven; but he that doeth the will of my Father which is in heaven."[2]

What does not lead to the Kingdom of God is calling Jesus "Lord, Lord,"—or perhaps calling anyone else "Lord, Lord." This in itself gives insight into where Jesus placed the emphasis, which was not on himself or any other religious figure, but on an attitude toward God. For how many years have we been taught that "to believe on him" as Lord is enough? The distinction between Jesus' own evaluation of himself and most later developments is indeed striking.

The outcome of the action described here is the entrance into the Kingdom of God. It does not seem strange to assume that entrance into the way of Life and entrance into the Kingdom of God would be describing the same thing. To be in the Kingdom is to have life. The new element here, the challenging one, is the statement of the Way, of

1. Mt. 7:24, 26; §38W.
2. Mt. 7:21; §38U.

something that can be done voluntarily, of something that is inclusive and not only specific. It does not deal with any one area of personality or behavior. It is qualitatively of a different sort. What is it?

To do the will of God implies certain assumptions. It assumes God has, or is, will; has intentionality; is characterized by purpose and meaning. God is a potentiality that wants to become active in history. This working of God in personal situations and in history, constantly intervening with challenge and demands for action beyond the natural choices, was not new to the Jew. In the books of Job, Jonah, and some of the prophets, this is a recurrent theme, yet what may Jesus have included that enlarges the totality?

The exhortation to do the will of God *assumes* that this will can be known, and can be acted upon if it is chosen. Three factors interweave and need careful scrutiny. These factors are choice to do the will of God, the knowledge of what that will is, and the doing of it. Which comes first? A central question. Do the specific moments of meaning, the insight into what the Will is, come before the choice to do it? Or must the choice to do the will of God precede the specific knowledge of what it is? If one takes the first position—that perception comes first—then every choice, every situation, has to be worked through in terms of whether one will do it. And there is not necessarily any clarity of perception as to what the will of God is, because the choice to do it has not been made. One's prejudiced, personal predilections will all color the choice.

The second way, that of choosing to do the will of God *before* one knows what it is in the specific situation, so alters the perception and so cleanses the personal desire that there is a much greater chance that the best and deepest value in the situation will be found. This act of all-inclusive choice demands utmost integrity and sincerity. It is to affirm in all situations that no matter what the content is—pleasurable or painful, easy or difficult—we will act out of what we see as the Will of the highest and deepest value, and that this also is to affirm intentionality in God at each moment of time. It is to say that no matter where the Will leads, we will follow. Desire becomes focused and single.

Why will this act lead to life? Why will this act prove to be the basic one for action on all the preceding laws? Why will this all-inclusive act of choice transform personality so deeply that it can be said one has entered the Kingdom of God, one has moved to a new realm? Instead of the egocentric will that dominates and pushes us into unfulfilled lives, it is possible now to see life lived in the new kingdom of "He/She." Instead of constrained sterility, futility, and unhappiness because we do not get our own way, there is a new blossoming, a rebirth, and a new purposiveness.

Again the laws *precede* the all-inclusive commitment to the will of God as discovered existentially. Are the two statements on doing the Will and fulfilling the five laws the same? Are the five laws the fruit of entering the gate, or the prerequisite to entering the gate? Perhaps the creative way is to see the five laws as signposts, guides for choice, but not giving specific instructions. They are fundamentally sound observations on ethical perceptions based on reality of psychic depths. These five laws would follow the commitment of entrance into the narrow gate and help in their transforming implementation. This concludes the first discourse.

A highly determinate question is now put to Jesus for the first time. "Now when John heard in the prison the works of the Christ [or Lord, in Luke] he sent his disciples, and said unto him, Art thou he that cometh, or look we for another?"[1] This had been asked explicitly by the demoniacs, and implicitly by the figure of Satan in the wilderness, but never to Jesus directly. Jesus' answer must have a deep hearing. It was to John's movement that Jesus had originally come, responding to the apocalyptic message. When John asked the question here, was he asking about an apocalyptic or a political Messiah?

Whatever John was asking, the answer of Jesus is clear in its ambiguity. He did not say yes and he did not say no. He answered in several stages, as was often his method. First he quoted Isaiah: "The blind receive their sight, and the lame walk, the lepers are cleansed, and the

1. Mt. 11:2-3; Lk. 7:19; §41A.

deaf hear, and the dead are raised up, and the poor have good tidings preached to them."[1] By pointing out the things that were happening, or had been promised and which obviously had happened at the time of Isaiah, this quotation linked Jesus directly to the prophetic tradition—as was also true in his first appearance in the synagogue. There was healing: blind, lame, deaf were being transformed and receiving new fruits. Jesus says, "It is happening, but I am not doing it." Implied also is that no one else is coming. (It is striking that the one phrase not in the original Isaiah but included here is the phrase " and the dead are raised up." This is obviously a Christian interpolation.)

The second stage of Jesus' answer is found in the enigmatic words "Blessed is he, whosoever shall find none occasion of stumbling in me."[2] The RSV translation has "who takes no offense in me." Strange and provocative statement, it reveals much of Jesus' insight into himself and into what he is arousing! It in no way pushes his answer into a yes or no. Could it mean, blessed are the persons who do not attempt to put me into categories, who do not find their estimate of me to be a factor in their own development, who are able to see clearly what role I am and am not playing, who are not caught in projection onto me which can cause them to stumble? Behind all possible interpretations, this much seems to be valid and true: Jesus is not making himself the center or decisive point for people's belief or reaction to him. Events belonging, perhaps, to the expectation of the Messianic age are happening around him, but he is not producing them, and in fact he is saying the person is blessed who does not attribute the events to the wrong source. He personally is not the source, but rather the channel through which something happens. This, then, is the really "good news"—that he is a catalyst in the divine-human process. This is a much harder role to maintain than identification with the power.

1. Isa. 29:18-19, 35:5-6, 61:1; Mt. 11:5; Lk. 7:22; §41C.
2. Mt. 11:6; §41C.

Jesus continued with his answer as John's disciples moved away. He spoke to the multitude. In rich and elaborate terms he praised John as being a prophet and "more than a prophet."[1] He was, Jesus said, no wishy-washy person in soft raiment, but a strong person not shaken by the wind. This was the first and only time Jesus praised the man who was the instrument of his own rebirth, whose movement formed the background of his whole life and teaching. John the Baptist is a strong, dynamic person, more than a prophet, the greatest person born of woman, but, Jesus continued, "yet he that is but little in the Kingdom of God is greater than he."[2] This appears a shocking statement and one may try to avoid what is said, not wanting to face the strong characterization that Jesus makes. But it is there, and I believe Jesus said it. Those in the Kingdom, as Jesus saw it, are greater than those born of any human, even greater than John of the prophets. There is the birth greater than the natural one through which there is entrance to the Kingdom. We do not yet know all that is involved in the price of the Kingdom, for the only statement so far has been "He who does the will of God shall enter the Kingdom." But, surely, did John not think he was doing the will of God?

What clues do we have at this point as to major differences between Jesus' and John's concepts? Three major areas present themselves for contrast: the nature of the Kingdom, the role of the Messiah, and the price of individual entry. With John, the Kingdom would be established through a cataclysmic, divisive act whereby the good would be saved and the evil burned up. For Jesus, the Kingdom would not come through an apocalyptic act of division, but would be inclusive as God was inclusive. For John, the Kingdom would be ushered in by the apocalyptic Messiah and the price to be paid was deep repentance and baptism. It was no longer enough only to be a good Jew. For Jesus, there evidently was a sense that the Kingdom was *now*, a present reality, and one could enter or not as

1. Mt. 11:7-9; §41D.
2. Mt. 11:11; 41E.

one chose. For John, it was achieved through repentance and specific acts.

These crucial and fundamental differences will become increasingly clearer. They form the core of the good news about the Kingdom that Jesus was proclaiming. Jesus continued, "And whereunto shall I liken this generation?"[1] He compared John as an ascetic with himself, acting out the Son of man as a "winebibber, a friend of publicans and sinners. And Wisdom is justified by her children."[2] Here again is a contrast. John acts from a harsh masculine principle, Jesus from a great Feminine divine reality which includes all. These two men stand as two men of great courage, as a bridge between late Jewish apocalyptism and new religious evolution.

1. Mt. 11:16; §41J.
2. Mt. 11:19; §41J.

III

"All Their Sins Shall Be Forgiven But One"

Who or what forgives?

Why is it that the prostitute responds?

What is the role of the human and of God in forgiveness?

Why is blasphemy the one unforgivable sin?

The incident of Jesus affirming the forgiveness of the man sick of palsy has been discussed—that amazing scene where Jesus out of his own knowledge of repentance and acceptance encompasses a new relation of human to God, different from the traditional Judaic concept.

Two scenes on forgiveness follow. The first incident[1] has a parallel account,[2] which raises the question of whether this is one incident repeated or two incidents. I would take this story in Luke as the primary story and treat it as historical, and agree with Perrin that whether these stories were exactly as told or not, they are true to Jesus' methods and beliefs. He states, "Although we are

1. Lk. 7: 36-50; §42
2. Mk. 14: 3-11; §137

not prepared to argue for the authenticity of any of the materials, we are arguing for the authenticity of such an element in the historical ministry of Jesus."[1]

Jesus had been invited to the house of a Pharisee, which in itself was unusual considering their continued criticism of him. However, all Pharisees were not the same. There were great differences among them. It was a festive time of eating and drinking. According to the customs of the times, the guests had "removed their sandals at the entrance, normally to wash their feet. This noticeably had not been done for Jesus."[2] Guests reclined like spokes of a wheel around a common dish in the center. In the midst of this scene a woman "of the streets" entered, "bringing an alabaster cruse of ointment and standing behind at his feet, weeping. She began to wet his feet with her tears, and wiped them with the hair of her head, and kissed his feet and anointed them with the ointment."[3]

To understand the intensity and the profound significance of her action and Jesus' response to it, something of the social milieu of the times must be seen, for every step she took was radical. At that time, because women were definitely considered inferior, they did not take part in collective social activities, nor was there a women's section in the synagogue. They were allowed outdoors only with their heads covered with a veil or with their hair arranged in a topknot. The word "harlot" meant "she who goes outdoors." This helps us understand her radicalism. She went where she was forbidden; let down her hair, which was the sign of prostitution; and went directly to Jesus, trusting him. Jesus had shown himself as one who was companionable with sinners and tax collectors and as one of whom it could be said, "He is a gluttonous man, and a winebibber, a friend of publicans and sinners."[4] And she was a child of Wisdom, "justified by her works,"[5] for Jesus received her

1. Norman Perrin, *Rediscovering the Teaching of Jesus*, (New York: Harper & Row, Publishers; London: SCM Press, 1967), p. 137.
2. Notes of Walter Wink, professor of New Testament Studies at Auburn Theological Seminary, New York.
3. Lk. 7:38; §42A.
4. Mt. 11:19; §41J.
5. Ibid.

and deeply appreciated her kissing his feet and anointing his feet with oil. Hers was an act of outpouring love, and his act was one of outpouring acceptance, despite all social barriers.

How did she come to act this way? From what in her did her actions spring? What gave her this courage? What is clear here about forgiveness? Who forgives? What is the role of God and human in forgiveness? All these questions and more pour in on us.

Is there any evidence that she had ever seen Jesus? No. My own conviction is that she must have heard of him, and knew something of what manner of man he was. Something she had heard or knew of him helped to arouse in her a new level of being. Her substance, which had been spent in the life of prostitution, now felt some stirring of Spirit that moved her to another dimension. Something moved in her, something from him during a meaningful coincidence, perhaps, stirred her. An encounter with a man such as she had never experienced before was now possible.

She came to Jesus across all social barriers and obstacles, out of some deep need or longing. She entered the room of the Pharisees, risking complete rejection by them and by Jesus. But she risked. She was compelled, driven by some inner force.

One can imagine, as she stood at the door, that she was undergoing a change. She brought her sin, but in a context of forgiveness. An anxious step. The palsied man in an earlier account had to take up his bed. It could not be left behind. Out of a life where her energy had been misspent due to her beauty and appeal to men, something happened inside her before she confronted Jesus, but not necessarily before she had heard something of him and his values. Perrin speaks of the table fellowship as one sure element that can be trusted as authentic, his consorting with those inferior people. This must have been known, and perhaps heard about, by her. Some new direction had been taken by her, some redemptive act had begun to be incarnated in her that moved her to this radical action and its results. The acceptance by Jesus helped her to her own deeper self-acceptance out of the encounter.

The reaction of the Pharisee, presumably known as Simon, could be expected: "This man, if he were a prophet, would have perceived who and what manner of woman this is which touches him, that she is a sinner."[1] All acts of touching were outside social custom, for they could be sensuous, even sexual acts, and to touch or be touched by a prostitute was to open oneself to uncleanness and defilement.

In response to this criticism from the Pharisee, Jesus told a parable.[2] The authenticity of this parable is questioned by some. However, it seems to fit. A man had two debtors, one owing more than the other, but the man forgave the debts of both. Jesus asked, "Which of them therefore will love him most?" And the answer came, "He, I suppose, to whom he forgave the most"; and Jesus commented, "Thou hast rightly judged." The greater the forgiveness, the greater the love, not vice versa. The inward act of stepping into forgiveness led to the release of love, which he recognized, not vice versa.

After the parable, Jesus turned to Simon, spoke of the woman's actions toward him, and said, "Wherefore I say unto thee, Her sins, which are many, are forgiven; for she loved much: but to whom little is forgiven, the same loveth little."[3] This is to say that forgiveness leads to love. That is what the parable is all about, and this statement is the conclusion from it. Jesus observed and was moved by the woman's outpouring love in all her gestures. Her feminine reality, which had been repressed in her life as a "woman of the streets," now found a new expression, a new outlet. Her own misguided side, a human nature flawed and wounded (in one sense, dead), had found some spring of action that led to repentance and possible response to a totality of value she had never known. This stepping into a new, totally transforming value showed the beginning of the act of forgiveness out of which love flowed. The first act of redemption took place within her, perhaps moved by what she had heard of this person who was breaking all the

1. Lk. 7:39; §42B.
2. Lk. 7:40-43; §42C.
3. Lk. 7:47; §42D.

taboos that kept her within her role. The next step was the actual movement with Love toward the Jesus who had helped constellate this value. And the last was the acceptance by Jesus, who perceived that because she came with such love, she had entered into the stream of forgiveness within; she had affirmed the possibility that the Yes in God can overcome the No. She would not have known this if Jesus had not already worked with his own answer to God. Her capacity for insight into her sin and her need for change meant she had moved out of subjection to pure substance into finding the Spirit within that substance. It was a movement into the process of God, where love overcomes all the negativities of repression.

But this inner act had to issue in outer actions, as it did, and to confirmation and acceptance by him who constellated the Value. Her act of loving spoke to Jesus of her inner change, and he could say what he did. The tears she brought were not the tears of self-pity or even just a release of feeling, but tears of repentance at the joy of a kind of conversion.

What went on in Jesus that enabled him to respond as he did? His encounter with this woman is not unsimilar to the incident with the man sick of the palsy, where he affirmed the forgiveness of sin. Jesus had learned at the baptism and wilderness that out of the act of repentance and the descent of the Holy Spirit into himself there was something of God within to help him be all-inclusive and to reconcile opposites, and that this something needed to be expressed in the Word as the Logos of Truth. Because he knew this as an objective reality where the Spirit in God touched and worked within the Substance of God in the psyche, he could become for this woman and others the articulation of this process. He knew the relationship between a will toward wholeness, born in substance, and the love derived from the Will. This meeting between the woman and Jesus is a significant one historically and symbolically. Because of what Jesus had achieved and was constantly becoming, he aroused in her unredeemed substance the potentiality of meaningful spiritual direction. This could happen because he had included darkness and descended into substance toward new revelation. This revelation was not just in or for him, but held within it a quality potential for all.

After Jesus said to her, "Thy sins are forgiven," the Pharisee reacted negatively, assuming Jesus had said that *Jesus* had forgiven sin. Jesus continued and concluded with the words to the woman "Thy faith has saved thee. Go in peace."[1] The word "faith" has appeared twice before and will appear again. In the incident with the palsied man, it is reported by the editors of the book of Mark that Jesus "seeing their faith, said unto the sick of the palsy. . . ."[2] This is obviously an editorial statement, not from Jesus. In the incident of the centurion,[3] the word "faith" appears on the lips of Jesus in what is probably a historical incident. A Roman centurion had come to Jesus to ask him to heal his servant from a distance. The centurion reportedly spoke in glowing terms of his understanding of Jesus because he, the centurion, also knew what it was to be under authority and thus recognized that the authority in Jesus was born from his own obedience to God. Jesus said, "I have not found so great faith, no, not in Israel." Nowhere, that is, had Jesus found anyone who expressed more deeply a recognition of the Source out of which he, Jesus, acted. The centurion distinguished between Jesus and the Source of his authority. This distinction and the man's response to it constituted faith.

The core of faith in his statement to the woman in the incident here is that it is an action, a response, an attitude toward something, not a belief. In the story, the process which had started in her, because Jesus had become a catalytic agent for God and of God in her, is the core of "faith." It was a response of an "I" to a "Thou." The Thou was not just the person of Jesus, but the Value he manifested to her as well. The conversion of her energy took her to Jesus, where acceptance completed a process. To this he gave the word "faith." The essence of forgiveness for us, then, is to be in contact with Something or Someone that symbolizes the healing factor. The significance of what this incident

1. Lk. 7:50; §42E.
2. Mk. 2:5; §29D.
3. Lk. 7:2-9; §39A-C.

says to us is great. Each must find his or her inner prostitute—that part not necessarily sexual but not excluding
it—which needs to turn in a new direction of transformative value.

There follows a report of women who followed him, including "Mary that was called Magdalene, from whom
seven devils had gone out."[1] This may be the basis for calling the woman of the streets Mary Magdalene. That
women followed Jesus in itself would have been most extraordinary, even dangerous, in his day. It served to stress
Jesus' relationship to the feminine: outwardly toward
women, and inwardly to the feminine component within in
terms of attitudes and symbols. His associations with
women helped counteract the strong masculine-dominat-
ed mood of his culture. Some scholars assert that Jesus' attitude to women may be one of the causes of his crucifixion.

Jesus then went to a house where there were so many
people they could not get to the food. His friends laid hold
on him, "for they said, he is beside himself."[2] This is one of
the very few instances where neither Matthew nor Luke
has the report. Does this point to its being inserted later or
omitted by both writers because of the content? Surely the
second position seems more probable. What does the incident reveal that these writers do not want to report? The
friends appeared to be saying Jesus was a little mad,
somewhat out of control. Out of love and caring they attempted to protect him. This seems more appropriate than
to assume that they were criticizing him. What was really
going on inside Jesus? Was he really out of control in some
awkward way, or was he spontaneous and perhaps a bit irrational, even playing a bit of the Fool, in its creative
sense?

The next reported incident is one of the most provocative in the gospels, because Jesus, who had been pronouncing the forgiveness of sin, now asserted there is one
sin which is never forgiven.[3] What is it? And by what right

1. Lk. 8:2; §43.
2. Mk. 3:19-21; §44.
3. Mk. 3:22-30; §45.

can he make this statement? Coming immediately after the incident with the woman, it forms quite a contrast.

The scribes who came down from Jerusalem accused him of being in league with Beelzebub, the prince of devils. It was out of this source, they said, that he himself cast out devils. This accusation is clear-cut, but their motive for making it may not be so clear. Did they really believe that he was in league with the devil? Was this a conscious attempt to deceive? Were they trying to trap Jesus? Some of the authorities had been determined to get him since the beginning of his revolutionary teaching, which upset their well-formed religious categories. Judging by his evaluation that this was blasphemy, the one sin "that hath not forgiveness," it must be concluded that he saw their accusation as a deliberate perversion of truth. They had stood in his presence, had heard what he had been saying, and had seen what was happening, but to defend their own rigidities they called his activities "of the devil." It is not, then, that they failed to see his truth, not that they ran from it, but rather, that seeing it they mislabeled it. To deny the value or to turn one's back on it is a totally different psychological and moral act from facing it and calling it evil. To do this is a perversion of moral discrimination. Pharisees and Jesus would have known the passage from Isaiah, "Woe unto them that call evil good and good evil."[1]

His answer moved step by step. First, he logically refuted the accusation with the questions "How can Satan cast out Satan?" and "How can a divided kingdom stand?"[2] If the Source of his actions were evil, he would not be casting evil out, but would be engaged in increasing it. Only the polar opposite to evil can cast it out. He continued that all sins, even all blasphemies, are forgiven, except blasphemy against the Holy Spirit; "but whosoever shall blaspheme against the Holy Spirit hath never forgiveness."[3] Clearly, in accusing his Source of being of Beelzebub, the scribes were blaspheming against the Holy Spirit. Why is this sin so destructive, so deadening to the person doing it? How does it preclude forgiveness?

1. Isa. 5:20.
2. Mk. 3:23-24; § 45E.
3. Mk. 3:29; §45I.

Because this act cuts off the very condition for forgiveness, the act of turning. And what is being assumed about Jesus and his relation to the Holy Spirit?

To look at something of unquestionably great value and grandeur and then to condemn it is to distort the moral discriminatory factor which is the essence of the turning that is forgiveness. The essence of the human being is the ability to know values, whatever their content. This is to eat of the Tree of the Knowledge of Good and Evil in the Garden of Eden. To cover over that knowledge by falsity is to do away with our humanness. "Hath never forgiveness" is a very strong statement. Does it mean "never, never" or "never until"? Is Jesus saying that human personality can be unalterably destroyed, become incapable of redemption? Or is he saying that there is never forgiveness while continuing in a state of blasphemy against the Holy Spirit, but that a turning is possible?

Whichever, a further observation is the striking assumption that Jesus makes about himself. He was able to affirm that he was so securely rooted in the Holy Spirit, or the Holy Spirit was so securely dwelling in him, that he could judge people by how they responded to him. After two thousand years of Christianity, where Jesus has been part of the Trinity with the Father and the Holy Spirit, it is not easy to be detached enough to be shocked by this statement, yet a more shocking statement of self-evaluation could hardly be made. Before moving to the Matthew account, it is moving and exciting to compare these two incidents of the woman and the scribes, for they are so absolutely opposite. Both involve response to Jesus' Value. With the woman, there is total outgoingness because the Source is tapped; therefore, salvation occurs. With the scribes, the response is not only rejection of the Value, but misnaming it in calling it evil.

Another interesting comparison is between Peter's earlier response by the sea and the scribes' response here. Peter says, "Depart from me because I am sinful."[1] The scribes say, "We hear you, but you are of the devil." The Mark account ends with the addition to "hath never

1. Lk. 5:8; §27.

forgiveness" of "is guilty of an eternal sin."[1] Although this may not sound different from what has preceded it, it has about it a later church feeling rather than the way Jesus spoke.

Matthew, following the Mark account, has woven it together with an account from Document P.[2] There, the report is that one may speak against the Son of man, but not against the Holy Spirit, without being blasphemous. The term "Son of man" again refers to an element in personality, not to the ego, nor to the Divine Center of the psyche. The Son of man is subject to criticism and is fallible, but the Source is another matter. This Son-of-man element in us can be killed, but the Holy Spirit as ultimate Source cannot be. Because this is true, it may form the basis for what happened after Jesus' death. The Holy Spirit, containing the ambivalences that make for discrimination, continues the function it began in the baptism and wilderness experiences. The other striking fact in the Document P account is the added statement about the function of the Holy Spirit in teaching, informing, and instructing at moments of crisis. When one is confronted by authorities, rulers—here, presumably actual, outer ones, but also perhaps inner ones—"Be not anxious, for the Holy Spirit shall teach you in that very hour what you ought to say."[3] To touch the reality of the Holy Spirit within is to go deeply into the objective depths of oneself, not just to one's own desires and subjective world, but to a level of objective, inner reality of truth. Here is where the Holy Spirit functions and the tremendous implication is that in the midst of crucial or desperate circumstances, the Holy Spirit knows what to say and how to say it. The Holy Spirit functions as the voice of God, not only within, but in relation to the actual situation. Its guidance is relative to the whole, and this returns us to the baptism and wilderness. How does one know whether the voice from within is in fact the Holy Spirit or ten other possible voices? Is it just an

1. Mk. 3:30; §45K.
2. Mt. 12:32; Lk. 12:10; §45J.
3. Lk. 12:11-12; §91I.

autonomous voice to be trusted, or must the ego play a part in checking this totality of the facts and what will make for the greater value?

What does the passage reveal of the greatness of Jesus? In direct confrontation with his enemies, he stood as a towering figure in the secure position of his relation to God. He answered logically and rationally and moved to a greater depth, where he saw clearly and cleanly that the scribes' estimate of him came from a corrupted place inside themselves. They had become so rigid about the minutiae of detail, so stiff-necked, and so corrupt that they could commit an act cutting them off from the inner change which is forgiveness. They had not stayed faithful to the Tree of the Knowledge of Good and Evil. This is to deny integrity. Jesus knew he had eaten of this Tree, and he had paid the price of using it in such a way that it led and can lead to the Tree of Life.

Here is, indeed, an individual. Here is a person whose identity is not with his conscious side or even with the Son of man, but whose identity is predicated on being a channel for the Holy Spirit in clarity and differentiation.

Jesus was then confronted by the presence of his personal family. His response to being told his mother and brethren were outside waiting for him was "Who is my mother and my brethren?" Looking around him, he continued, "Behold, my mother and my brethren! For whosoever shall do the Will of God, the same is my brother, and sister, and mother."[1] Luke has "My mother and my brethren are these which hear the word of God, and do it."[2] At a later point, when a woman praised him, saying, "Blessed is the womb that bore thee, and the breasts which thou didst suck," his response was "Yea rather, blessed are they that hear the word of God, and keep it."[3]

Here Jesus does not seem necessarily to repudiate his family, but to add a family not of natural but of supranatural origin. Based on flesh and blood and emotional bonds, the natural family is not the true family. The new

1. Mk. 3:31-35; §46.
2. Lk. 8:21; §46E.
3. Lk. 11:27-28; §87.

family, based on common loyalty to a greater Value of the will of God, need not exclude members of one's natural family. This bonding loyalty, the complete commitment to act at all times on what one perceives to be the greater value, requires inner and outer searching. The more one knows of oneself and can bring that Self to the commitment in openness and nonegocentricity, the more one can perceive the dynamic value and potential in any situation.

What is the difference between the two versions: doing the will of God and hearing the Word of God and keeping it? "To do" and "to keep" are surely comparable; both imply action following insight into content. The second statement is perhaps more definite, for it spells out a precondition of "doing" or "keeping," namely, hearing. Jesus affirms the reality of the Word of God, here understood as a truth in any situation that can be known, as an ever-present process. Later, he will have more to say on the significance of hearing and on the necessity of clearing our ears.

Still later, Jesus said, "If any man cometh unto me, and hateth not his own father, and mother, and wife, and children, and brethren, and sisters, yea, and his own life also, he cannot be my disciple."[1] These statements all add up to his definition of true relatedness, its ultimate basis and source. It is clear that *he* is not the center or core around which people are related; rather, all people who relate to the same center he does are, like the spokes of a wheel, in authentic relationship. This community of the new family, resting on the center of God, will have power and meaning of a unique sort.

Jesus' declaration of the need to hate one's family is a strong, radical statement, especially for a Jewish person. Psychologically, it cuts the umbilical cord. It marks a major break with his background in which the commandment "Honor thy father and thy mother" demands a contrary attitude to what Jesus said here. Is it really so contrary? What is there intrinsic to the natural blood ties that keeps people bound to them, that keeps them in a state of unawareness of deeper values, that keeps them uncon-

1. Lk. 14:26; §104B.

scious rather than working for consciousness? It is the
work of Dr. Jung that has helped us understand the deep
pull and containment of the archetypal world. To hate is
not to have a hostile reaction to, a repulsion or negative
emotion toward. Those are superficial attitudes compared
to the intentional severing of the umbilical cord that ties
each of us to the parent or parental images. If those images
continue to dominate us as adults, we never get to ourselves. To take this step is to take on oneself the burden of
guilt when established patterns are broken. What is called
for is an attitude of detachment from the natural ties and a
redirection of energy toward the value found in Jesus'
way. It is to be wed to the principle of increasing consciousness and not to the pull of unconsciousness, to move
from the biological to the spiritual level.

Blood relationships are fact, and without the natural, instinctive libido there would be no procreation and ongoingness. However, evolution is not served by procreation
only, for it is the transformation of libido into a single goal
that produces the next step in evolution. And undoubtedly, natural relationship would be better served by this new
step of transformation of libido into a single goal. Instead of
becoming regressive pulls, as they so often do, blood relationships could flow into a new reality. This call to hate
mother, father, brother, sister, is not against Love. Rather,
it is for Love that people move from the limitations and
egocentricities of a narrow love into a deeper, more inclusive Love that would transform the narrow into the
deeper. This is part of the purpose of God. This is God
manifest. In fact, the freedom from the old patterns of the
natural may be just what enabled Jesus to relate as deeply
as he did to the whole feminine side of life through his
creative use of feminine symbols and in his attitude toward
women.

IV

"How Shall We Liken the Kingdom of God?"

Where and under what conditions is the Kingdom manifest in society and in our lives?

What is the price to be paid by an individual for entrance into the Kingdom?

What is the nature of God as revealed in the parables on the Kingdom?

What is the role of Jesus in the Kingdom?

Jesus' central religious message is contained in his concept of the actualization of the Kingdom of God, the realm where God, He/She, reigns. Where and how does God reign? The birth of the Kingdom out of potentiality into a new reality, in the individual and in society, is the major thrust and dynamic of his message. He chose parables as the most appropriate form to express it.

A long discourse on the theme of the Kingdom of God[1] is followed later by several other significant passages, which will all be included in this chapter. The total body of

1. Mk. 4:1-34; Mt. 13:1-53; Lk. 8:4-18; §47-48.

teaching on the Kingdom—expressing urgency, offering an invitation, and making a claim—is considerable and challenging.

Prior to this discourse, what has Jesus said about the Kingdom of God? The first reference, "The time is fulfilled, the kingdom of God is at hand,"[1] is a summary statement by the editor of Mark that has been questioned as being too close to John's message to be authentically from Jesus. Luke added to Mark that the content of Jesus' message is teaching the good tidings of the Kingdom of God.[2] In another place in Matthew, doing the will of God as a prerequisite to entering the Kingdom of God is surely from the lips of Jesus.[3] Then, in the Beatitudes, there is "Blessed are ye poor, for yours is the Kingdom of God."[4] What impression do these few statements make? Certainly they convey the sense of the great value of the Kingdom; that the good tidings have to do with achieving that value; and that a state of inner poverty as well as outer poverty and need may be central to the achievement of that value.

What the expectations of his people were regarding the Kingdom, how it was to come about, how and what God would do, what role the Messiah would play, and what, if any, price the human would have to pay for entrance have all been dealt with in Chapter I. The content of these expectations must be clearly kept in mind as the new material is examined.

In the discourse, seven parables on the Kingdom are given, and interspersed throughout is the refrain "Who has ears to hear, let him hear."[5] Why this refrain? What does it convey about the nature of what Jesus is about to say? We hear with our ears; words spoken by others come to us through our ears. Granted, we also communicate by non-verbal gestures. Words filter through our preconceptions of what we think we will hear, or what we want to hear. Both these aspects of thinking and wishing contaminate the objective world where people speak to or with us. To be able

1. Mk. 1:15; §21C.
2. Lk. 4:43; §26C.
3. Mt. 7:21; §38U.
4. Lk. 6:20; Mt. 5:3; §36B.
5. Mk. 4:9,23; §47F,S; Mt. 13:43; §48M.

to speak is an art; to be able to hear is another and possibly a more subtle one.

What, then, do we learn from this refrain of Jesus, this exhortation, this warning even? It is as if he were saying, "Beware what you hear, for it will not be what you are used to hearing, or even what you want to hear!" This is a clue that the nature of what he may be going to say will not be the old, currently held ideas. His message will contain new ideas or be totally new. Earlier, he said, "For to this end came I forth."[1] To proclaim something new about the reign of God to his people emerges again as in the earlier discourse. And to us, two thousand years later, the same refrain may be as relevant as then, but for different reasons. He was tellings his *Jewish* audience to clean out their ears and to be rid of what they wanted to hear. He could be telling his contemporary *Christian* audience to be sure to clean out *their* ears so they can listen to him and his real message without two thousand years of Christian accretion and dogma. For our Christian heritage can blind us as much, but differently, from the way his people were blinded. Jesus and his message are not necessarily what Christianity has taught.

The setting of the discourse is striking. So great a multitude followed Jesus that he got into a boat while the people stayed on shore. This can be taken simply as an objective reality, or its symbolic meaning can be seen in that his place of speaking came from his relationship to the lake, to water, so often the symbol of the unconscious. It is dramatic to see him in the boat, the container, the vessel that held him while he spoke the Word.

He began with a parable which, unlike the seven which followed, did not start with the phrase "The Kingdom of God is like unto. . . ." A parable tells a story which turns upon a single point having its parallel in the situation. The words symbolize a deeper spiritual and psychological reality. It may be assumed that this first parable is something in the nature of an introduction to what he will say about the reception of his message. In this, Jesus spoke of four kinds of ground into which a sower sowed his seed, each

1. Mk. 1:38; §26C.

ground yielding different results from the seed.[1] The relationship between seed and ground is crucial, for the seeds all have the same potential, but the state and condition of the ground determine their growth or nongrowth. What is the truth that Jesus talked about behind this imagery? There are four kinds of ground, three of which are negative, and one which is positive. Behind the image is the deep reality that the seed may be the word spoken by him, the ground the condition of the hearers. The ground on which the words fall, then, is more apt to be negative than positive. This is a sobering warning, one more insight into the realism of this man. Three kinds of ground illustrate the obstacles that prevent real hearing; the fourth kind of ground, the good ground, yields fruit plentifully.

If one maintains the single dynamic point—the fact of relationship between seed and condition of ground, or between word given and received—one has great responsibility as hearer. For anyone, even Jesus, to speak means nothing unless there is receptivity to the word. Words, the most human attribute we have, are spoken forms which reach consciousness out of the unconscious. They come out of depths and can only be received by depths of openness in the ground on which they fall. The I that speaks out of an ultimate I-Thou needs a human Thou to hear. Implicitly, Jesus is affirming something about himself: not only that his words will be new, radical, fresh, but that they are worth listening to because of the Source within him out of which they come. It is easy for us to assume this, but entering into the moment of history, this man stands alone, fresh from his baptism experience, facing his people's central religious hopes for the Kingdom.

Next he spoke to some who were with him and the twelve, and who asked about the parable and why he had spoken it. He replied,"Unto you is given the mystery of the Kingdom of God: but unto them that are without, all things are done in parables: that seeing they may see, and not perceive; and hearing they may hear, and not understand."[2] This reply, coming from Isaiah, has been a center

1. Mk. 4:3-8; §47B-E.
2. Mk. 4:11-12; §47G,I.

of much controversy.[1] To speak of the Kingdom of God as a mystery conveys a numinous, awesome sense. In dealing with the Kingdom of God, we are not dealing with the obvious, the purely rational understanding of things, but with something from irrational depths of Being.

Certainly, Jesus wants and expects those closest to him to understand, but for the rest of the world he speaks in parables just so they will not understand and perceive. The "that" in Greek is "in order that." Why does this come as a shock to so many? Why should it not be accepted that Jesus knew exactly what he was doing with his message and its dynamic nature, and that he was realistic about his people's point of view? In its stark simplicity it may be too hard to face due to our own picture of Jesus. The mystery was to be known to those inside; it was not yet to be revealed to those outside. Why, perhaps, was this necessary? What would have been the result if the mystery had been understood immediately? There were enemies already plotting to get rid of Jesus. To have immediately proclaimed his content could have led to an earlier death. Jesus was a strategist, in the best sense of the word, who knew the time was not right to take this chance before he had really conveyed his message. The meaning of the parables was to be hidden for now, but was to be revealed later.

"Lest haply they should turn again, and it should be forgiven them,"[2] the second part of Jesus' explanation of why he used parables, does not seem consistent with the first part. If one compares the Mark account with the two copyists, it is significant that Luke does not have this part about the forgiveness. Either it was not in the Mark that Luke had or Luke omitted it because it went against his idea of forgiveness. Even more instructive is seeing, when we compare Matthew, that he has a quotation from Isaiah[3] from which the statement about seeing yet not perceiving and hearing and not understanding comes. At the end of

1. Isa. 6:9-10.
2. Mk. 4:12; §47J.
3. Mt. 13:14-15, §47J; Isa. 6:9-10.

the quotation from Isaiah is a statement on turning and being healed. It would seem wise to conclude that Jesus originally spoke what is in the first part, Mark 4:12, but then Matthew, in copying it and adding the whole Isaiah passage, gave basis for a later addition of the second half of verse 12 in Mark.

Still bearing on this point is the fact that it is immediately reported that Jesus went on to elaborate his first parable on the sower.[1] His explanation becomes allegory, different from parable, which makes it highly suspect. The fact of what he has just said about the nature of parable would make it very unlikely that he would explain it. And the nature of the explanation has in it elements not consistent with what Jesus has said so far about Satan. Altogether, a large question mark needs to be put by this exposition. Therefore, after eliminating this questionable material, we come to the words

> Is the lamp brought to be put under the bushel, or under the bed, and not to be put on the stand? For there is nothing hid, save that it should be manifested; neither was anything made secret, but that it should come to light.[2]

Everything that is hidden is eventually to be brought to light and made clear. Whatever the reason for the hiddenness of the parables, the ultimate aim is the proclamation of their truth, their revelation in the light.

All this helps us to approach the parables on the Kingdom of God with their newness, freshness, and divergence from currently held concepts. Is the interpretation we shall find each time radical enough to meet these criteria? This is why it has been so vital to understand what were the current Jewish Messianic hopes, and to free our minds from cherished Christian conceptions of what Jesus said about the Kingdom. With free eyes and ears, let us look at each of the seven parables, asking, What is the central, dynamic new point about the Kingdom? One dimension to be constantly kept in mind must be whether the parable is dealing with only the personal aspect of the

1. Mk. 4:14-20; §47M-P.
2. Mk. 4:21-22; §47Q-R.

Kingdom (one person's relationship to it) or with the social aspect (its growth in society). That is, are the Kingdom parables descriptions of a process pervading society or of a process within one person? Those issues would probably have been important to Jesus. Considering the attitude of his hearers, one would expect him to meet their questions first—which would have been, *When* would the Kingdom come, *how* would it come, *who* would bring it, and *what* would be its sign? To these questions Jesus would surely have first addressed himself, and his answers would have emerged in total contrast to the answers his hearers would have given.

The first parable is the story of the seed planted in earth, growing slowly, and by its own power coming into the full grain in the ear:

> So is the kingdom of God, as if a man should cast seed upon the earth; and should sleep and rise night and day, and the seed should spring up and grow, he knoweth not how. The earth beareth fruit of herself; first the blade, then the ear, then the full corn in the ear. But when the fruit is ripe, straightway he putteth forth the sickle, because the harvest is come.[1]

Is the single central point the slow growth of the Kingdom, or the cutting at harvest time? The latter is reminiscent of John the Baptist; the former describes the possibility of the Kingdom of God growing slowly in a natural, evolutionary way. This was totally different from the contemporary expectation that the Kingdom would come in a cataclysmic way, brought in by a political and apocalyptic Messiah. Today, evolution and gradual growth are not new to us. Two thousand years ago, to the people whose God intervened in dramatic, catastrophic, or beneficent ways, the idea that the Kingdom must be the outcome of gradual development would seem drastically new. There is no mention here of any Messianic agent, which throws great light on the Messianic function as process, not as a "who."

The second parable is that of the mustard seed:

> And he said, How shall we liken the Kingdom of God? or in what parable shall we set it forth? It is like a grain of mustard seed,

1. Mk. 4:26-29; §48D.

which, when it is sown upon the earth, though it be less than all the seeds that are upon the earth, yet when it is sown, groweth up, and becometh greater than all the herbs, and putteth out great branches; so that the birds of the heaven can lodge under the shadow thereof.[1]

What is the newest element here? In contrast to the idea of a cataclysmic beginning there is the radically different idea of a very insignificant beginning that has within it the capacity to envelop all.

We begin to see how and in what way God works in the thought of Jesus as the dynamism of the wilderness decisions manifests itself here. Concepts of God and the Kingdom coming to birth begin to emerge that are very different from what his contemporaries thought. God's mystery is there, but differently; the scope of the way God works takes a new form. The Kingdom will grow in a natural way from very small beginnings to an all-encompassing reality. It will be mysterious, once started; minute in origin, but powerful in its dynamic effects. Jesus will later address himself to the question of the actualization and growth of the Kingdom in one person, but now he is speaking to their questions as to when, where, and how the Kingdom will come in their midst.

Matthew has five more parables on the Kingdom interwoven from his Document M. The first one is on the wheat and the tares:

Another parable set he before them, saying, The kingdom of heaven is likened unto a man that sowed good seed in his field: but while men slept, his enemy came and sowed tares also among the wheat, and went away. But when the blade sprang up, and brought forth fruit, then appeared the tares also.

And the servants of the householder came and said unto him, Sir, didst thou not sow good seed in thy field? whence then hath it tares? And he said unto them, An enemy hath done this. And the servants say unto him, Wilt thou then that we go and gather them up? But he saith, Nay; lest haply while ye gather up the tares, ye root up the wheat with them. Let both grow together until the harvest.[2]

1. Mk. 4:30-32; §48E.
2. Mt. 13:24-30; §48A-B.

One can emphasize the fact that the wheat and the tares must grow together for a considerable time, or the fact that at the end they are divided and spread apart. The second alternative is almost exactly like John the Baptist's teaching of the apocalyptic nature of the Kingdom. The first, much more likely to be from Jesus, suggests that there will be tares, weeds, problems, and evils from enemies in the Kingdom, but their presence among the wheat must be accepted for a time lest one should pull out the wrong thing. What does this assume? That there is, along with the potential for growth or good, an enemy, a power against growth—the ambivalence—and that the distinction of which is which is not always easy and one must be careful. Here again, the slowness of development cuts across the idea of a sudden, clearly distinguished beginning. One may wonder whether the end of the parable about the harvest and the saving of the wheat may not have been added later. Much of Christianity, and aspects of Judaism also, has split good and evil and confined the Kingdom to the good only. In both these trends the Tree of the Knowledge of Good and Evil in the Garden of Eden reminds us of a Unity that contains opposites, but does not split them.

Matthew's second parable about the Kingdom is very similar to the second parable in Mark. "For the kingdom of God is like unto leaven, which a woman took, and hid in three measures of meal, till it was all leavened."[1] What is the truth here? Compared to the truth of Mark's two parables, the central point here seems to be the potency and pervasiveness of the Kingdom, which is hidden and small to begin with, but which eventually infuses the whole. The whole impact of these parables cuts across the dominant religious concepts of the time.

We come now to the two best known, most often interpreted of Jesus' parables: the two about "selling all" for the Kingdom, using the image of the treasure in the field, and the image of the pearl of great price.[2] It is illuminating to remember that a pearl is slowly built by the oyster

1. Mt. 13:33; §48F.
2. Mt. 13:44-46; §48N-O.

around an irritation inside its body. Surely we have arrived at Jesus' contribution, not as to how the Kingdom grows in society (as in the earlier parables) but how it comes to be born and grows in the individual. What must the individual do to enter into the Kingdom? For the Kingdom is here, present, to be actualized in and by individuals. Until now the Jews were chosen; now each individual must choose. So far there has been one statement on entering the Kingdom of God by doing the will of God; now the condition in both parables is stated as "selling all." In one parable, the man seeks goodly pearls consciously; in the other, there is a sense that the man comes by chance upon a field where a treasure is hidden. In one there is an active looking or searching for the value of the Kingdom, symbolized by the pearl; in the other, the treasure symbolizing the Kingdom has been planted in a field—shall we say by God?—to be found by someone there. In both parables there is instant recognition of the value and a willingness to pay the price. Because the Kingdom surpasses everything in its value, there is motivation to sell all to achieve that value. In the case of the man who found the treasure in the field there is the added statement that he goes in his joy and sells all. The vision of the fruits perhaps is compelling enough to induce immediate joy.

The crucial and central meaning of "selling all" has been interpreted through Christian history in many forms. How must it be seen to be consistent and true to the totality of Jesus' religion? It is, in fact, the most authentic action on which he based his life and teaching, which is death-rebirth.

"To sell all"—three simple words; really two: one verb and one noun. Let us start with the noun, the "all." What does a human being possess that could be called one's "all"? Is it one thing, many things, or one and many? The interpretation has often been taken as leading to the ascetic life, referring purely, entirely, to physical possessions. But are possessions the main thing? Are they in themselves the "all," or is there something behind them? Are possessions wrong, or the attachment to them wrong? Do they bind us per se or does an attitude bind us? What do we own behind possessions? All sorts of attitudes, pride, achievements, self-glorifications—those things in the eyes of others and ourselves which make us feel good. Are these the core of the "all" or is there something behind them? If we choose to give up all the egocentricities we could dream of having, have we reached this "all"? Behind all these—physical possessions, attitudes, and egocentricities—there lies a core of reality which can be called negative self-will, the determination to direct our own life the way we want to, the effort to personally control things as we want and to dictate things. Freedom of choice distinguishes us as humans from animals. This ability to choose life or destruction, good or evil, one direction versus another, enables humans to become co-creators. Thus, the right to have things our own way seems to be the most precious possession one has, for it can and does determine everything else.

This "all," then, is one thing, yet has many parts; one bundle and many bundles; and the discovery of the content and number of the bundles occupies a lifetime. To sell the "all," the one thing, means to renounce that right to choose specificity of one's own desire and to let oneself be molded by the Patterning of the moment. Through such conscious choice we give back to its true owner what we have been given. It is as if our life were on loan. We either take it and run away to shape it as we will, or we turn it back to its Source in a volitional act of choice which makes us co-creators with the process of God. Is the selling a single act, or is it a single and yet continuous act? On the one hand it is a complete act as far as one's consciousness encompasses it, but on the other hand it must be renewed as new areas of the psyche are discovered. Perhaps it is always, again and again, an expression of the death-rebirth archetypal myth.

To whom do we sell? To God as Will, intentionality, desire to be discovered in all moments. Selling all to God requires a once-and-for-all affirmation that includes every known area of one's Self and that needs constantly to be repeated as new areas of Self are found to bring into the single act. This means, then, a stripping away of self-directed will. Is it a sacrifice? What is the real motivation for it? Sacrifice is renunciation; yet what one receives through selling all to God is infinitely greater and richer than what one sells. Motivation in that sense is creatively selfish: the Self-regard within comes to birth and exerts itself.

Four later parables complete the affirmation of the Kingdom and enrich its meaning.

One Kingdom of God parable centers on "a certain king" who condemned a servant who owed him money and then, "moved with compassion," released him and forgave him the debt. (The love of God supersedes the first response of wrath.) The servant, however, went out and cruelly treated persons who owed him money. The king then called the servant to him and severely punished him until all was paid.[1]

What is the essence of this parable? The Kingdom of God requires not only that God's light or loving side overcome His/Her dark side, but that God's grace and love then be manifested by the person who has been the recipient of the love. The fact that the servant could still act so negatively after benefitting from the king's grace attests again to the ambivalence in human nature and in God.

Another parable, the one often referred to as the Parable of the Great Feast, was recounted by Jesus when he was a guest of one of the rulers of the Pharisees at a Sabbath meal:

> And when one of them that sat at meat with him heard these things, he said unto him, Blessed is he that shall eat bread in the kingdom of God. But he said unto him, A certain man made a great supper; and he bade many: and he sent forth his servant at supper time to say to them that were bidden, Come; for all things are now ready. And they all with one consent began to make excuse. The first said unto him, I have bought a field, and I must needs go out and see it: I pray thee have me excused. And another said, I have bought five yoke of oxen, and I go to prove them: I pray thee have me excused. And another said, I have married a wife, and therefore I cannot come. And the servant came, and told his lord these things. Then the master of the house being angry said to his servant, Go out quickly into the streets and lanes of the city, and bring in hither the poor and maimed and blind and lame. And the servant said, Lord, what thou didst command is done, and yet there is room. And the lord said unto the servant, Go out into the highways

1. Mt. 18:23-35; §78W.

and hedges, and constrain them to come in, that my house may be filled. For I say unto you, that none of those men which were bidden shall taste of my supper.[1]

What is the central point here? God wants His/Her food eaten, faces resistance from some people who do not come to the feast, keeps calling people in order "that my house may be filled," still has more than enough food and space at His/Her table, and is wrathful with those who refuse. In essence, then, this is a parable on the two sides of God: the love of God when there is human responsiveness and the anger when there is not. The opposites are as intrinsic to the nature of God as they are to human nature. The desire of God is that in the eating of bread there be participation and co-creation, and there is deep wrath when this does not occur. "For I say unto you, that none of those who were bidden shall taste of my supper." On the human side, the first group invited—"for all things are ready"—had excuses as to why they could not come to the feast. All the excuses were natural and good: taking care of one's fields, taking care of oxen, being with one's wife. None of these things could be considered strange or out-of-the-way, but the very pull of the natural kept those people from accepting new, supranatural calls when they came. It is not that response to the supranatural is good and concern for the natural is bad. Rather, it is a question of appropriateness and timing. "For everything there is a time," says Ecclesiastes 3:1-9. To take care of animals or human relationships is appropriate at times, but at other times it may conflict with deeper, higher demands of the moment. The value is to choose the deepest specificity that is appropriate. No one can decide for anyone else. But the master, being angry that those invited did not come, sent the servant into the streets to bring the poor, maimed, blind, and lame to his table. They came, but still there was room. So he again sent the servant out to constrain others to come, "that my house may be filled." Why did this group of wounded and sick respond so quickly? It is just because they were sick and wounded that they had

1. Lk. 14:15-24; §103D-H.

92

nothing to lose and everything to gain by accepting the invitation. What does it mean inside us that the well-established conforming part hears but does not enter the Kingdom? The contrasting responses of these opposites show the amazing realism of this man.

Two more parables on the Kingdom of God again bear on the theme of God's desire for, and response to, human reactions and recognition. They depict the urgency of God's longing for human reactions and the consequences when human responses are present or absent. When present, there is unqualified joy on His/Her side; when absent, there is equally strong anger and condemnation.

In the first parable, the emphasis is on the need for the human to be ready with enough oil for lamps to burn and to give light when the "bridegroom" comes, the bridegroom being, perhaps, the Holy Spirit:

> Then shall the kingdom of heaven be likened unto ten virgins, which took their lamps, and went forth to meet the bridegroom. And five of them were foolish, and five were wise. For the foolish, when they took their lamps, took no oil with them: but the wise took oil in their vessels with their lamps. Now while the bridegroom tarried, they all slumbered and slept. But at midnight there is a cry, Behold, the bridegroom! Come ye forth to meet him. Then all those virgins arose, and trimmed their lamps. And the foolish said unto the wise, Give us of your oil; for our lamps are going out. But the wise answered, saying, Peradventure there will not be enough for us and you: go ye rather to them that sell, and buy for yourselves. And while they went away to buy, the bridegroom came; and they that were ready went in with him to the marriage feast: and the door was shut. Afterward come also the other virgins, saying, Lord, Lord, open to us. But he answered and said, Verily I say unto you, I know you not.[1]

There is emphasis also on the need to be ready to enter into the celebration of the feast, the celebration of the conjunction of spirit and matter, when it occurs. There are ten virgins waiting to meet the bridegroom. Five are wise and have enough oil for their lamps; five are foolish and do not have oil. Consequently, when the bridegroom comes at midnight the wise virgins have enough light to meet him and to go to the wedding feast. Thus, they, as in virgin

1. Mt. 25:1-12; §136E-F.

birth myths, are receptive to the Spirit when it comes. The foolish virgins, having first to replenish their oil, arrive at the feast late. They ask that the door be opened to them, but it remains shut.

The next parable is the one on the talents.[1] Before embarking on a journey, the master gave five, two, and one talent to his three servants. Those who were given the five and the two talents invested them, and repaid them with gained interest when the master returned. The servant given the one talent buried it, and thus repaid nothing. The use of individual energies, especially latent ones, was highly pleasing to the master. To those who used the talents he said, "Enter into the joy of the lord," while for the one who did not use the talent, his wrath was great, and he said, "Take away even that which he has."

In these last three parables the duality of God's two sides is clear, as opposed to John the Baptist's dualism and split. Which aspect of God is evoked is entirely dependent on the human attitude. Interdependence characterizes the relationship.

Finally, there is a parable which has been the subject of much controversy of interpretation. Early in the morning, the owner of a vineyard hired workers at the marketplace for an agreed wage. At four other times during the day he hired more laborers. At the day's end he told the paymaster to pay first those who had come last and to give them the wage for a full day. When each laborer received the same amount, those who had worked longest protested. But the master said, "I do you no wrong. . . . Is it not lawful for me to do what I will with mine own?"[2] If this parable is looked at without preconceptions it may not be so complicated. Behind the story, what happens, what is the symbolic meaning? God's concern is that the vineyard be worked to produce grapes, to produce wine, to create spirit. This progression illustrates how and why God needs human cooperation for the fruits to come. He/She cannot do it alone; cooperation is needed.

In virtually all of his parables about God's Kingdom, Jesus spoke as a prophetic eschatologist, not as an

1. Mt. 25:14-29; §136H-P.
2. Mt. 20:1-16; §118.

apocalyptist. "God's sun rises on the just and the unjust," he said. "Live in the now," he said. "This day is the daily bread." "Lead us not into temptation but deliver us from evil," he said. No apocalypse is in these words. This day is the *eschaton*. It is always so for Jesus, whether it has to do with imprudent virgins, talents not risked, or work in the vineyard rejected. "Today is all there is," he reiterated. God's needs are always urgent and always now.

What is the standard by which the householder judges? The criterion is not the length of time, but the fundamental attitude of willingness. Being willing is the divine standard whereby the individual is judged by his or her response when called, not by the length of time of work. To put it differently, the Eternal wants response in time, intensity of involvement, and quality of being, rather than the extension of time, quantity of involvement, and amount of being. The workers were in linear time; Jesus was speaking in cyclic or eternal time. To some the irrationality and seeming injustice of God are a problem. It may be that this only deepens an understanding of His/Her nature.

In addition to the parables, several single statements throughout the *Records* enrich the meaning of the Kingdom. Jesus had said that John was the greatest person born of woman, but "he that is but little in the kingdom is greater than he."[1] In Luke, Jesus sent his disciples forth to preach "the kingdom of God," and in Matthew, he told them to preach that "the kingdom of heaven [God] is at hand."[2] Another account in Luke reports that Jesus told the disciples to say to people, "The Kingdom of God is come nigh unto you."[3] These instructions would surely be from Jesus—to preach what he had come to say: that the Kingdom is available in a new way for those who will pay the price.

Regarding the futility of anxiety about material things, Jesus added, "Seek ye first his kingdom and his righteousness and all these things shall be added unto you."[4] The

1. Mt. 11:11; §41E. See Chapter II, p.62.
2. Lk. 9:2; Mt. 10:7; §56F.
3. Lk. 10:9; §82I.
4. Mt. 6:33; §38D.

first priority is the Kingdom—other things follow.

In another instance, Jesus said to the rich young ruler who asked the same question as the lawyer earlier—"What shall I do to inherit eternal life?"—to be willing to give up his material possessions. When the man's "countenance fell," Jesus replied in three sentences, all of which express the difficulty of anyone having riches entering the Kingdom of God.[1] The possession of things offers a primary attachment very difficult to renounce.

Again, one of the scribes asked Jesus what was the first commandment. After the scribe expounded on the answer given by Jesus, Jesus said, "Thou art not far from the kingdom of God."[2] Discernment of the process, understanding the condition, conceptualization of what the human and God need is a significant step before action on it.

Possibly the most radical statement about the Kingdom to his hearers was made in response to the question of the Pharisees about when the Kingdom of God would come. Jesus answered, "The kingdom of God cometh not with observation: neither shall they say, Lo, here! or, There! for lo, the kingdom of God is within you."[3] Or, as in alternative readings, "the kingdom of God is in the midst of you," or "between you." The first alternative presents the deepest and newest possibility and may, in my opinion, have been the source of the greatest opposition to him by his people. What was he saying? What did it come out of? Notice, he did not say "only within you," but "within you," leaving the presence of the Kingdom of God as a Transcendent reality expressing itself in the social. This reality, he was saying, also has its counterpart inside the psyche. What is behind the perception of the Kingdom of God in the world or society is an archetype of wholeness that is potentially realizable in the person. This archetype of wholeness within the person is a finite expression of the Kingdom of God that enables one to serve the Kingdom in its outer form and to actualize it internally. Thus, all the

1. Mk. 10:23-25; §117G-I.
2. Mk. 12:28; §130L.
3. Lk. 17:20-21; §112A.

qualities that characterize the Kingdom as social or outer community also describe an inner reality. The social reality of the Kingdom also has a parallel in the psyche. The Kingdom is not only in Spirit, but in Substance. The core of this teaching came, of course, from the baptism, when the Transcendent moved into Immanence. This immanent quality, the indwelling of God in the psyche, the *imago dei*, the Self as the holy Other within, marked the beginning of newness of Jesus.

The last places where the phrase "Kingdom of God" appears are in the Passover supper accounts. In four places, two in Document J and one in Mark, also copied by Matthew, the phrase is used by Jesus when he asserts he will or will not drink or eat "until it be fulfilled in the Kingdom of God,"[1] or "until the Kingdom of God shall come,"[2] or "when I drink it new in the Kingdom of God."[3] The Passover supper will, of course, be dealt with later at length, but suffice it now to say that all the references to the Kingdom of God during this event seem to refer to Jesus' sense that his own completion of the Kingdom of God would come about through the act of his final manifestation of loyalty to the God-process.

What can be summarized from all the indications of what Jesus experienced, felt, thought, and knew about the Kingdom of God? It was present for him in a new way, but not as many scholars (Dodd, Jeremias, and others) would affirm that it was—namely, that *he* was the Kingdom. People taking this position see Jesus putting himself at the center and thus identifying his power with the power of the Source, with God. This is totally contrary to all that is stated here.

If his presence as such was not the presence of the Kingdom, what was being affirmed by Jesus about the Kingdom? That its value is ultimate, unquestioned, and worth everything. That this value of the Kingdom forms the core of the invitation to enter it.

The Kingdom is present potentially, to be actualized

1. Lk. 22:16; §138G.
2. Lk. 22:18; §138H.
3. Mk. 14:25; §138J.

by each person as he or she pays the price of entrance, which is to "sell all," "to do the will of God."

The outer Kingdom will not come about in a cataclysmic, apocalyptic way, nor will it be ushered in by a Messiah; it will grow imperceptibly from small beginnings to huge proportions.

God's urgency about the Kingdom is shown in the parables of His/Her responsiveness to human response, and in His/Her wrath at lack of response. He/She wants the Kingdom to Become.

The Kingdom is outer and inner. What is possible about the reign of God in human society also has its counterpart in the individual psyche. This may have been the most radically new thing that his people would not accept.

Jesus saw the process of his own life as the fulfillment of the Kingdom of God for himself. His total commitment to the Kingdom was his completion, lived to the bitter and glorious end. This was his message then and now.

V

"There Shall Be No Sign"

Out of what in Jesus did this statement come?

What is the reality behind these extra-ordinary events?

What is the place and meaning of "syn-chronicity?"

What role did Jesus play in the heal-ings?

Healings and exorcisms considered as natural events, and incidents usually considered miraculous or super-natural, now occupy the center of the stage. Whether these events occurred in exactly this sequence[1] or not can never be known. However, the interpretation and understanding of them are certainly independent of sequence.

1. Mk. 4:35-8:26; §50-70.

In the wilderness experience Jesus rejected the use of miracles, or supernatural means understood as the performance of actions outside the natural sphere. Was this limited to things he could perform for himself only, or was it born out of a new concept of God? The series of incidents under consideration in this chapter requires careful scrutiny of the accuracy of report and open-mindedness about explanations. It would be as harmful to reject the so-called miracles as to accept them uncritically. The discourse on the Kingdom of God in the preceding chapter ends with the two parables on selling all for the treasure in the field and the pearl. For Jesus, this must have been the climax of what he had to say and teach. After dealing with these revolutionary and evolutionary concepts of how the Kingdom was to come about, he stated the primary personal condition for its achievement. Each person must sell all for the new Kingdom to be born in persons and in society. As he talked to his disciples, might he not have hoped that they now truly grasped his message and its significance? Was this hope justified by the events that followed?

After this discourse, Jesus and his disciples got into a boat to cross over to the other side of the lake.[1] Outwardly, this journey across the lake occurred after a tiring time, and Jesus had a human need for rest; inwardly, it was a journey of the disciples of Jesus across the waters of the unconscious, a journey from a known to an unknown side. This is a familiar motif in myth and history. Jesus slept in the bottom of the boat, obviously trusting his disciples to handle the boat. The sudden squalls and unexpected storms on the Sea of Galilee could not have been unknown to any of them, so he relaxed, rested, and slept. It was dusk.

Suddenly a storm arose. How serious we cannot know, but strong enough to alarm the disciples. Fright, terrible fright, sprang up in them. They awoke Jesus and the situation changed. Why the fright, the natural, instinctive response? Not Why? so much as Why in them? When physical life is threatened and when the possibility of being

1. Mk. 4:35-37; §50A, C.

overcome by forces over which one has no control exists, fear is not unnatural. One might ask, Why were the disciples not beyond the natural response? What had they been hearing from Jesus? What had they heard, and did their actions and attitudes reflect that?

What did they expect Jesus to do or be as they awakened him? They said, "Master, carest thou not that we perish?"[1] Was it to save him or themselves that they awakened him? Or was it the natural thing to do because Jesus embodied all the values he did for them? Obviously, the storm was not bad enough to awaken him, for he slept right on until the disciples called. This gives pause to wonder how bad the objective storm was, and whether it became intimidating because something was aroused in them. For the perception of the size of storms varies tremendously according to inner attitudes and tension. The implication seems to be that the disciples expected Jesus or his presence to help them in some way, for it is natural in dangerous situations to want a leader to be present. However, if they had truly understood and were living the process of "selling all," they probably would not have awakened him. It takes a suprahuman attitude to overcome natural things.

The report in Mark:[2] Jesus awakened, rebuked the wind, and said to the sea, "Peace, be still. And the wind ceased, and there was a great calm." And he said, "Why are you fearful? Have you not yet faith?" Matthew and Luke have virtually copied Mark in a slightly different order. Mark's text has the disciples asking each other, "Who then is this, that even the wind and the sea obey him?" This is striking because it shows they did not awaken him with the hope or expectation that he would perform some miracle. What happened came as a surprise to them.

What are the possible interpretations of the reported events? Did Jesus do or say something expressing supernatural power? Did this sudden squall and storm just die

1. Mk. 4:38; §50D.
2. Mk. 4:39-41; §50F-H.

naturally, which would not have been unusual on that lake? Was it a synchronous event? Did the storm die because he commanded it to? Or did something happen inside the disciples when the person who carried all their values was awakened and his presence was felt? Is it possible that Jesus even told the discples to be still, and a calm came over them? An inner attitude can have a tremendous impact on fear, in this case on the perception of the size of the storm. His magnetism for them, his expression of numinous power, his words as expressions of the Word, would have carried their centeredness so that when he was asleep they were overcome by the threat of nonexistence. Their existence in a meaningful way was projected and carried by him. When he was awake beside them, the truth of the situation changed for them, and they were no longer threatened.

What then can we say was the role of Jesus here? What was it he did or said that made the change? He did not exert or express supernatural powers; he did express by his very living the transformative, supranatural reality of God growing within him since the baptism. He was related to his center, to that new reality of his being which rose above the purely natural. This is no small achievement. This, then, was a supranatural event because he aroused a central Reality for them that dispelled their fear. We are so embedded in the identification of Jesus with God and with the Messianic that it is hard to strip that identification away and see the man stand out, rooted in something larger than the moment. Part of his achievement, then, was not only what he did, but his clarity about his role, and what he could do.

He said to them, "Have you not yet faith?" "Faith" is a word that has come to have certain meanings to us. What did it mean to Jesus here and on other occasions?[1] Here, it is as if Jesus were saying, Why are you so frightened? Have you not understood and responded to what I am teaching? If you are open to the Will of God in the moment, if you

---

1. Mk. 4:40; §50G.

have sold all, you are not bound to certain outcomes but can respond to what comes in a meaningful way. Then you will not fear. Faith in this sense removes fear, not because there is a specified, preconceived outcome, but because life depends on how one responds to what is in existential realities and the meaning of it.

Two aspects of the meaning of this incident of the storm have personal application. Each person can and must know the situations in actual life which most seem to threaten physical life. For one person it is storms; for another, being devoured; for another, heights; for another, depths. These actual situations threaten the natural desire for survival and produce fear until one has moved beyond the natural desire for survival to a greater desire for fulfillment. Symbolically, the rising of the waters could mean the arousal of the unconscious. Fear does arise from that part of us which is like the disciples, and just as their fear was dispelled by the presence of Jesus, so our fears can and will be dispelled when we make conscious in ourselves the dormant value which Jesus has carried for us, but to which we must ourselves relate. Take the whole incident as symbol and it becomes a beautiful statement of the existential possibility of meeting the contingencies of life by constantly reawakening in ourselves the value from God beyond, Transcendent but Immanent, as *imago dei*, and giving peace even in the midst of turmoil.

That there were healings throughout the ministry of Jesus there can be no question, but how they occurred and how they were perceived by Jesus may cast much light on the dynamics of healing for us two thousand years later. We need to understand the real happenings, how they were produced, and how they were perhaps exaggerated. Are physical healings even dangerous sometimes? What is the relationship between physical, literal healings and psychic or spiritual wholeness?

Close to the beginning of his ministry, it was said that people sought Jesus because some healings had occurred. "All are seeking thee." Jesus' response was, "Let us move to the next town that I may preach there, for to this end came I forth."[1] He did not deny that there were healings, but he made a definite statement of priorities. At the beginning of his ministry, healings happened. He did not make them happen, but they happened. The questions: Were healings ever sought after by Jesus as central to religious wholeness? What was his attitude toward them and his role in them? What was the function of the attitude of the person seeking healing? Behind these questions lie the possible explanations of the happenings. In all these incidents, those wanting healing sought Jesus. This is central. He did not initiate the healing. The sick came to Jesus, who had become a healing symbol for them. When asked if he were the Christ by the followers of John the Baptist, Jesus answered with a quotation from Isaiah which included healing as a happening, but not necessarily one he sought.[2]

It is striking that one way Jesus attempted to deal with the phenomenon of people seeking healing from him was to ask questions which located the answers within persons, and this placed the cause of any healing also within.

> And as Jesus passed by from thence, two blind men followed him, crying out, and saying, Have mercy on us, thou son of David. And when he was come into the house, the blind men came to him: and Jesus saith unto them, Believe ye that I am able to do this? They say unto him, Yea, Lord. Then touched he their eyes, saying, According to your faith be it done unto you. And their eyes were opened. And Jesus strictly charged them, saying, See that no man know it. But they went forth, and spread abroad his fame in all the land.[3]

His question "Believe ye that I am able to do this?" and his words "according to your faith" place the discriminative and healing factor within the blind men. Later, he asked blind Bartimaeus, "What wilt thou that I should do unto thee?"[4] Here also the blind person's attitude is central.

Another incident which throws light on the dynamics of the healing process, as seen by Jesus and further inter-

1. Mk. 1:37-38; §26B-C.
2. Mt. 11:2-6; §41C.
3. Mt. 9:27-31; §53A.
4. Lk. 18:41; §121D.

preted by the gospel writer, revolves around the woman with the issue of blood. In this account a most interesting small point reveals the shift from Jesus' point of view to what the later writers wished to make of it.[1] "And straightway Jesus, perceiving in himself that the power proceeding from him had gone forth, turned about him in the crowd, and said, Who touched my garments?" This is the editor's statement that Jesus perceived power, but when one turns to the account in Luke, Jesus said, "Someone did touch me: for I perceived that power had gone forth from me."[2] The inference in Mark as editor becomes an assertion by Jesus in Luke, a striking example of how religious bias shapes facts. At the end of this incident we have the the story of the twelve-year-old girl aroused probably from a coma. She is supposed by some to be dead; Jesus tells the parents of the child that "no man should know of this."[3]

So the evidence accumulates that Jesus recognized himself as a figure who constellated possible healing in people. Whatever he was in touch with in himself could affect others. He moved with compassion for sick persons, and with understanding of himself as symbol rather than producer of healing. The power that was generated through him was not his power, nor did he identify with it. When the distinction between him and the Source was lost, Jesus himself was regarded as the healer. What does this mean and imply?

A significant incident which occurred in his own home town may help us to understand better Jesus' attitude toward this healing factor.[4] When he taught in the synagogue of his home town, the reaction was what one might expect from one's townspeople. The scene in Mark suggests mutterings among the crowd, some praising his words and the authority by which he spoke; others asking, "Is not this the carpenter, the son of Mary, and brother of James, and Joses, and Judas, and Simon? and are not his

1. Mk. 5:25-34; §52D-J.
2. Lk.8:46; §52H.
3. Mk. 5:35-43; §52I-T.
4. Mk. 6:1-6a; §54.

sisters here with us? And they were offended in him."[1] It was a limited but very natural reaction, not necessarily negative, of people who had stayed in their familiar patterns and their own little worlds. But one of their townspeople had moved into the world that was new and unfamiliar to them, and had moved into God's world, God's Kingdom, where a New Birth had been experienced by him. On the part of the villagers there was, perhaps, pride, but mostly a kind of unconscious envy, a feeling of being challenged beyond their limitations. No poet has expressed this problem better than Josephine Johnson:

> You who fear change are like those sheep that turn
> Back from cold mountain creeks, and drink
> Only in familiar pools, or suck
> Green milk of those marshy ponds that lie
> Round and unmoving in a valley's palm.
>
> O slow and complacent muzzles, does it mean
> Nothing to you that dust and drought
> Shrivel the little pools, and dung
> Stains the warm stagnant water where the steers
> Follow your little pathways to the pond?
>
> Time fouls still water and slime lies
> Mucous and soft above all ponds.
> The lake by living springs unfed
> Shrinks to a caking slough.
>
> Blind is the shepherd who would lead his sheep
> Back to those steer-trampled waters![2]

When a person like Jesus (or anyone who has taken the step of entering the narrow gate and finding a new family) acts, it will appear strange, different, and challenging to those who remain in old patterns. So the reaction to Jesus in his home town was expressed as genuine ambivalence: response to or withdrawal from.

Jesus perceived their ambivalent reaction and said, "A prophet is not without honor, save in his own country, and

1. Mk. 6:3; §54D, F.
2. Josephine Johnson, "You Who Fear Change," in *Year's End* (New York: Simon and Schuster, 1937).

among his own kind, and in his own house."[1] As always, Jesus placed himself in the prophetic tradition of his people and recognized the truth that it is those closest who cannot perceive change and transformation. They remain blind just because the instinctual responses are so deep, and so they fail to see the newness manifested in their friend or townsperson.

The account is concluded in Mark with, "And he could there do no mighty work, save that he laid his hands upon a few sick folk, and healed them. And he marvelled because of their unbelief."[2] Matthew has, "He did not many mighty works there because of their unbelief."[3] In Mark it is clear that Jesus *could* not do any mighty works; in Matthew that he *chose* not to. Doing mighty works in Mark is involuntary and outside his choice, while doing mighty works in Matthew is a volitional act of choice. What is accomplished by Matthew's obvious editorializing? It changed the role of Jesus from one who participates in a process of rebirth with those wanting healing to one who has power entirely within himself to do as he chooses. The Mark account depicts Jesus as co-creator with the healing process, while the Matthew account depicts him as an independent chooser with power to manipulate the Source of healing.

If we take Jesus as a miracle worker, then he is not holding for us a process for us to learn from. Also in Mark, the statement "save that he laid his hands upon a few sick folk, and healed them" contradicts the previous sentence, and it seems to be a later insertion because the early church could not quite accept the radicalness of Jesus' position that the power was not his.

What was being asserted by Jesus in the light of all the reported healings? Out of what does the possibility of physical healing come? We are in the presence of a mystery, and a new learning that focuses on the question of spirit and matter, their interaction, and what lies behind them. The one thing that seems certain, from the incident

1. Mk. 6:4; §54H.
2. Mk. 6:5; §54J.
3. Mt. 13:58; §54J.

here and from healings known to have happened and to be happening at centers such as Lourdes, Einseideln, and Epidaurus, is that no healing in substance occurs without an external catalytic agent being a symbol for healing. There must be a healing symbol, someone or something to which the sick person is bound, an outer reality which constellates the healing factor within the seeker. The symbol can activate the archetype of wholeness or healing within the sick person. The unanswered mystery is why one person responds to one symbol, one to another, and some respond to none.

Throughout Christian history Jesus himself has been identified as the singular carrier and representative of the healing Source. Why do people want someone else to be the healer, rather than to relate themselves to the healing process? Because it seems easier to have the healing power invested in another person than to participate in a healing process oneself. "Believing on" Jesus has produced endless healings, but the significant thing is that Jesus never identified himself with the Source. He was the vessel, a container of the power, and thus a symbol for people responding to him. It is basic to remember that he meant, "You can say what you want to about me or the Son of man but not about the Holy Spirit in me." Another incident, to be discussed later, is where the leper who was healed made the discrimination between thanking Jesus and glorifying God. A misleading aspect of the current emphasis on physical healings is that physical healing may be equated with psychic healing, and they are seldom the same. A positive aspect of the emphasis, however, is the realization of the powerful interrelationship between psyche and soma. This raises the question of interaction between psyche and soma. Are they parallel, independent forces, or are both expressions of the Something more, the *unus mundus*?

Now comes the first report of Jesus sending out his disciples, the third discourse in Matthew.[1] The difficult critical question is, How much did Jesus actually say to his disciples, and how much reflects early Christian commun-

1. Mt. 9:36-11:1; Mk. 6:7-11; §56C-K.

ity when the disciples did in fact go out to spread the message? What may be the minimum that could actually describe the Jesus of history with his followers? There is also a report in Document P where Luke has extended statements on the same theme. Matthew combines what he finds in Mark with some of his Document P report and statements found elsewhere. That he had twelve disciples seems clear. (The word "disciple" usually designates followers other than the twelve who were called "apostles.") The Mark account states, "He called unto him the twelve," and Document P says, "The Lord appointed seventy others, and sent them two and two before his face into every city and place, whither he himself was about to come."[1] The setting of the Document P account where Jesus is en route to Jerusalem is totally different from the one in Mark.

What are the features of the Mark account of the Mission Discourse to the disciples? Jesus gives them "authority over the unclean spirits"[2] and advocates no possessions or worldly goods. He tells the twelve to stay in any house they enter, and lastly, that if a place or house does not receive them, they should "shake off the dust that is under your feet for a testimony unto them."[3] Is any of this from Jesus or is it all a reflection of later development? He could have said it, but it does not quite ring true or consistent with his message. It does ring true with much of what the disciples actually did when, after his death, they started to proselytize. Within this discourse there is in Luke the statement "And he sent them forth to preach the Kingdom of God, and to heal the sick."[4] Matthew has a statement with the same import which is preceded by, "Go not into any way of the Gentiles, and enter not into any city of the Samaritans: but go rather to the lost sheep of the house of Israel."[5] The statement on the Kingdom of God is not surprising, but the statement on limiting the message to the Jews is somewhat startling.

1. Lk. 10:1; §82A.
2. Mk. 6:7; §56C.
3. Mk. 6:11; §56K.
4. Lk. 9:2; §56F.
5. Mt. 10:5-6; §56E.

After their first mission, when the disciples returned to Jesus to report their activities, Jesus suggested they retreat into a desert place for a rest. But the multitudes saw them and ran to them. This is the setting for the first of the two accounts of the feeding of the multitude.[1] At the end of the first account he sent his disciples away and "departed into the mountain to pray." At the end of the second report he sent the multitudes away and got into a boat with the disciples to move toward Dalmanutha. Whether we have one incident reported twice or two incidents is a matter of individual choice. I favor one incident told twice. In both cases, Jesus was moved by compassion at outer pressures and demands at a time when he was seeking rest and withdrawal and desired to be alone.

In the light of all that has preceded, we would hardly take these accounts to be supernatural events of a concrete, literal nature, yet it seems clear that the writers of the gospels wanted to present another picture of the miracle worker. Out of what could the accounts grow, and what could their meaning be for us today? The situation is simple: there were multitudes of people following him, people hungry for what he had to offer; people wanting him as a shepherd, wanting him to teach them. They pressed hard on him and at the end of the day the disciples wanted him to send the people away, but he refused.

Were they hungry just for food? Certainly it is so presented. To be sure, the problem of physical hunger probably was there after the long day of listening, though hunger often seems worse than it actually is under certain circumstances. And they were with a man who held great power, great *mana*, for them. Whatever he touched bore the mark of him. What did he do? He commanded his disciples to bring the limited amount of what was available and to spread it out.

What exactly went on in the thought or heart of Jesus at this time we can never know. How conscious was he of the result of what he did ahead of time, or was it an entirely fortuitous outcome? After he blessed the loaves and the fish, as the host or family head did at each meal, their ac-

1. Mk. 6:32-46, §60; Mk. 8:1-10, §67.

tual quantity seemed changed, and there was enough for all the people to eat.[1] The literal miracle would be the expansion of the physical properties of the food to include enough for all. The deeper miracle could be one of two things, or some of each. Perhaps the food was, in fact, more than anticipated when broken into parts and the number of people was exaggerated. But more significant was what happened to the food and the people when the food was blessed by one who held the value that Jesus did for them. In blessing he brought spirit, an attitude of calling up or down that of God which changes, transforms, and heals. The substance seemed different after the blessing. No longer just physical food, it was imbued with the blessing of Jesus and his Source. The attitude of the people was changed, too, and what was poverty before now became plenty. A new sustenance had filled them—"spirit food," as the Navahos call it. What was required to fill them was now much less, yet they went away satisfied.

Just what was this blessing and how relevant is it today? Not in outer social situations where real food is needed, but in personal ways, we are more aware of inadequacies that can be changed to plenty. Jesus blessed the loaves and fish and there was a change, but no such change could have occurred through a casual blessing of the food or with only the conscious ego side. Such an event could happen only when one was in touch with the resource of transformation as Jesus was. Perhaps we can evoke the values incarnated in him which can permeate the situations of our need. This would be to arouse the presence of the values seen *in* him, not him, and to let these values come to bear on any situation of poverty or psychological inadequacy. What happens when one comes in contact with the blessing, the emanation from a holy center such as Jesus touched? The phenomenon of multiplication in alchemy deals with it. Things change, multiply, according to what is brought to bear. The vitality inherent in things, the properties of matter, may have potency when touched by Spirit, or whenever Spirit in them is released.

1.   Mk. 6:41; §60G.

One of the strongest statements on human nature and its religious problem is found in the next incident, where Jesus was criticized by Pharisees, who had come from Jerusalem, because his disciples ate their bread with unwashed hands.[1] That the Pharisees came from Jerusalem shows how much fame surrounded him and how concerned they were to catch him on some small point. The law concerning eating with undefiled hands was a man-made law, not a law of God, and Jesus answered them first with an apt quotation from Isaiah, criticizing them for worshipping God with their lips, "but their heart is far from me." He continued, "Ye leave the commandment of God, and hold fast the tradition of men."[2]

One example of this was the law of Moses concerning the treatment of mother and father. Once again, the first stage of Jesus' answer was a logical reply or a historical example. Then he turned to the multitude to expound on the real core of the matter. He penetrated directly the crucial issue of defilement with, "There is nothing from without the man, that going into him can defile him: but the things which proceed out of the man are those that defile the man."[3] What was Jesus doing here to the problem of defilement or contamination? Of those things that can hurt persons and dirty them, Mosaic law listed sexual intercourse—especially adultery; childbirth; sexual or other issues from the body (semen and menstrual blood are unclean); animals regarded as sacred in other religions; leprosy; and dead bodies. Jesus changed the whole focus of the source of defilement from outer to inner. No laws, taboos, or strictures in themselves save from contamination. We do not become guilty by association. The outer situation, though it may be wrong or evil, cannot in itself corrupt us, for corruption comes from attitudes within us.

Such realism and insight into human nature separated Jesus from much of his tradition, which was filled with laws intended to keep the person from contaminating factors. They also separate him from much of the Christian tradition, which follows closely the Jewish attitude. The

1. Mk. 7:1-23; §63.
2. Mk. 7:8; §63G.
3. Mk. 7:15; §63I.

fundamental issue here is *where* evil resides. The tendency to want to project it, to see it outside instead of seeing it as part of one's own self, is very great, as has been seen. We are split people who do not want to include the darkness within, so we see it externally in others. Because we project, the split becomes worse. Jesus goes back to the heart of the issue.

When Jesus moved away from the multitudes, his disciples went with him and asked him about his statement. One almost feels his exasperation when he said, "Are you so without understanding also?"[1] The mood here is comparable to when he asked the disciples, when they aroused him in the boat, "Have you not yet faith?" He might have expected these disciples to be more with him in spirit and understanding, but they had not gone through his depth of repentance in the experience of the baptism and wilderness. Moved by the Spirit of God, Jesus was following the will of God as he perceived it. The disciples were following Jesus, not his way. This distinction between the objects of devotion of the disciples must never be lost sight of, because it determined later events in the life of each of them, and in the whole historical thrust following the life of Jesus.

He explained that nothing from without can defile one. But, he said:

> That which proceedeth out of the man, that defileth the man. For from within, out of the heart of men, evil thoughts proceed, fornications, thefts, murders, adulteries, covetings, wickednesses, deceit, lasciviousness, and evil eye, railing, pride, foolishness: all these evil things proceed from within, and defile the man."[2]

For the third time he repeated that all evil is from within. Surely it may reflect an actual outer evil, but the source of evil is the heart of the person. The heart (the word was used by the Hebrews of that time to mean mind or will) can produce evil as well as good. It is, in other words, a symbol of ambivalence. One is reminded of the commandment to love God with all one's heart, soul, strength, and mind,

1. Mk. 7:18; §63K.
2. Mk. 7:20-23; §63L.

which comes later in the account.[1] To love with all one's heart, then, is to include loving God with our darkness, too.

Earlier, Jesus had said, "Remember your anger at the altar," "Resist not evil," and "Sufficient unto the day is the evil thereof." Here the source of evil within ouselves becomes clearer. Why is it so hard to accept this? Why so much easier to see evil in others and not in ourselves? To claim our own evil or darkness is to alter our one-sided picture of ourselves as good, rational, and civilized beings. We are, in part, all of these things, but under the surface in the unconscious also lurks the great shadow part of ourselves which is dark, unknown, and full of demons and angels. Much that is positive and repressed from childhood is there, but the negative and destructive is also there and if not faced and integrated comes out in the symptoms Jesus described. We are nowhere near as good as we think we are. Our world wars and the violence in racial, economic, and ecological areas all testify to the cruelty and insensitivity which dominate us. Paul Tillich said that the worst evil is done by good people. What does it require to look at one's own evil, and how is one to do it?[2]

Beyond this, there is the question of what the source of all evil is, a question that has taxed theologians, philosophers, and thinkers through the ages. Not what we today think is the root of evil, but rather, what evidence we have as to what Jesus, the Jew in his tradition emerging into newness, thought was the root of evil. Orthodox Christianity has assumed evil comes from humans. "All good from God, all evil from man" (omne bonum a Deo, omne malum ab hominem). One finds this stated over and over in Christian thought, but the fact is that in Isaiah, Yahweh says, "I make peace, and create evil."[3] And even more significant is the fact that in the creation myth of the Garden of Eden, Yahweh plants the Tree of the Knowledge of Good and Evil. The opposites of good and evil are there from the beginning as part of the Godhead. The question of whether evil comes from God or humans was addressed in conversations and correspondence between Dr. Jung and

1. Lk. 10:27; §83A.
2. See Appendix II for techniques to deal with evil.
3. Isa. 45:7.

Father Victor White. They also dealt with the problem of whether evil was the absence of good (referred to theologically as the doctrine of *privatio boni*) or had its own reality.[1]

Does it make a practical, as well as psychological and religious, difference which way we choose to answer the question of the origin of evil with integrity? Yes. For many of us, the struggle to overcome and transform our own evil is deeper, more valid—even easier—if it is seen as part of the Divine Process. Somehow, to see one's own struggle with darkness as part of the struggle of God to unite His/Her opposites into a whole lifts the burden of negative self-judgment and invests one's personal efforts with more depth, wholesomeness, and dignity. It was very meaningful to hear Reinhold Niebuhr say, "I did not create myself," and "I must move without that sin of pride as an evasion."[2]

The Pharisees, many of whom constantly opposed Jesus because of the revolutionary stands he took on the status quo religion of the day, now asked for a sign.[3] They wanted to catch Jesus, but to be able to turn him over to the Romans, they had to prove that he was a political threat. Only if he claimed to be the Messiah would the Romans have any interest in him. He had already spoken the parables of the Kingdom of God and had definitely stated his new dynamic concept. He had evaded the Messianic question by his answer to John's disciples. That the Pharisees asked for a sign indicates that nothing of a miraculous nature, as they understood such things, had occurred; or that if miracles had occurred, they had not heard of them. The latter possibility hardly seems likely. Much more probable is that we have here one more piece of evidence that no miracles had happened. Their request for a sign obviously implies there had been a dearth of supernatural events that could be considered signs.

At this request for a sign, Jesus "sighed deeply in his spirit and said, Why does this generation seek a sign? . . .

1. Gerhard Alder, ed., *Letters of C.G. Jung*, 2:52-53.
2. Fletcher Farm, Vermont, seminar, 1936.
3. Mk. 8:11-13; §68.

"There shall no sign be given unto this generation."[1] Matthew's account has Jesus saying, "An evil and adulterous generation seeketh after a sign; and there shall no sign be given unto it, but the sign of Jonah."[2] In Luke's Document P account of the same incident, Jesus asserted that it was an evil generation which sought for a sign and no sign would be given it but the sign of Jonah.[3] The sign of Jonah is defined in Luke's Document P in terms of Jonah's prophetic function of preaching repentance to the people of Nineveh. Here Jesus added another dimension to "Son of man" by likening it to Jonah's function. At another point, Matthew mentioned the sign of Jonah, and the emphasis was not on Jonah as preacher of repentance, but on Jonah's being three days and nights in the belly of the whale.[4] Clearly, that was a reference to the resurrection.

Critically, then, we have many reported answers from Jesus to the request for a sign. What may have been his most authentic answer? In Mark it is clearly "no sign;" in Matthew "no sign" is qualified by "but the sign of Jonah;" and in Document P "the sign of Jonah" is understood in Luke as preaching and in Matthew as a resurrection symbol. Which way is tradition most likely to have moved? From Mark to the resurrection symbol, or from the resurrection symbol to Mark? There seems to be no question that the movement would have been from the simple, unambiguous account in Mark to the later addition of the repentance motif and then to the early Christian image in Matthew of the resurrection symbol. How may the later traditions have developed? Perhaps the most likely way would have been then for the answer of the sign of Jonah as preacher of repentance to have appeared first, and then as resurrection motif.

The answer of Jesus in Mark is, by implication, one of the most stunning and clear statements on the nature of the Kingdom of God, how God works, and Jesus' own self-estimate. Jesus affirmed here that God does not work through miracles as we have defined them, and the

1. Mk. 8:12; §68C.
2. Mt. 16:4; 68C.
3. Lk. 11:29; §88B.
4. Mt. 12:38-40; §45R-S.

Kingdom of God is not going to come through supernatural signs. These are not insignificant statements! Ever since the wilderness experience we have seen how Jesus' self-estimate clearly eliminated miraculous elements and wonders. The thing he rejected is a "sign" understood as a miraculous intervention by God into the natural order of things. That is not the way God works; that is not what should be looked for in Messiahship. Not only does it not work that way, but it could not work; it is not the way things are. The Kingdom of God, the way by which God's reign will come, will not be an outer event. This completely refutes the apocalyptic concept and invalidates looking to Jesus or to any person for a Messianic sign. His answer originated in his own baptism and wilderness experience, in which God moved from the apocalyptic in John to the deep inner recess of Jesus' being. There was no possible answer to the request for a sign except the one he gave.

If the so-called miraculous events prior to this scene had happened in some form, or had some historical basis, and were not pure fabrications of the author, how can they be interpreted? Some surely were imaginative enlargements of the editors which make them seem miraculous. But behind even these, what could have happened? Do they express Jesus' relationship to a supernatural power which he had previously rejected, or do they in varying degrees express his relationship to some aspect of the power of God, taken not as supernatural, but as supra-natural? Did Jesus' experience in the baptism and wilderness expand the meaning of how God works in situations and in the psyche? Were there new laws at work in these so-called miracle accounts which Jesus tapped, and how available are they to us? Whatever he was doing or helping to happen, he did not consider it a sign, nor, since they requested a sign, must the Pharisees have considered his activity a sign. Yet much of what Jesus is reported to have done has been proof to Christians of his supernatural power!

What would Jesus say of the two thousand years of history since his life? He wanted people to relate to the central reality of God and to know the power of that, not to project that power onto him. In his lifetime to his followers,

118

and since to Christians, he has been a symbol. It might be helpful to explore and relate to the archetypal reality available behind that symbol now.

Where does the longing for sign come from? Are not *we* part of that "evil and adulterous generation?" In what ways do we long for a sign? Often we have spoken of the projection of negative elements onto others; now, we also face how much we project hoped-for positive things which may save us. We long for a political or social savior "out there" who will do the task for us, instead of ourselves actualizing the saving element within, bringing it into fullness of manifestation.

In the incident immediately following the Pharisees' request for a sign,[1] a careful analysis is necessary. The disciples and Jesus left the scene in a boat. They had very little bread. Jesus first said to the disciples, "Take heed, beware of the leaven of the Pharisees and the leaven of Herod." The disciples were puzzled by this and said, "We have no bread." To what, in fact, did Jesus refer when he said "leaven" and why did he say it? In light of the preceding incident, could he not very naturally have been referring to the Pharisees and Herodians who were trying to catch him on questions related to the Messianic hope so as to do away with him? When the disciples said, "We have no bread," Jesus asked, "Why reason you, because you have no bread? Do you not yet perceive, neither understand? Have you your hearts hardened? Having eyes, see you not? and having ears, hear you not? and do you not remember?" This was a very natural response of Jesus, a reaction of anguish to their lack of understanding. They had taken the "leaven" to mean "bread," even though that was really ridiculous in light of the reference to the Pharisees and Herodians.

Then, according to the text, Jesus pointed out the fact of the feeding of the five thousand as if he were saying, "Do you not remember that I produced bread before? I can again." Again, he asked, "Do you not yet understand?" which makes no sense in light of his relation to the feeding

1. Mk. 8:14-21; §69.

of the multitude and the miracles in general. But if one eliminates the words referring to this feeding, or considers that they may have been added later, then the words "Do you not yet understand?" follow very naturally and logically. This possibility is further confirmed perhaps by the way Matthew, following Mark, ends his account:

> How is it that you do not perceive that I spake not to you concerning bread? But beware of the leaven of the Pharisees and Sadducees. Then understood they how that he bade them not beware of the leaven of bread, but of the teachings of the Pharisees and Sadducees.[1]

Luke has, "Beware you of the leaven of the Pharisees, which is hypocrisy."[2] If we consider the section on the feeding of the multitude as later addition, then the scene offers one of the most anguished accounts between Jesus and his disciples. That he could hope they would understand him seems a very natural and legitimate expectation. The fact was that they did not, that somehow they were so blind about him that they could not separate him from what was behind or in him. He became the value, not the representative of it, and thus this becomes even more crucial and may be behind the next step he took.

---

1.   Mt. 16:11-12; §69C-D.
2.   Lk. 12:1; §91B.

VI

"But Who Say You That I Am?"

Out of what does this question come?

How does Peter respond?

What so far is Jesus' Messianic self-consciousness, if any?

Why does a statement on the Son of man follow in Jesus' answer?

Now one of the most crucial dialogues in the gospels, a dialogue between Jesus and Peter, took place. When Jesus finished the conversation with the disciples on signs, he went forth to the villages of Caesarea Philippi, near Jordan's source. On the journey he first asked them, "Who do men say that I am?" The disciples' answer was a threefold one: John the Baptist, Elijah, or one of the prophets.[1] It is conspicuous that the Messiah is not included in the answer, although the answers of Elijah and John the Baptist had Messianic overtones. Jesus proceeded to the second stage with the question "But who say you that I am?" Peter answered, "Thou art the Christ," and Jesus

1. Mk. 8:27-33; §71-72.

"charged them that they should tell no man of him."[1] This conversation occurred shortly before Jesus was turning his face to Jerusalem. The questions came after some discouraging times with the disciples due to their lack of understanding of what he was really teaching. Naturally, he would have wondered what they were seeing and putting on him, what their image of him was, and what they hoped for from him.

Behind these two questions, was Jesus really asking a third question: "Who do I say I am to myself?" Did he ask the first question—"Who do men say that I am?"—because he did not know what the people thought, or because it naturally led to the second question, which was his real focus? Or did he know who people thought he was, and did he want to correct those misconceptions? Or was it a mixture of all these things? We see a man deeply puzzled, burdened with new realities and messages, struggling to clarify for himself and others, and perhaps for God, concerns not in his head but in his heart and at the core of his being. Luke says that Jesus was praying alone.[2]

Surely this was a time of ultimacy. What were the people thinking? What were those closest to him thinking? These are questions that seem to be outer, but perhaps the root of them was a moment of deep interiority. He was searching for God's meaning for him in the depths and heights. Multitudes were following, full of praise and commendation, but enemies, the authorities, were pursuing in disapproval of his activities. And his disciples were following, perhaps blindly, perhaps helping, perhaps hindering the birth of the new Kingdom. It was an agonizing inner-outer time, and we can see the true stature of this human becoming ever clearer. His life was to be lived, in one sense, without reference to any outer authority, but in another sense the God to be served was in human history. His space was filled with the "Thous" of every moment of choice. Responses, acclaim, hostility, and being persecuted were part of the reality of the situation where he was to find the will of God.

1. Mk. 8:30; §71G.
2. Lk. 9:18; §71A-B.

Looking back before this moment, the demoniacs had called him the Messiah, the Holy One of God, and Jesus had told them to be quiet and not to tell anyone. The disciples of John, when he was in prison, had come and asked Jesus, "Art thou the Christ?" Obviously, whatever John had heard about Jesus evoked that question and did not answer it for him. Clearly, whatever Jesus had done was not in accord with John's Messianic hope. At that point, the simple, stunning answer of Jesus was "Go tell him what you see happening. Much is going on toward healing and there is good news." And he added, "Blessed is he, whosoever shall find none occasion of stumbling in me,"[1] that is, do not misinterpret or let your own preconceptions stand in the way of objective looking and judging. By quoting Isaiah the prophet and by warning not to stumble, the anwswer was neither a yes nor a no. Jesus did not affirm or deny the Messianic role. This would be his continuing, challenging attitude even at the trial. What is behind this way of dealing with this question constitutes one of the central points in the life of Jesus and in this book. Why did Jesus not say, "No, I am not the Christ, but a prophet"? That is a more startling question than, Why did he not say yes?

Peter's answer to the second question on the journey to Caesarea Philippi could hardly be clearer: "Thou art the Christ."[2] Luke adds, "the Christ of God,"[3] while Matthew has, "Thou art the Christ, the Son of the Living God."[4] What content did Jesus put into these replies and why did he say not to tell anyone, then proceed to speak of the Son of man,[5] and to continue the dialogue with Peter?[6] Peter

---

1. Mt. 11:6; §41C.
2. Mk. 8:29; §71D.
3. Lk. 9:20; §71D.
4. Mt. 16:16; §71D. See Appendix I regarding Matthew's addition in 16:17-19 of the one extended statement attributed to Jesus on the church and the role of Peter. Matthew's earlier omission of all the references to demoniacs calling Jesus the Christ may be because he saw them as detracting from this statement by Peter.
5. Mk. 8:31; §72A.
6. Mk.8:33; §72B.

here articulated the deepest longing and, perhaps experience, of the group as a whole. What Messianic content did he express? It is unlikely Peter hoped for an apocalyptic Messiah. He could have been affirming the hope that Jesus would be the political redeemer who would free them from bondage to Rome, or he could have been sensing something new in Jesus that he did not understand and yet which aroused the numinous value. Even if the sense of something new was true, Peter was certainly seeing it manifested only in Jesus. The meaning of the saving element behind savior, redeemer, was felt by Peter to belong only to Jesus as the Christ. Up to this point Jesus had in no sense affirmed or denied he was the Christ. In fact, he had tried to avoid the question. He did not identify himself with the Messianic role, nor did he want others to identify him with the Messianic role. He wanted his disciples and the people to know what he had known since the baptism-wilderness: that God functioned in the psyche as well as in history; that God could be experienced in the human soul as immanent Reality.

It is evident why Jesus charged them not to say anything to anyone. He did not say yes to Peter's affirmation, but even more conspicuously, he did not say no. He simply said to be quiet and them continued with his implicit answer in what follows. This was a great moment. Why was he not direct about his relationship to the Messianic role? Either is was not yet clear to him, or it was clear but there was no yes-no answer, or it was clear but he was not willing to say it to the people. The last seems more subtle, more difficult to comprehend, but truer. To have said yes would have been to lie; to have said no would have been equally untrue because what lay behind the hope of the Messiah was a Reality that he could not refute or refuse. The roots of the Messianic longing and the specific longing for a Messiah had been discovered in a human by Jesus and understood to be part of God's intent.

He, Jesus, knew himself now to be a vessel, a container of newness of God, yet he hardly knew what to do with it. So to have said no would have denied this new archetypal Reality within, now in a birthing process. To have defined it either way would have damaged the vitality of the image.

With directness he went on to speak again about the Son of man. "And he began to teach them, that the Son of man must suffer many things, and be rejected by the elders, and the chief priests, and the scribes, and be killed, and after three days rise again."[1] The phrase "Son of man" has appeared before this as a potential forgiving factor, as being the basis for authority and decision making, and as a human factor, separate for Jesus from the Holy Spirit, capable of being blasphemed against. The previous statement about the Son of man is repeated with variations in two later places, and it is the only one that appears three times in almost the same form. We may have a formulation here that represents a later Christian development, but this does not eliminate the possibility or the probability that Jesus spoke something like this. That Jesus should choose to move directly from the issue of whether he was the Christ or not to a discussion of the Son of man reveals deep self-insight. Having not answered yes or not to the Messianic question, he replaced the Messianic-Christ image by using the "Son of man." In doing this he came closer to defining what "the Son of man" might refer to. He described the suffering of the person choosing the individual way and being rejected by collective opinions and the authorities. The Messianic-Christ image here moved from archetype of the indwelling Self to that of Self-in-action making a choiceful moral decision to face evil as part of totality. "Messiah" was redefined in terms that bridged the gap between unconscious and conscious.

That Jesus anticipated his possible rejection and death does not seem strange. The plot had been growing since it was first stated that the Pharisees and Herodians were out to get him. It does not take any superhuman insight to predict his suffering and death, but that he would refer to the resurrection is new and of a different quality. This is the first time any reference to the resurrection has been made, and on the basis of critical grounds is suspect. It is startling in light of his statement about miracles and signs and strange that Peter should rebuke him for a prediction of such a glorious outcome. It is not strange if we see it as a

1. Mk. 8:31; Mt. 16:21; Lk. 9:22; §72A.

·

natural addition to the text, the reference being to the early church's belief in the resurrection and whatever lay behind it.[1]

Let us return to the dialogue between Jesus and Peter. Peter rebuked Jesus because he predicted his probable rejection and death. "And Peter took him and began to rebuke him." Jesus turned and rebuked Peter before the disciples, saying the famous words "Get thee behind me, Satan: for thous mindest not the things of God, but the things of men."[2] Why did Jesus rebuke Peter? Because Peter had called him the Christ or because Peter did not accept the reality of Jesus' prediction of his rejection and death? Was Jesus stating the probable fact, the hard reality, and was Peter so blinded by his own preconceptions and desires that Jesus should be the Christ that he could not listen to the truth? Peter is addressed by Jesus as Satan, and as one who minds the things of men, because his attitude is one of narrow, egocentric wishes. He, Peter, lived in a world where the focus was on his own natural predispositions and longings and not on the supranatural forces of the will of God. Satan was depicted earlier as a potential prodder to consciousness, one who brought the fact of the regressive or lesser alternative to consciousness and thus offered a choice. Peter offered the most regressive choice here by saying, in essence, "Do not go the way of the Son of man." But Jesus had to go the way of the Son of man as being the way of God's will.

It may be asked if Jesus was here tempted by Peter to choose the lesser way. No, not in the sense that there was any real desire not to go the way of the Son of man. For Jesus, the "things of God" came first even if pain and death were involved. Jesus was strong in his affirmation that the lesser way is always there in the alternatives within the Godhead. For Jesus, the Satanic way was for human consciousness not to become actualized. Peter was in this condition. If we use the dialogue as a possible form for our own inner growth, it would mean including considerations like this: Jesus, or that in Jesus which is in us,

1. See Appendix I for all references to the resurrection in the gospels.
2. Mk 8:33; §72B.

would choose value even when it entails great pain. Peter's denial would parallel that side in us that wants to hold on to the good and the comfortable and to avoid darkness. Peter in us cannot let go of preconceived images in order to face reality, and protests the choosing of the other side. In our reality, the question of where the ego, our conscious side, stands, determines whether we hold on to old images or choose new ones.

Earlier, a third question was suggested: What would Jesus have answered to, "Who do I say I am to myself?" He might have said he saw himself as a describer of a Process that led to Life, that he was faithful to the message of seeking and sharing the Way to the Kingdom.

Following this extended dialogue with Peter, Jesus called his disciples together and said, "If any man would come after me, let him deny himself, and take up his cross, and follow me." Luke adds, "take up his cross daily."[1] The Greek meaning of "deny himself" is not to deny *to* himself, the basis of most ascetic practices, but to deny himself in the sense of egocentric self, that self that wants to have things its own way, to be lord of the universe.

This is the first time "cross" is used by Jesus as a symbol. It comes at about the halfway point of the story, shortly before he moves toward Jerusalem. He did not say, "take up *my* cross;" he said, "take up *one's own* cross." What could be the meaning of taking up one's own cross daily? The cross represents an intersection of opposites, any number of opposites. To take up the cross may be to shoulder responsibility for the integration of our own opposites. Dr. Jung has this to say:

> Instead of bearing ourselves, i.e., our own cross ourselves, we load Christ with our unresolved conflicts. We "place ourselves under *his* cross," but by golly not under our own. . . .The cross of Christ was *borne* by *himself* and was *his*. To put oneself under somebody else's cross, which has already been carried by him, is certainly easier than to carry your own cross amid the mockery and contempt of the world. . . .

1. Mk. 8:34; Lk. 9:23; §73A.

> We imitate Christ and hope he will deliver us from our own
> fate. . . .No talk at all of uniting our Above and Below! . . .
> Have your congregations understood that they must close their
> ears to the traditional teachings and go through the darknesses of
> their own souls and set aside everything in order to become that
> which every individual bears in himself as his individual task, and
> that no one can take this burden from him?[1]

Jesus continued with what A.E. Housman, the poet, has said is the most profound statement ever uttered, the paradox of losing life to save it. Why did these words follow the dialogue of ultimate conviction and precede the so-called transfiguration experience? Whether this was the actual sequence or whether it was the editors' choice, it is highly dramatic that the paradox statement is placed between these events. There are several reports of this saying. Which is most apt to be the original? The simplest form is the one in Document P, Luke, which says, "Whosoever shall seek to gain his life shall lose it: but whosoever shall lose his life shall preserve it." The Matthew account in Document P has "for my sake."[2] The more complicated and questionable form in Mark includes the phrase, "for my sake and the Gospel's;" Matthew and Luke have just "for my sake."[3] My choice is to take the account in Document P as the simplest, possibly most authentic form. The assumption is that "for my sake" and "for my sake and the Gospel's" would both be reflections of early Christian thought. Much clarity can be gained if we take this statement and divide it into two halves, and for each half ask what is the *motive*? the *process* to be followed? and the *outcome* to be achieved?

Let us subject the first half of the paradox—"whosoever shall seek to gain his life shall lose it"—to this kind of analysis. In the words of the text, the *outcome* is losing life and the *process*, or the way leading to that, is seeking to gain life. The implicit *motive* would be to gain life, or the desire for life. Thus, *if* that is the motive, the way of seeking to gain is a negative one which leads not to finding life but

1. *Letters of C.G. Jung*, 2:76.
2. Lk. 17:33, §112J; Mt. 10:39, §57O.
3. Mk. 8:35; Mt. 16:25; Lk. 9:24; §73B.

to losing it. In the second half of the paradox—"whosoever shall lose his life shall preserve it"—the *outcome* is preserving life and the *process* is losing life. The implicit *motive* here is the desire for life. Thus, the second half of the paradox describes the method or process for achieving the outcome of Life.

The distinction between motive and process is seldom made, but it seems absolutely crucial to the whole thought of Jesus. The words are simple; the meaning the most profound possible. Examine the first half of this statement. One wants life. What might be other words for that? Fulfillment; capacity to grow; spontaneity; courage; ability to suffer and to have joy, to love in the richest sense, to respond creatively in all situations, to be authentic, to have integrity. And what is the *wrong* way to go about this so that life is lost as an outcome? The wrong way is to seek to gain by holding on, to protect, to predetermine one's responses, to try to control and to manipulate, to exert power over. It is little wonder that such an attitude is totally self-defeating, yet it is the principle on which the world acts and on which the structures of society are built. This seeking to gain constitutes the problem of "structural evil," a term Walter Wink uses in his seminars to describe what happens when collective groups organize into idolatrous power structures which seek their own good at the expense of the good of the whole.

The second half of the paradox completely reverses the process in the first half. With the same motivation or yearning for Life, the process is one of losing one's life, which paradoxically leads to preserving it. What does it mean to lose one's life, to let down the protective walls around the psyche, or soul? It is an individual, voluntary act whereby one gives over the mastery of his or her life to Something greater within and without. There is a striking assumption here, different from earlier statements on the way, that that Something must lie *within* the psyche. Here is one of the first statements of a divine Immanence, of Divinity within, of Something wanting to live in the human but needing the human to break the barriers and defenses of egocentricity that have grown around it. The sacrifice of

130

these boundaries allows something new to be born. This can be understood as the Self or *imago dei* which expresses God in the psyche.

The Greek meanings for these words provide further insight. The word for "life" in all cases is *psyche*;[1] the word for "shall lose it" as outcome in the first half is the same word as "shall lose his life" as process in the second half, and is the same word Matthew uses when describing how the broad way leads to "destruction."[2] This lends a very potent meaning to "lose" in the two halves of the paradox. Finally, the word in the first half for "seeking to gain his life" has the connotation in Greek of "building a hedge about" and is totally opposite to the meaning of "seeking to preserve it," the outcome in the second half, of bringing forth a living reality. These words, then, suggest a powerful contrast. There is a way of self-protection which hedges in the vital spark of being within by defenses, evasions, and excuses. This leads to futility.

The second way of being willing to let these defenses fall, to open oneself to vulnerability, to penetration into Substance, is to discover the living Spirit within wanting birth and rebirth.

Following the narrative, six or more days had passed since the strong impact of questions and answers, and turnings. There had been Caesarea Philippi and the encounter with Peter, followed by some of the most profound statements we have from Jesus. One may wonder what was going on in the minds and spirits of his disciples. What had they heard him say? Had they understood him or not? Had his teaching penetrated their consciousness or perhaps invaded their unconscious and there affected them? They had heard Jesus deny their hope that he would be their long-hoped-for Messiah, the glorious one to fulfill their dreams and those of Israel. Instead, he stated a new and unwelcome truth about the Son of man, that strange, compelling image from the intertestamental period that he transferred from vision and hope to an ex-

1. Lk. 17:33; §112J; Mk. 8:35; Lk. 9:24; Mt. 16:25;§73B; Mt. 10:39; §57O.
2. Mt. 7:13; §38M.

istential Reality in himself and to potentiality in others. He had said the Son of man must meet rejection and suffering and possible physical death, and for this Peter had rebuked him. They had heard him speak of the price of losing all for the sake of Life, not for his sake, or God's sake. His were words that challenged to the core of being. Were the twelve disciples discouraged, or were they stimulated? Was their vision and hope for him gone? No later evidence suggests that. Did they perhaps still cling to some hope of theirs, in spite of his words, or were they even more in awe of him? What did his being feel like to them, in them? Was anything new being born in them from him, for him, of him?

Now Jesus went to a high mountain with Peter, James, and John. There they—the three—had the so-called transfiguration experience:

> And after six days Jesus taketh with him Peter, and James, and John, and bringeth them up into a high mountain apart by themselves: and he was transfigured before them: and his garments became glistering, exceeding white; so as no fuller on earth can whiten them. And there appeared unto them Elijah with Moses: and they were talking with Jesus. And Peter answered and saith to Jesus, Rabbi, it is good for us to be here: and let us make three tabernacles; one for thee, and one for Moses, and one for Elijah. For he wist not what to answer; for they became sore afraid. And there came a cloud overshadowing them: and there came a voice out of the cloud, This is my beloved Son: hear ye him.[1]

What may be the reality of what went on with the disciples? What led them, out of all that has just been speculated on, to see Jesus this way? There may have been a deep archetypal experience in which they saw Jesus as Messiah, related to Moses and Elijah. That these two figures should have been part of their experience is not strange in light of the history of these two. Both had powerful experiences on a mountain top—Moses at Sinai, Elijah at Mount Carmel. Both experienced God in a cloud. These experiences combined the sense of the *tremendum* and a still, small voice. Both were moving from old patterns

---

1. Mk. 9:2-7; §74A-E.

to new, and both were said to have been transported to heaven. Does the light around Jesus serve as a compensatory experience to the darkness they had heard him proclaim about the Son of man in himself, and in the paradox, or is there some other explanation? The statement that they heard the voice affirming that he was beloved son suggests the possibility that this might have been the time Jesus shared with them his experience at the baptism. If this was true, the connection of Moses and Elijah is clearer. (It would also account for its becoming known.) In the telling, Jesus must have seemed numinous to them, and this could be the explanation of the light that surrounded him. His report of his experience to them in words would come to them as the Word, the Logos Incarnate, because of what he carried for them. What Jesus himself experienced as he reported the baptism was probably Something very numinous, so he seemed transformed to them. But it may be he aroused the Self in the three disciples through his report to them.

An incident of a type rare in the gospels follows the transfiguration experience, and shows great humanness and humor. (Many scholars feel this is an early Christian story.) Peter was asked if Jesus paid the half-shekel Roman tax, and he answered, "Yes," and then went to Jesus. Jesus then asked Peter:

> The kings of the earth, from whom do they receive toll or tribute? from their sons, or from strangers? And when he said, From strangers, Jesus said unto him, Therefore the sons are free. But, lest we cause them to stumble, go thou to the sea, and cast a hook, and take up the fish that first cometh up; and when thou hast opened his mouth, thou shalt find a shekel: that take, and give unto them for me and thee.[1]

What is Jesus really saying here? Is this a very human moment when he is saying, "We should not pay, for we are free; but in order not to confuse the authorities on an issue that is not too central, go get a fish and sell it and pay the half-shekel"? Compromise? No. To me it seems creative strategy and discrimination. A stunning reply.

---

1. Mt. 17:24-27; §77.

VII

"He Steadfastly Set His Face Toward Jerusalem"

Why did Jesus make the choice to go to Jerusalem at this time?

What did Jerusalem most mean to him?

Whom did he encounter?

What do you perceive to be his innermost attitude?

Jesus began a new phase of his journey, determined not by outer facts but from an inner determination in facing outer events. He moved, according to the story, from Galilee to Judea, a region he had not returned to since the baptism. By law, he would have gone every year. But we have no record of the length of time of his ministry (in the Gospel of John, three years are indicated). This journey would take him to Jerusalem and to the events of the last week of his life, his trials and death, and subsequent events whatever their nature. In Mark there is a simple statement of his movement out of Galilee into the borders of Judea beyond the Jordan, while Luke states, "He steadfastly set his face to go to Jerusalem."[1] Even though that may well be

1. Mk. 10:1; Lk. 9:51; §79.

a later way of stating it, it carries something of the sense of the inner dynamism, of the passion and conviction of Jesus at this time.

Why did he choose to go? Out of what did this choice come? What probabilities did he face? Why to Jerusalem, the focal point of his people's religion and of his own, a city that he loved deeply? Could he have avoided the choice? Could he have stayed where he was and evaded the potential changes to his life and beyond his life to his message? Is there any evidence that he thought of his death as redemptive? What did he bring with him to this possible encounter with the authorities that could mean death? What could the outline of the cross begin to mean? What kinds of answers to God were shaping in him? Was he driven or led by the Holy Spirit?

Jesus could have stayed in the country, or in the outskirts where there was more safety, even though there was opposition. People were hearing his message, responding—was this not enough? Evidently, no. Further depths of confrontation were needed at the root place, Jerusalem, the center of the religious and temporal law. Here the sacred laws, the sacred realities of his people, were centered. And here the Jewish and Roman laws were defended and could be violated. The Covenant was to be most fulfilled here where all that was good and all that was negative, everything light and dark, was centered. Here is where the Jewish people renewed vows and where the religious laws and practices became entrenched, rigid, and bound. Here he must go to meet the realities and the redemptive possibilities of the religious and political power structures. In Jerusalem was the Temple, the holiest of places, the bulwark and rock on which his people had built and nurtured their Covenant with Yahweh. Here was the House of God, the center of their worship, God's supreme dwelling place. All the forces and dynamics of the people and their God were focused in Jerusalem, along with the negative forces that were and are most potent and destructive shadow elements. All the opposites were constellated here. In choosing to go to Jerusalem, Jesus went to the heart of the religious problem of his people. Jerusalem was also the focal point where he met God's opposites in his own religious depths.

Those in power, the Pharisees and religious leaders, holding to tradition perhaps out of necessity, did understand all too well at one level what was being said by Jesus. They understood by not understanding. They chose unconsciously to remain blind guides. To have opened themselves to what he said and meant would have been radical beyond their comprehension. The only alternative was to build their defenses against him, to protect themselves and the God whom they served as they knew Him/Her. As we saw, the Son of man within Jesus had to face rejection, hatred, and death. Darkness was gathering, and his God was not One who saved him from the darkness, but One who asked of him to face His/Her totality, including darkness.

That Jesus knew about the dark, not only as the unknown, but as evil, is seen over and over again. He knew its potentiality within the human and as a good Jew he knew it was in the God of the *Tremendum*, who had both wrath and love within Him/Her. In many passages Jesus showed how one must work at the transformation of darkness, must go to the heart of it, to confront it and deal with it. His passionate concern for this transformation within God and human was the great burden he carried with love and even joy, but a burden because there was so little response from others. At this juncture the choice came not to continue where he was, but to move to the center, Jerusalem. If he avoided the choice, he must remain where he was. The fact that Jesus later said of his death, " 'til it be accomplished,"[1] which he understood as an act of "being perfected,"[2] or made whole, shows that this conscious choice to go to Jerusalem was for him the outcome of his total commitment and could not have been otherwise.

In going to Jerusalem, the greatest threat was not so much the loss of his own life, however great that personal aspect must have been, but the loss of his message, the end to the carrying forth of what had so significantly been born

1. Lk. 12:50; §95A.
2. Lk. 13:32; §101A.

in and through him. His people had not heard and Jesus still hoped they would. What would his death do? I see no indication that he thought his central message would go on, be carried by others, or that his death would in itself be redemptive.

Here it is important to separate later developments from the historical existential significance of this man's life. Now, in facing Jerusalem, Jesus was facing the fulfillment of his life and God's life in him through the possible experience of total abyss. The paradox never shines through any clearer than here. Death becomes a possibility of the achievement of wholeness through the incorporation of the opposites Spirit and Substance. Death here is not only of the body, but the death of the message, death again as the descent that leads into rebirth. Only dimly can we imagine something of what death might mean in the mind of Jesus. Later, when the disciples argue about who shall sit on his right and left hand and share in his glory, Jesus responds, "Are you able to drink the cup that I drink, or to be baptized with the baptism that I am baptized with?"[1] He knows with full consciousness the suffering potential that is ahead, yet he does not pursue a martyr's role. As in some of the passages where the Son of man is seen, the same archetype, that of the suffering servant, is here at work in the awareness of Jesus. Isaiah says:

> Behold my servant, whom I uphold,
> My chosen in whom my soul delights.
> I have put my spirit upon him,
> He will bring forth justice to the nations.
> He will not cry or lift up his voice
>   or make it heard in the streets;
> A bruised reed he will not break,
> And a dimly burning wick he will not quench.
> He will faithfully bring forth justice.[2]

He chooses what he has to choose, not out of blind obedience or resignation to God's will, but out of the continual operative dialogue between himself and God moving to more consciousness. What the cross could mean to him,

1. Mk. 10:38; §120C-D.
2. Isa. 42:1-4.

what inner reality led him to it, what happened on it and afterwards, will condition what this symbol may become for us. The cross and the man on it has certainly been a central symbol to orthodox Christianity. In the context of the point of view throughout this book, the cross obviously will assume new meaning.

Some of the finest teachings of Jesus are given on the last journey to Jerusalem. All of them cannot be dealt with. The sequence chosen is from Luke[1].

Jesus started the journey, and some of his disciples moved ahead of him into a village of the Samaritans. When these people would not receive Jesus, the disciples, full of wrath and as if they were apocalyptists, wanted to bring down fire to consume the village. But Jesus rebuked them and with amazing objectivity moved on to another village.[2] It was as if he expected this kind of response and was not surprised. Once again Something inner overcame the wrath of God and of people. It is fascinating that this first incident on the journey should touch the core of his teaching: the acceptance of darkness as well as light in the nature of things and the need in the human not to be dominated by it. Here, transformation is realized again.

In going on his way Jesus encountered three persons, and with each one he moved into dialogue. Each of them, obviously moved by his impact, asserted the desire to follow him. In two of the three encounters, this desire originated within the person; in the third, it was implanted by Jesus. But Jesus, the realist as always, put to each one a challenge, a condition to be met.

In response to one who would follow him, Jesus added richly to the phrase "Son of man." "The foxes have holes, and the birds of the heaven have nests; but the Son of man hath not where to lay his head."[3] Animals and birds live and are protected by nature. Instinctively they reside in established patterns beyond which there is no freedom and therefore no conflict, though they move with freedom in their containment in behavior patterns of cyclic rhythm.

1. See Appendix I.
2. Lk. 9:52-56; §80.
3. Lk. 9:58; §81A.

But that which is the Son of man inside us does not and cannot rest within the natural. Yes, it emerges from the natural to thrust into the supranatural. It is the restlessness of consciousness itself, always moving, always pushing to growth. It presents a paradox of being rooted and secure in oneself while one is always moving, facing the unpredictable will of God.[1] The Son of man within is a paradox of a sense of home, yet a continual flexibility of movement. It states a stability that moves into mobility.

To the second person, Jesus said, "Follow me," but the man protested that he must first go and bury his father. Jesus replied, "Let the dead bury their own dead; but go thou and publish abroad the Kingdom of God."[2] It is perhaps to be questioned whether Jesus did initiate the conversation without some previous expression on the part of the man, because it was not like Jesus to put himself at the center. The excuse the man gave of needing to bury his father seems so natural, and yet Jesus had some indication from this man that he needed to do something different—a hard message indeed.

In the third instance, when one person indicated he wished to follow Jesus after he had said farewell to those at home, Jesus said, "No man, having put his hand to the plough, and looking back, is fit for the kingdom of God."[3] He again forces the man out of a natural desire—to bid farewell—into a reorientation toward the Kingdom. This is a radical step beyond the story in 1 Kings 19:19-22, where Elisha is permitted by Elijah to return to say farewell to his mother and father before following Elijah.

What is the essence of these last two confrontations that is different from the one on the Son of man? Either they represent Christian accretions at the later time of making converts, or they are genuine. I incline toward accepting them as expressions of Jesus' passion that his message be understood and carried to more people. Sacrifices did have to be made, even of seemingly sacred ideas about family ties. This surely broke the fourth command-

1. For further discussion of the meaning of the Son of man, see Howes, *Intersection*, pp. 171-97.
2. Lk. 9:60; §81B.
3. Lk. 9:62; §81C.

ment: "Honor thy father and thy mother." Later, Jesus made an even stronger statement: "If any man comes unto me, and hates not his own father, and mother, and wife, and children, and brethren, and sisters, yea, and his own life also, he cannot be my disciple."[1] Here "hate" must be interpreted as "break from," "detach from." This was radical but emphasized the positive value of the Kingdom of God over old ties. The renunciation is not demanded for its own sake but for the sake of the evolution of consciousness which the Kingdom represents. Family ties are deeply ingrained archetypal patterns, the very lifeblood of natural existence, but the tie to God and the Kingdom is also a deep archetypal pattern, on the whole unactualized, but the core of a new step for persons and for society.

The next absolutely central encounter[2] occurred when "a certain lawyer stood up and tempted him, saying, Master, what shall I do to inherit eternal life?" Jesus responded with another question: "What is written in the Law? how readest thou?" which the lawyer answered by putting together two laws from the Hebrew Scripture, one from Deuteronomy and one from Leviticus.[3] To this Jesus replied, "This do, and thou shalt live," and the lawyer asked still another question: "And who is my neighbor?" Jesus then told the well-known parable of the Good Samaritan,[4] at the end of which he asked the lawyer, "Which of these three, thinkest thou, proved neighbor to him that fell among the robbers?" When the lawyer said, "He that showed mercy on him," Jesus concluded the encounter with, "Go, and do thou likewise."[5]

To take this dialogue step-by-step as an actual historical happening and then to understand its inner psychological dimensions is to encompass the total perspective with which Jesus viewed life and the working of God. As a parable about the existential dilemma of evil and the nature of healing, it encompasses the full nature of

1. Lk. 14:26; §104B.
2. Lk. 10:25-28; §83A.
3. Deut. 6:5; Lev. 19:18.
4. Lk. 10:30-35; §83C.
5. Lk 10:36-37; §83D.

the problem of freedom in the human and the divine. The question "What shall I do to inherit eternal life?" may from the standpoint of the asker be concerned with the continuance of life beyond death. But whatever the man's concern, Jesus takes it immediately into a definition of life here and now, a life lived with the quality of the eternal giving depth, meaning, and purposiveness. This he does with the statement "This do and thou shalt live."

Eternal life becomes a volitional act capable of achievement here and now. The "this do" refers to the two commandments the lawyer quoted when Jesus asked, "What is written in the Law? how readest thou?" Jesus' first step, then, is to return the question to the lawyer, because he knows that the answer to the lawyer's question is known already but needs to be brought into consciousness. It becomes obvious that the fulfillment of the two commandments ensures the achievement of eternal life, a life of mysterious dimensions.

The commandment from Deuteronomy says, "Thou shalt love the Lord, thy God, with all thy heart, and with all thy soul, and with all thy strength, and with all thy mind," and the second commandment adds, "And thy neighbor as thyself." There is here, then, an object of devotion—the Lord God—to which all of oneself can turn in love. What can "love" mean here? The fact that, following this, Jesus says, "This do," puts it within the area of choice and volition. This is not love of an emotional, spontaneous kind beyond conscious eliciting. Hundreds of definitions of "love" do not belong here; one does. It is to relate to, to serve, to be devoted to, to bring all energies to. To whom or to what? To the God of his Jewish background, the transcendent God of purpose, ever being manifest in the flow of events through His/Her mighty will and power. Here is where Jesus shows the Jewish roots he had brought to his baptism experience.

And with how much of oneself should one choose to love this God? With all, with every facet of personality. Nothing is left out, especially if one includes bodily realities under "strength" and if one notices a striking thing about "heart." Earlier, in the incident about defilement, Jesus said, "Out of the heart of man, evil thoughts proceed, for-

nications, thefts, murders, adulteries, covetings, wicked-
ness, lasciviousness, an evil eye, railing, pride, and
foolishness."[1] To love, therefore, with all one's heart is to include all the negatives that one could imagine. It is to bring
the totality of being, not to split off and repress the
darkness and bring only the shining, bright side. A Jewish
midrash says to "bring your evil as well as your good inten-
tions"—to bring, in other words, the totality within the heart.
All four facets of the human are to be centered in the single
devotion to the reality of God. "To love with all" means to
know all the areas of oneself, conscious and unconscious.[2]

What is to be understood by the second commandment, "Love thy neighbor as thyself"? To love your
neighbor as yourself implies that you do love yourself, and
out of this comes love of neighbor. This is a very true statement but leaves the question open as to whether we do today love ourselves. Have we not tended to love or to try to
love our neighbor and God, but omitted the love of ourselves? It is more than possible that our love for the other
would be much greater if it rose from the wellspring of our
real Self, which would come more into being if we loved it
and nourished it. This is not selfishness; it is the tension of
including and caring for the core of our own soul so it can
move freely into relationship with others.

By quoting the commandments to love God with one's
total being and to love one's neighbor as oneself, the
lawyer revealed his understanding of the way to inherit
eternal life. Jesus affirmed this understanding with, "You
have answered right: this do, and thou shalt live." But,
"desiring to justify himself," the lawyer asked, "And who
is my neighbor?" Jesus fashioned a model for "neighbor"
in the parable of the Samaritan. This parable and the one
of the prodigal son may be the two most existentially valid
parables of the gospels.

As a Samaritan went along the road between Jerusalem and Jericho, he saw a traveler, nearly dead, who had
been robbed and beaten. A Levite and a priest had already

1.   Mk. 7:21-23; §63L.
2.   Some tools for working toward such self-knowledge are found in Appendix II.

passed on the opposite side of the road to avoid involvement and possible contamination. The priest and Levite performed the religious duties in the Temple, and contact with a dead body demanded ritual purification. But this compassionate man of a despised race tended the traveler's wounds and carried him on his beast to an inn, where he left him with the innkeeper after paying, and promising to pay whatever more would be needed when he returned. He gave the utmost he could have given. Jesus asked who had proved neighbor to the wounded man and advised the lawyer to go and act the same way.[1]

Why did Jesus choose the Samaritan as the healing factor in the story? The Samaritan, as an outcast knowing rejection, was himself a wounded figure and was not allowed in the Temple. In this story he had come to terms with his own wounds and therefore was able to show compassion and mercy to another wounded one. The wounded one became the healer through his own transformation. This is one example of the Wounded Healer archetype. His attitude in the parable is distinctly opposite the attitudes of the priest and Levite, who, as good religious figures, were too preoccupied with or scared of defilement to deal with the wounded one. They were not really in the situation, and therefore it did not become an event for them.

The man wounded and beaten by the robbers can symbolize all persons ever wounded by oppressors, the people of the world who have suffered from evil, consciously or unconsciously, inflicted in war and peace. They are suffering humankind, and no one of us is free from guilt for letting such sufferings happen. They also are the parts of ourselves that have been hurt by parents, substitute parents, peers in our childhood. Here is the mystery of evil done to others: people are wounded and become split where there may or may not be objective reason. They then become robbers themselves and do to others what has been done to them.

The Samaritan is very impressive in his willingness not only to bind the wounds, to put the wounded one on his animal to take him to the inn for rest, and to pay, but also

1. Lk. 10:30-35; §83C.

in his willingness to pay more if needed when he returns to the inn. This willingness to return affirms the necessity of remembering what needs healing. He puts oil on the wounds. He is the answer to the question of who is the neighborly one, for he can show mercy because he acts from his own hurt and healed center. Only by this process, where the Samaritan grows in us through specific hurts and healing, can the mercy be shown that the world needs so urgently. The Samaritan as the healing factor will grow in us each time we face a hurt, a rejection, or a nonacceptance, and work through it to love. The potential is there, but practice is needed to bring its energy into actuality. The priest and Levite are caught in power only and have no freedom; the Samaritan acts in love and uses his freedom creatively.

This parable has tremendous possibilities of personal meaning if we internalize the whole thing. As already said, it is the most complete statement of the religious existential situation of good, evil, and freedom. It states the way it is inside us if we can but find all the parts.

Jesus and his companions went on their way, and Jesus entered a certain village where a woman named Martha received him into her house. She had a sister, Mary. These two sisters treated their visitor in totally opposite ways and received opposite reactions from him.[1] Martha was very busy preparing for the guest, hectic and distracted by much serving. To her, Jesus said, "Martha, Martha, thou art anxious and troubled by many things, but one thing is needful." Hers was an attitude of wanting to please, to have everything just right—perhaps not just to seek the approval of Jesus but to meet her own standards of perfection. She was not able to hear the Word or to be in dialogue with Jesus. This story applies equally to men, just as all the stories told about men apply to women. These may be feminine attitudes, but they are in all of us. It was not what Martha was doing that was the mistake but *how* she was doing it. Caught in the patterns of egocentricity, she bustled about, probably making everyone nervous, and finally said to Jesus, "Dost thou not care that my sister

1. Lk. 10:38-42; §84.

did leave me to serve alone?" In contrast, Mary sat quietly at the feet of Jesus, listening to him. This in itself was violating her proper role, which forbade women to sit at the feet of a rabbi. She was attentive to the value of the moment which appeared to be present through a guest with the wisdom and stature of Jesus. She could hear and she could be in dialogue. This sense of presence on the part of Mary was an expression of the kind of attitude Jesus was always speaking of. Mary is a manifestation of centering on the creative value, in this situation represented by Jesus. It could be manifested in other places and Mary could be doing the dishes and setting the table, but she would do it with a totally different attitude from Martha. What makes her so different is indicated in Jesus' response to Martha: "But one thing is needful: for Mary has chosen the good part, which shall not be taken away from her." Martha had not chosen; Mary had. This choice is what Jesus labeled the one thing needful. Martha remained at the level of unconscious, compulsive action, helpless as to what to do except to please and appease the drives of her own being. Mary chose to respond to real value, especially when expressed in the word spoken by Jesus. She is therefore a more developed side of the Feminine, and willing to go *contra naturam*. Later statements on anxiety will intensify and enlarge this.

The account continues with a statement that Jesus "was praying in a certain place" and the disciples asked him to teach them to pray. From this we have the so-called Lord's Prayer,[1] repeated over the years by millions who have received numinous value from it without consciously understanding what they are praying. The prayer's form and content give depth and structure to the religious impulse of confrontation with God, but one can remain very unconscious in the process. To relate to meaning behind words, especially religious ones, is to move from the unconscious to the conscious. It is necessary to bring the Lord's Prayer into focus so that it is consistent with the total thought of Jesus, a task of rendering the familiar into something truly mysterious in the pray-er. The prayer in

1. Lk. 11:2-4; §85B.

Luke is simpler and probably more authentic than other versions. The two exceptions will be to add from Matthew, "Thy will be done" after "Thy kingdom come," and "but deliver us from evil" after "And bring us not into temptation."[1] Prior to this time, Jesus' only references to prayer have been at the baptism and in the discourse on standards of righteousness, but no content is given at those points.

This prayer is addressed to the Father—*Abba*, the word "Father" as used later in the Garden of Gethsemane. *Abba* is an intimate form of address, the diminutive of "father," and brings the presence of God close for Jesus. "Father" would have been said in Jesus' day as the natural masculine. Today it is possible to understand that for Jesus the concept of Creator, Father-Mother, Source, Giver of Life, Ground of Being, would be more total. "Hallowed be Thy name"—may your name be holy, be blessed, be above all, be known as all-inclusive, be reverenced and held in awe.

"Thy Kingdom come. Thy will be done." Taking all that Jesus ever said, who is responsible for the coming of the Kingdom and the fulfilling of the Will? Is this phrase a command that God bring this about? Does it rest on His/Her action? If so, what is the need of human creation? Or has the whole emphasis of the teaching been on the responsibility of the human inner and outer actions that must be taken for actualization? If it is the latter, then this prayer is not petition but affirmation of one's own intention to help bring about the Kingdom by individually doing the will of God. The Kingdom is the result of individuals co-creating with God in establishing relationship and social structures making for mutuality and love. It is a social fruit of the personal fulfillment of the Will. Utter seriousness and sincerity are demanded of the pray-er in this affirmation of the intention to help fulfill and actualize the vision.

"Give us this day our daily bread" stands exactly in the middle of the prayer. This petition to God to be given the sustenance for each day does not refer primarily to physical bread, for Jesus had said in the wilderness, "Man

---

1. Mt. 6:10, 13; §37W.

shall not live by bread alone, but by every word that proceedeth out of the mouth of God."[1] Could the prayer here be
not to give us what we *want* today, but to give us the word
from God's mouth which we may hear and be ready to act
on, for it is of such substance that Life comes and the
Kingdom is manifest? To hear, from outward and inward
realities, the meaning most wanting to be born is to incarnate the Word of the moment.

"Forgive us our sins, for we ourselves also forgive
everyone that is indebted to us." Prior to this, three great
statements on forgiveness are found in the incident of the
palsied person, in the Mary Magdalene story, and in the
parable of the unforgiving servant.[2] These three statements
together stress forgiveness as a process into which one is
free and able to enter if the power of the healing symbol is
present to enable such movement, as was the case with the
paralytic and the woman who was a sinner. The sequence
and nature of this sentence in the Lord's Prayer hold one of
the crucial elements of the teachings of Jesus. The first action before God is acknowledgment of our sins, of the
negative things we have in fact done to others, ourselves,
and to the Life process itself. "Sin" may be defined as missing the mark, partial response; a violation of something or
someone; or a profanation of, or damage to, others. These
sins need to be brought into consciousness before God.

What attitude is necessary to do just this? The needed
attitudes are humility to see oneself as one really is behind
defenses and persona, and openness especially to the dark
part of oneself. These sins are brought into the open to see
where they have hurt others. At the same moment we
stand needing forgiveness we must acknowledge that we
too have been hurt by others. The wounds imposed on us
from the past become the sins that we do to others, unless
we have taken care of them and healed them. Thus it is
that the forgiveness of God is sought in standing before
God and seeing what we have done to others because of
what people have done to us. It is not a causal relationship,
but a process.

1. Mt. 4:4; §20B.
2. Mk. 2:1-12; Lk. 7:36-50; Mt. 18:23-34; §29, 42, 78W.

We must enter the process of forgiveness by standing in the Presence, looking at what we have inflicted and at what has been inflicted on us. Participating in this flow is the basic condition for experiencing forgiveness and perhaps is the very definition of forgiveness. It is the healing process that God and human enter together to transform wound, hurt, flaw, and division into a new integration. Forgiveness comes from the continual action of the human and God when the mercy overcomes the wrath.

The forgiving of those who have hurt us must extend to the most basic wounds in our being. It is not just what someone did yesterday or last week to me, but centrally where the first hurts were. Fritz Kunkel[1] often asked the question "Where were you first killed?" This puts as dramatically as possible how severe childhood hurts are.

"Bring us not into temptation, but deliver us from evil." The shocking observation about this phrase is that God can lead us into temptation and into evil. Most Christians seem to overlook this fact, for it does not accord with the concept of an all-good God. Once again, we see here the two sides of God, and see also that, in fact, God's dark side can pull us into regression and make us not do the will of God. One might wonder about the phrase "Bring us not into temptation" when the whole teaching of Jesus has been on the fact of continual choice. It could be read, "Bring us into the temptation of choice, but do not let us be overwhelmed by the dark possibility, or do not let us be enfolded by regressive pulls." The prayer seems to say this. It attests to the strength of the pull of the dark side, but it also affirms that the task of consciousness is to face this polarization and not to let one side alone prevail.

In essence this prayer to God by the pray-er can be made by the ego, the conscious part of the personality, and be sincere but partial, or it can be prayed from the deeper Self and, therefore, be more total, more effective for change in the pray-er, in his or her total relationship to the totality of God.

1.   Fritz Kunkel, M.D., a German psychiatrist and author of many books, came to the United States at the time of Hitler. He was close in spirit to the Jungian tradition and was a founder with me of the first seminar center, The Pines.

Immediately following and obviously connected with this prayer is a parable on importunity. A man came to his friend's home at midnight, hungry after his journey. The host had no food in his house and went and knocked at the door of a friend, asking for bread. This friend at first refused, for his family was in bed and would be disturbed if he arose and unbolted the door. However, when the host continued to plead, the friend gave him what he needed.[1] What seems to be the central dynamic truth of this parable seen as coming after the Lord's Prayer? The giver of bread, of Substance, the sustaining power, gives bread on one condition. He/She is asleep with children, and is aroused by the knock at the door, and gives bread not because she/he is a friend, but because She/He is importuned by the one seeking bread.

Importunity signifies insistent persistence. It is this attitude on the part of the seeker that finally arouses the giver of bread, perhaps the feminine side of God. And the seeker, it must be noted, is not seeking bread for him- or herself, but for a hungry friend who has come at midnight, the darkest time, the time of the unknown, often the time of crisis. The host, knowing he does not have bread on hand, does know where to go for it, which is an immense knowledge and wisdom. He realizes that he must be importunate in seeking the bread, and is impelled to do this because of his concern for and relationship to the one who came at midnight. The fact that the seeker uses the term "friend" about the one who comes at midnight shows a prior relationship. The question of why the giver of bread has to be importuned raises for many a shocking question: Who is this sleeping God, or this concealed God? There are references to the sleeping God in the Psalms, especially 44:23, where it says: "Rouse thyself! Why sleepest thou, O Lord? Awake, do not cast us off forever." The psalmist is dealing here with co-creation, as Jesus does.

This is also an impressive parable about the meeting of psychological and religious insights. The journeyer who comes at midnight can be seen as some part of ourselves, some autonomous complex that has been cut off from consciousness. At "midnight" hours such parts come into the

1. Lk. 11:5-8; §85C.

area of conscious awareness and need attention, but the conscious side does not have the wherewithal to feed these parts, although it does know where to go, and that is considerable knowledge. The importunity is the constant activity of the ego to mediate between unconscious needs and the Source which can fulfill them. The parable also points up the need for psychological techniques with which to recognize these repressed, hungry parts, and for religious techniques to know how to go to the Source. The feminine elements in this parable lead one to say that this is not just the Father-Parent God, but Mother-Father-Parent God. That is, the masculine and feminine aspects of the deity are brought together, as in the Genesis creation story.[1]

There is now a short parable of great psychological significance which Matthew has placed at the end of the account on the unclean spirits. An unclean spirit, when it had left a man, wandered through waterless places seeking rest and found none. It said, "I will turn back to my house whence I came out," did return, found the house swept and garnished, and took in seven other spirits more evil than itself. "And the last state of the man became worse than the first."[2] What are the warnings here? There are several. The unclean spirit is not easily gotten rid of and has the power to collect more evil spirits to itself. If it goes through waterless places, it obviously is not cured. The house can be swept and garnished and yet be ready to entertain and harbor the unclean spirit again. Evidently great care is needed to deal with one "evil spirit," our unhealthy neurosis. A superficial cleaning of the house does not suffice, nor does ignorance of the unclean spirit's power help. Realism, self-knowledge, and integrity of intention are essential for real change.

Continuing in Luke, we come to an image about the light needing to be put on the stand "that they which enter in may see the light." Then comes the statement "The lamp of thy body is thine eye: when thine eye is single, thy whole body also is full of light; but when it is evil, thy body

1. See Introduction.
2. Mt. 12:43-45; Lk. 11:24-26; §45W, 86I.

is full of darkness. Look therefore whether the light that is in thee be not darkness."[1]

What is the eye as a physical organ? It is the organ of perception, the sense within us by which we perceive and comprehend the reality of the Thou of the outer world. Earlier, Jesus warned of the danger of beams and motes in our eyes, which distort reality. Here there are again two processes and two outcomes, but the striking thing is the contrast between single and evil which are not natural opposites, while the outcomes of the two states of the eye—the whole body is full of light or of darkness—are natural pairs of opposites. What meanings or alternate words can be used for "single" and "evil?" Single, centered, focused versus multiple, dispersed, unfocused. Evil as destructive, disintegrative, fragmenting, versus good as constructive, integrative, unifying. And it is the eye and its condition which yields such different outcomes. The injunction "Look therefore whether the light that is in thee be not darkness," warns against a tremendous danger of self-deception. There are, indeed, so many ways to fool oneself about the light within. From the total teaching of Jesus perhaps the most common self-deception he refers to is to confuse part of the whole with the whole, to assume that because one does have some virtues and is in part good, that therefore there are no other parts of oneself which may be repressed and full of negativity, hidden from one's conscious perception. This split is something Jesus continually dealt with, as part of his concern for the God-human dialogue. In two other places the term "evil eye" has come from the lips of Jesus—in the list of defilements in Mark[2] and in the parable in Matthew where the householder says, "Is thine eye evil, because I am good?"[3]

In the following instance, one of the multitude said unto him, "Master, bid my brother divide the inheritance with me." Jesus responded with a question, again revealing his own self-insight: "Man, who made me a judge or divider over you?" He used the situation in which he found

1. Lk. 11:34-35; §89B-C.
2. Mk. 7:20-23; §63L.
3. Mt. 20:1-15; §118.

himself as an opportunity to teach and to convey his concern.[1] Again, Jesus raised a question that put authority not in himself but in the other.[2] He detected, in the man who asked him to make the division, an attitude of greed and covetousness about possessions and proceeded to tell a parable on this theme.

He spoke of a "certain rich man" whose ground yielded such a plentiful harvest that he had no place to keep it. The man decided to build bigger and bigger barns for all his goods and said to his soul, "Soul, thou hast much goods laid up for many years; take thine ease, eat, drink, and be merry. But God said unto him, Thou foolish one, this night is thy soul required of thee; and the things which thou hast prepared, whose shall they be?" Jesus concluded the parable, "So is he that layeth up treasure for himself, and is not rich toward God."[3] The parable reveals what a futility it is to lay up treasures, achievements, all sorts of things—practical or psychological—because one never knows when the moment of death may come and these things cannot be taken along. This is a commanding statement, a rude awakening to the finite nature of things and to the unpredictability of the finitude of one's own life. Opposed to this is a life where richness consists not in what one has, but in one's attitude of turning everything to God. Such richness is the consequence not of holding, greed, possessiveness, but of lavish openness of all that one is or has to the central object of devotion—God.

To bring all of oneself, known and unknown, and free of all attachments, to God, the supreme deepest value of each moment, is a unique gift of the human. It assumes a new direction, a new mystical possibility, one might say, where the flow of the God-human co-creativity can happen.

1. Lk. 12:13-14; §92A.
2. For a discussion on Jesus' use of questions, see Joan Lyon Gibbons, "A Psychological Explanation of Jesus' Use of Questions as an Interpersonal Mode of Communication" (Ph.D. diss., Graduate Theological Union, Berkeley, California, 1979). To be published in 1985 as *The Courage of Questions* (San Francisco: Guild for Psychological Studies Publishing House).
3. Lk. 12:16-21; §92B-C.

The ability to do this with such great fruit contrasts with its opposite, the Luciferian power drive, where we hold on. To lay up treasure for oneself leads to destructiveness and ultimate loss, an outcome that parallels loss of life in the first half of the famous paradox on building walls around one's psyche.

Matthew has a statement earlier about laying up treasures in heaven, not on earth, "for where thy treasure is, there will thy heart be also."[1] Whatever we do with our treasures, whatever direction we turn them, will determine the validity of our feelings. Subjective feelings are not the main criteria, but are conditioned by the central direction of our soul. The Value is primary and the heart is directed by it. The objective Reality of the ongoing process is to be served first.

The teaching on anxiety has great variations in Matthew and Luke.[2] Jesus spoke of the futility of anxiety and then said, "But seek ye first his kingdom, and his righteousness; and all these things shall be added unto you."[3] What things? Material objects or lack of anxiety? He continued, "Be not therefore anxious for the morrow: for the morrow will be anxious for itself. Sufficient unto the day is the evil thereof."[4] The ever-present possibility of evil is in the nature of freedom of choice and assumes the duality we have seen. Earlier, Jesus had said to Martha, "But one thing is needful."[5] Perhaps the two statements together point to the one thing needful, which is constant choice in the light of this omnipresence of evil. Already it has been said: Be open and ready to face evil; resist it not; have the courage to acknowledge it; face that all the evil things in humans proceed from and defile the heart; and finally, include evil in loving God with all one's heart, soul, strength, and mind. These are strong admonitions to face our own

1. Mt. 6:21; §38A.
2. Although Luke has been followed throughout this chapter, there are many questions concerning some of the sections of Luke such as §93H-K (12:32-34). In these cases the Matthew parallel (6:34, 19-21) seems truer and more authentic and will be followed.
3. Mt. 6:33; §38D.
4. Mt. 6:34; §38E.
5. Lk. 10:41-42; §84.

shadows. "Sufficient unto the day is the evil thereof" is a sobering reminder that each day and hour has within it the potential for evil, from within and from outside ourselves. This is of the very nature of God and human. *To be* in today is to pay attention to all potentials. Regression, possible wrong choices, and destructiveness are plenteous each day.

Jesus continued the journey to Jerusalem, and in the course of it made one of his most personal and poignant statements: "I came to cast fire upon the earth; and what will I, if it is already kindled? But I have a baptism to be baptized with; and how am I straitened until it be accomplished!"[1] There are few times when there is chance to see so deeply into this human, Jesus, as here. He asks three questions aloud, yet it is as if he were pondering them to himself. These questions center on his "I" and his vocation with God, not on himself self-centeredly, but on himself as a vehicle of a destiny he is committed to pursue. They are self-reflective questions, not to be answered easily, questions that put his deepest passion and conviction into the context of inner-outer dialogue with his destiny. Because of the nature of these questions and the way he deals with them, these few words provide one of the most self-revealing passages of the quality of this man and his innermost being where God has come to reign. They have the poignancy of fierce tenderness toward his own past. Here is no weakling and no stoic, but a man fully human, fully alive in his being, moving in the only direction he can see as God's will for him, yet fully aware of the suffering this will entail. Suffering is not sought for its own sake. It is experienced by Jesus because it is the inevitable consequence of fully embracing a passionate individual choice.

The first question was, "I came to cast fire upon the earth; and what will I, if it is already kindled?" What fire is Jesus referring to? Where did the fire come from? Jesus is not the fire; rather, the fire in some way is in his hands to be kindled. This is his form of eschatology. It has been his fire and where has it led? Here is the anguish of the fire being transformed by an individual. The fire has been seen in

1. Luke 12:49-50; §95A.

the flaming sword at the entrance to the Garden of Eden, where Yahweh placed it as something to be taken hold of by humans when they returned to the Garden after the expulsion. The flaming sword and the cherubim must be confronted before reentry into the Garden of Eden to find the Tree of Life. Jesus has made, is making, this journey. The sword combines fire and decision.

At his original baptism experience, the elements of earth, air, and water are all present, but no fire—except within. The fire that Jesus is transforming and individualizing is the fire of judgment inherent in John's preaching of the coming of the apocalyptic Messiah. John has said that the Messiah would bring the fire of judgment, of separation. If Jesus himself came to John's movement as an apocalyptist, believing with John that the Messiah would bring the fire of judgment, then Jesus went into the water with the image. One might say it descended within Jesus into the water and became transformed within him. The fire that was to destroy and separate became a centered, inner fire!

The new fire is no longer the destructive fire only; rather, it becomes a transforming element of a deeper Messianism experienced first in Jesus and then in others. This new fire, by which the redemptive function of the Messiah becomes a redemptive will within every person who is committed to doing the will of God, is the fire Jesus ardently endeavored to cast upon the earth. (I am indebted to Luella Sibbald[1] for the emphasis on the fire here as the Will.) Why has this fire produced a conflagration that impels Jesus to ask, "What do I do now that all things are aflame?" Jesus knew what the outcome of this new fire would be, but here it is in reality upon him. Vision and concretization are different. Here is reality. The fire is aflame and will in all probability produce his death.

Jesus continued with his second concern: "I have a baptism to be baptized with; and how am I straitened till it

1. Luella Sibbald is an analyst and seminar leader with the Guild for Psychological Studies.

be accomplished!'"[1] The weight of this thought is very heavy. The meaning of his baptism is to be carried through to its ultimate end. It is also unimaginably difficult. The total experience of Jesus at the baptism already prefigured the journey that led to the end. Here is a man whose destiny was to carry the movement of the God-Process from Transcendence to Immanence in the Self, to incarnation, and it exacted everything. Two thousand years of Christianity have dulled the perception of the magnitude of this task, because it has primarily emphasized the incarnate. There is no possibility of turning back, no regrets, no regression on his part, but a marvelous new insight into the particular demand of the eternal upon him and us. The word "straitened" conveys the burden of his destiny. It was used earlier in connection with the entrance to the narrow gate and the straitened Way to Life.

Jesus went on to ask his third question: "Think you that I am come to give peace in the earth? I tell you, No; but rather division."[2] Here is the man who has been called the Prince of Peace announcing that he will bring division, at least initially, especially between generations in families. His function is to stir things up and to help people to face outer and inner confrontations. Out of division or disagreement within families, perhaps based on response to his teaching, newness and a more lasting and true peace can come. It is interesting that the division is between older and younger persons of the same sex: father-son and mother-daughter. May it be that if the way of Jesus were to be taken more seriously, genuine disagreement and division would arise out of which new understandings could emerge in the way the division was met consciously? As it is, the Prince of Peace is apt to reside in us as an image of singleness without multiplicity, a forced cohesiveness without differentiation.

Jesus continued and spoke to the multitude, pointing out that they knew how to read the signs of danger, knew when a storm or wind would come, but did not know how

1. Lk. 12:50; §95A.
2. Lk. 12:51-53; §95B.

to read the signs of the times. "How is it you know not how to interpret this time?"[1] Why was this true then, and why is it true now? To read the signs of the times then would have been to face what was happening in the country because of the increasing unrest against Rome, and this would have challenged the belief that the theocratic ideal and spiritual freedom could come only through political freedom. But they did not so read them. To face social and political reality now or at any time requires a radical openness to where one has been wrong and where change is possible. Nowhere is human blindness so apparent. This is where our social ideals are held onto. Jesus asked the multitude a second question: "Why even of yourselves judge ye not what is right?"[2] He suggested the importance of agreeing with one's adversaries, in this case Rome. If his people did not, the situation would be much worse for them and far more damaging because they did not change their social-religious point of view. The kind of "knowing" about clouds and wind is a deep instinctual knowing that includes accepting fate as it is. To "know" the "signs of the time" requires clear, conscious perception which is able to cut through projections, face shadows, and assume responsibility for moral choices. It may mean facing inner as well as outer "iron curtains." Today the issues are different, but the attitudes remain the same; the challenge is always there.

Continuing with the same line of thought, Jesus called for repentance, "or you shall all likewise perish," and added a parable about a man who had a fig tree which yielded no fruit. The man suggested to the vinedresser that the tree be cut down because there was no fruit, but the vinedresser asked that the tree be left one more year while he tended it and that it be cut down after that if it still did not yield.[3] Does one detect here a struggle within Jesus between the side that despaired of his people and the side that wanted to hold hope that the wrath would not overcome mercy?

1. Lk. 12:56; §96A.
2. Lk. 12:57; §96B.
3. Lk. 13:6-9; §97C.

In the next incident, some scholars have stated that Jesus most definitely broke a law that was sacred to his people. Earlier, on a Sabbath, he had responded to a man with a withered hand, saying, "Stand forth. . . . Stretch forth thy hand. And he stretched it forth: and his hand was restored."[1] Here, in responding to a woman who had suffered a crippling infirmity for eighteen years, Jesus stunningly manifested his radicalism. What could be more natural than to use the Sabbath for its restorative function? Now, for the third time, Jesus was criticized for healing on the Sabbath. To this criticism, he replied logically, humanly, and compassionately, "Don't you water your oxen and asses at Sabbath? So why shouldn't this woman be helped on the Sabbath?" And all his adversaries were put to shame."[2] This same kind of incident is soon repeated, with an interesting difference. When at the house of one of the rulers of the Pharisees on a Sabbath, Jesus took the initiative in saying to the Pharisees who were watching to see what his response to a sick man would be, "Is it lawful to heal on the sabbath or not?" The Pharisees did not reply, and after healing the man, Jesus asked, "Which of you shall have an ass or an ox fallen into a well, and will not straightway draw him up on a sabbath day?" Again, the Pharisees did not reply.[3]

A brief dialogue now occurred with certain Pharisees. He was moving on the journey, and some of them warned him to get out because Herod wanted to kill him. It is significant that certain Pharisees would do such a thing. Remember, too, the Pharisee who bade him to his house in the scene with the prostitute. It is an indication that not all the Pharisees plotted against and continually harassed Jesus, and that not all Pharisees were criticized by him. Therefore, one must speak of *some* Pharisees when referring to them as enemies of Jesus. To this warning Jesus replied in terms that show depths of self-revelation. He said, "Go and say to that fox, Behold, I cast out devils and perform cures today and tomorrow, and the third day I am

1.   Mk. 3:1-6; §33.
2.   Lk. 13:10-17; §98.
3.   Lk. 14:1-6; §102.

158

perfected"[1] The alternative reading for "perfect," as noted before, is "all-inclusive," so Jesus was saying, in essence, "Go tell that fox that I must go on until all has been included in my life that needs to be, or until the time of my death, which is my final act of commitment." Paradoxically, Jesus is choosing life, not death, but through that choice he will probably die. To the Pharisees, he added, "I must go on my way . . . for it cannot be that a prophet perish out of Jerusalem."[2] Jesus had to go against his instinctive natural reaction to raise it to choice and self-reflection. He saw himself in the prophetic tradition and needing to face the ultimate reality of what Jerusalem stood for. Caught up in this realization, and apparently oblivious of the Pharisees' presence, Jesus continued, "O Jerusalem, Jerusalem, which killeth the prophets, and stoneth them that are sent unto her! How often would I have gathered your children together, even as a hen gathers her own brood under her wings, and you would not!"[3] So Jesus revealed his tender, feminine, passionate love for his people and his country. Nothing could be more apt than his image of the hen in expressing his desire to protect and to give. How ardently Jesus longed for his people to understand his new message that could save them. All this was in Jesus as he approached Jerusalem. It was not what would happen to him personally—although that suffering was deep enough—that would matter. What his people and his country were doing to themselves in their refusal to hear him were his deepest concern. In this scene on the threshold of Jerusalem, the most intimate, personal aspect of his religion expanded into its largest social dimensions. His whole nation and people were involved by their reaction to what his message carried.

Jesus continued his journey and his teaching in the company of great multitudes, to whom he emphasized the need to count the cost before starting the journey of being

1. Lk. 13:31-32; §101.
2. Lk. 13:33; §101A.
3. Lk. 13:34; §101B.

his disciple.[1] Again, Jesus with a fine sense of logic, pointed out that no one would build a tower, or want a king to go to war, without some reckoning of cost. In the case of following the conditions Jesus asked for from all those following his way, all must be counted and sacrificed. Perhaps this is a strange inconsistency. On the one hand, yes, the cost must be counted as best one consciously can; at the same time, it must be recognized that one can never know at the beginning what the "all" will ultimately include. One can count the cost of all if one is aware that much of it is still unknown and will be already sold by prior commitment when known.

---

1. Lk. 14:28-33; §104D.

VIII

"The Kingdom of God Is Within"

What kind of teaching was Jesus giving en route to Jerusalem?

What indications are there of Jesus' sense of impending death?

What is added to the understanding of the total death-rebirth process?

What does the "within" add to the dimension of God?

The parable of the prodigal son and the storm at sea incident form the most important pair of teachings in the gospels on the meaning of the journey into the depths, and on the death-rebirth archetype. Preceding the prodigal son parable are two short parables which center on a lost part: one sheep out of a hundred and one coin out of ten.

A man who had lost one sheep left ninety-nine in the wilderness while he searched for the missing sheep. When he found it, he returned home with joy.[1]

1. Lk. 15:3-6; §105B.

A woman who had lost one of the silver coins from her dowry lit a lamp and swept the house until she found it. She then called in her neighbors to rejoice with her.[1]

Because one part of the whole is lost, the owner leaves the rest and seeks the lost part. In each story something negative could have happened while the owner was occupied in the search for the missing part, but the risk was taken because of the need of redemption. Why such concern for one out of many? Why not forget it? Why not let it go? Just because it is part of the whole. Ten and one hundred are both significant numbers. When their totality is broken, the restoration of wholeness is central, and the owners know this, as does Jesus, the teller of the parable.

Much is spoken today about the holistic point of view. It is to be found in the thought of this person Jesus. Here the wholeness concept refers to the efforts of the person and to the description of things as they are, to the nature of reality. In these parables the owner has ten coins or one hundred sheep and places great value on this fact, so much so that each owner goes out in search of what is lost. We likewise must cherish and protect the totality of what is given within us. Loss of any part of our wholeness will damage the whole and therefore the lost must be redeemed. Psychologically this involves pursuing unconscious parts of ourselves that have been split off from consciousness and could remain quite autonomous and not contribute to the whole. Each parable probably ended with the joy of the finding—but the extensions of such natural endings to "even so there shall be joy in heaven over one sinner that repenteth" and "even so there is joy in the presence of the angels of God over one sinner that repenteth" seem not to be related to the thought of Jesus but to reflect later Christian ideas.

The next parable, about the Prodigal Son,[2] further develops this theme of wholeness. In the parable there were two sons. The younger one asked his father for his inheritance and the father gave it to him. The son went to a far country where he spent his inheritance in riotous living until a great famine arose in the land and his hunger and

1. Lk. 15:8-9; §105C.
2. Lk. 15:11-32; §105D.

need forced him to become a swineherd. At the bottom of the pit, he came to himself and realized his father's servants had more than he did. What he touched in the depths led him to realize his life was not complete and to remember his inheritance. When he returned to his father to serve him as a servant, his father greeted him joyously, having assumed him to be dead. In his joy that his son was alive, the father asked that a feast be prepared for him. In the meantime, the older son, who had stayed home, was very irritated when there was a feast for the younger brother and not for him. This, then, is the essence of the story of the son's journey away from and back to the father.

What is the psychological-religious meaning of this parable? The younger son first asserts his independence and desire to take something of religious value from his inherited concept of God and to use it as he wishes. Is this irresponsible rebellion, or is it a step in finding one's own way and individuality? If the latter, it may seem to be erroneous, but judging by the final fruits of where this action leads it may also be a step of unconscious but necessary wisdom. The first step, then, is a choice to claim what he had inherited from the father, to use in his own way. The father agrees. Freedom of choice is obviously not only congenial to God, but may even be desired by Him/Her. The younger son moves to a far country, to unexplored areas of depth within himself, and through this step faces the possibility of an expansion of consciousness. In this new territory the son expends all and goes to extremes, as is likely to happen when new vistas are open. It must never be forgotten that what the son is using all the time is his inheritance from the father, which is not only monetary, but involves relationship. He may exploit and misuse the God-given energy in him but this is not to deny his reality. Freedom of choice, taking individual responsibility—these may be what the father longs for in him, and in us.

What does "riotous living" mean? The older brother assumes it refers only to living with harlots. Indeed this may be part of it, but there is no reason to limit it to that. "Riotous living" can refer to any activity that is totally contrary to our own expected and established patterns. Out of this extremity the younger son falls into dire need and eventually decides to return to his father as a servant. Going deep within, he finds a place where it can be said, "He came to himself." What does this signify? He found something of the central Self and was immediately reminded of the original contract with the father, understood as a God figure. Today, the notion of the Self as a religious factor within is acknowledged, but the fact that the Self is the *imago dei* is not taken seriously enough. For Jesus there was no question that God was behind the Self, ever-present and operative.

So the son returns as servant. "While he was yet afar off, his father saw him, and was moved with compassion, and ran, and fell on his neck, and kissed him." Why the ecstatic, eros-filled* response of the father to the one who returns? What has happened to the father, in whom there is now so much feminine dimension? May it be that Jesus here described a radical transformation of the image of the Jewish God into one that affirmed the feminine? Both father and son are changed and now enter into a relationship that was impossible until the son had made his journey. Consciousness is expanded by the son taking the father's inheritance into new territory. Many myths and legends about journeys deal with this central motif of death and rebirth. And it is Jung's contribution to explore this inner land to be lifted into consciousness.

There are folktales and myths from many cultures which set forth this same story of a younger child who wastes an inheritance from the parents and, after a harsh time of deprivation, returns to and is welcomed by the parents. The "prodigal" spends, wastes, suffers, and eventually returns to serve. The "prodigal" in these tales—as in this story told by Jesus—finds a newer, richer, and more conscious relationship with the parent figures. The Prodigal Son story told by Jesus contains the great rejoicing response of the father when his son returns from a long journey. He has an elaborate feast prepared for the son, and the father himself announces joy over the son "who was dead and is now alive." Assuming that Jesus is not speaking of a literal father and son but of the God-human dialogue, what has happened to the father through the journey of the son that moves him to run to greet his son with compassion?

The older brother had stayed home with the father, remained dutiful and orthodox, and resented deeply a feast prepared for the returned younger brother. The older brother protested that he had always been a good boy yet had never received such a feast. To his complaint, the father replied, "Son, thou art ever with me, and all that is mine is thine." Even though this was true, in fact the older son did not experience all that was in the father because he never experienced the joy of the father's fulfillment as the younger brother did. There was an expansion of personality in the younger son and in the father—the Godhead—that the older son never realized because of his limited experience.

The interaction between each of the humans with God is totally different in this parable. Therefore, the question of which fulfilled the will of God in the deepest sense arises. Which son most helped the being of God to Become? Certainly in the thought of Jesus there is no question. The journey of the younger son helped God who, in the words of Jacob Boehme, is the Nothing that wants to become Something.[1] A new creation has happened.[2].

Next, Jesus contrasted the love of God to the love of mammon (money or material possessions) and insisted that one cannot serve two masters. It is significant to note that it is not money as such that is wrong but love of money. The Pharisees reacted to this teaching by scoffing at Jesus. He replied, "That which is exalted among men is an abomination in the sight of God."[3] Again an upside down statement, a reversal of values. The satisfactions derived from attaining ordinary riches are not valued in the sight of God. At the same time, we do live in the material world.

Another parable soon follows which startles, even amuses, for it condemns or questions the wisdom of duty. A servant, when he reported to his master after work in the

1. Franz Hartmann, *Personal Christianity: The Doctrine of Jacob Boehme* (New York: F. Ungar Publishers, 1957).
2. For a more expanded interpretation of this story, see Luella Sibbald, "Experience Becomes Journey," in *The Seeded Furrow* (San Francisco: Guild for Psychological Studies, 1977), pp. 11-26.
3. Lk. 16:13-15; §107A-B.

field, was given further tasks. So it is "when you shall have done all the things that are commanded of you, say, We are unprofitable servants; we have done our duty."[1] The attitude here reminds one of Martha, and of the older brother in the prodigal son parable. Where does Jesus, therefore, place duty, or why does he place it as he does? Duty is needful both for the person and for the job to be done. Duty is a necessary reality but is limited and by itself uncreative. Yes, the garbage must be dumped each day, and to neglect it is very serious, but to do only duty is not to fulfill either the needs of the person doing it or the demand of reality. The acceptance of necessity is part of freedom and maturity.

Continuing his journey to Jerusalem, Jesus entered a certain village in Samaria where ten lepers called to him, "Master, have mercy on us."[2] Jesus told them, "Go and show yourselves unto the priests," the usual and orthodox procedure. "And one of them, when he saw that he was healed, turned back, with a loud voice glorifying God; and he fell upon his face at his feet, giving him thanks: and he was a Samaritan." What is the meaning of this scene? All ten lepers recognized some value in Jesus which they expressed by calling him Master. Surely they believed they were suffering the wrath of God as punishment for some sin, but Jesus constellated something of the quality of healing. What caused the healing then? As has been seen before, that which was alive in Jesus in the core of his being aroused in sick, fragmented people the possibility of integration. The presence of Jesus himself sparked this potentiality, as any healing symbol does.

One leper returns, the Samaritan. Why was it only the Samaritan, or as Jesus said, the "stranger," who returned, just as it was only the Samaritan who stopped to aid the wounded man in the earlier parable? He is the one outside the status quo. The wounded stranger in us often becomes the helper or healer. Only the stranger, who knew more of healing and its process because he had suffered, glorified God and thanked Jesus. To this Samaritan Jesus re-

1. Lk. 17:7-10; §110.
2. Lk. 17:11-19; §111.

sponded, "Were not the ten cleansed? but where are the nine? Were there none found that returned to give glory to God, save this stranger? And he said to him, Arise and go your way: your faith has made you whole." This response by Jesus reveals much about his attitude to himself, to God, and to human beings. "Where are the nine?" has a poignancy not often found in the gospels, and indicates how deeply Jesus wanted people to become whole and not just healed. The cry of God is in Jesus as the desire for consciousness beyond healing whereby a new birth of God takes place. It was the stranger, the Samaritan, who made a connection between the human and the divine longing for a new evolutionary step.

Why did Jesus commend the Samaritan? He had stopped long enough to reflect on what had happened to him. He had not just been absorbed in the experience of being healed—with all its attendant emotions and possible subjective reactions. No the Samaritan had somehow been moved to know the Source of healing and the channel through which it had come, and something of the wisdom of bringing this into consciousness. Of course this was not a rational choice, but something that arose from the depths of his soul and needed an expression which involved discrimination between glorifying God and thanking the human vehicle, Jesus.

What did the Samaritan do to call forth such a moving response from Jesus? He discriminated between the roles of God and Jesus. Jesus himself never failed to make this distinction, and it cannot be made without a sense of discrimination between the healing Source and the channel. Wholeness involves a level of consciousness *about*, rather than just a happening *to*. The "happening to" is not to be belittled, but in a world where there is today much emphasis on healing, the distinction is crucial. Self-awareness, understanding of the movement of the psychic contents and the symbolic role in bringing the conscious side to an understanding of the archetypal movements are necessary transformative elements. It is especially important that the role of Jesus in all he has constellated for two thousand years be understood. Healing may and does occur through projection onto him, but wholeness may be possible only if there is consciousness of what value is behind the projection and integration of that value.

Another question that can be posed is why the articulation is so central. Dr. Jung said, "Interpretation is absolutely necessary before the meaning of a thing can be grasped. The naked facts by themselves mean nothing."[1] "It is not really so much words, or only words, as it is the conceptualization process which in part uses words but which is intrinsically deeper than the words."[2] May it be, then, that articulation is so central because it serves consciousness in the person using the words and more concretely manifests the reality of God as unconscious and conscious come together?

Toward the end of his journey to Jerusalem, Jesus was again asked when the kingdom would come, and he answered, "The kingdom of God comes not with observation: neither shall they say, Lo here! or, there! for lo, the kingdom of God is within you."[3] Alternate translations of this are "kingdom of God is in the midst of you" or "between you." "The kingdom of God is within you" is, as I have said before, by far the most radical statement for his contemporaries. "The kingdom of God is in the midst of you" could be interpreted as referring to Jesus, but that would be contrary to all his teaching. "The kingdom of God is between you," between persons, would have been a profound expression of the central Jewish concept of God who intervened in history and who was actualized in the human-God, I-Thou dialogue.

"The kingdom of God is within you" is a statement of the deepest truth Jesus knew out of the baptism-wilderness experience, for it was there that the God Jesus knew as a Jew—the transcendent process of the restless, wandering God—came into his being. From God, something of the Spirit descended, activating the Self which had been projected by the people into the Messianic hope. Now it was enlivened in the psyche as immanent and incarnational. An inner archetype was alive and experienced by Jesus, and history began to change. After the baptism the

1. Quoted in Howes, "Son of Man," p. 68.
2. Ibid., p. 76.
3. Lk. 17:20-21; §112A.

Messianic is taken within by Jesus, and the Holy Spirit also is known as an inner reality. The later Christian experience of "Christ within" has its origin in Jesus' own experience at the baptism. Since then the *imago dei* within is consciously realized as the Self. It also represents the Messiah-Christ within. And this indwelling God-image becomes available in the psyche because of the consequent experiences of Jesus and the early disciples.

Two short parables follow. The essence of the first is that a widow kept importuning a judge to avenge her of her adversary. The judge would not listen to her at first but finally said to himself, "Though I fear not God, nor regard man; yet because this widow troubles me, I will avenge her, lest she wear me out by her continual coming."[1] We have seen this motif before in the parable about the man who importuned his friend for bread after midnight.[2] What is Jesus asserting here? A quality of pleading for justice on the part of the feminine is needed. Jesus is here adding, as so often, a feminine, feeling element to his patriarchal Jewish orientation.

The second parable clearly reflects the total thought of Jesus in its contrast between a Pharisee praying in the Temple in self-righteousness and publican praying, "Be merciful to me a sinner." The publican received a sense of blessing.[3] So again there is the paradox: to exalt oneself is to be humbled, to humble oneself is to be exalted. Behind this paradox is the psychological reality of how one has dealt with one's shadow. The Pharisee asserted that he was glad he was not like others, thus putting his shadow outside and inflating his own self-image. The publican, on the other hand, knew that he was a sinner and humbled himself.

Before reaching Jericho on the journey to Jerusalem, Jesus was confronted by some Pharisees concerning divorce. They asked, "Is it lawful for a man to put away his wife?" The divorce laws stated that a man could "discharge" his wife at any time, even if he had to pay her

---

1. Lk. 18:1-5; §113A.
2. Lk. 11:5-8; §85C. See Chapter VII, pp. 148-149.
3. Lk. 18:9-14; §114.

money. What did he answer or comment? He said, in essence, that divorce laws were given by Moses, "for the hardness of your hearts"; that from the beginning male and female had been created equal by God; and that "what therefore God has joined together, let not man put asunder." Marriage was and is for the purpose of the two elements—male and female—coming together. If, in fact, a marriage is one where God has joined people together, no one can put them asunder, but how many marriages are so based? It is a rare situation where God is truly consulted as a basis for relatedness. Later, the disciples asked Jesus again about this matter and he said that if either husband or wife put away his or her spouse for the sake of remarriage, that was adultery.[1] That Jesus included women as possible initiators of divorce and remarriage was extraordinary for those times. Jesus' earlier definition of adultery as looking at persons to lust after them seems consistent with his definition of adultery as putting away a spouse for the sake of remarriage. Undoubtedly, many divorces for the sake of remarriage constitute a lustful attitude, but not all. Matthew adds the fact that a woman who has been put away will make the man who remarries her an adulterer.

Some children were brought to Jesus, who held them, spoke about their significance, and blessed them. But the disciples rebuked them.[2] Who are the disciples in us who rebuke the childlike? What can be said of the meaning of the child? The child is innocent, spontaneous, full of every kind of response, unspoiled by the egocentricity of parents and the world, and a potential energy field not yet directed. One of the main symbols of the Self has been the divine child which represents the Beginning and End. It is the original entelechy of wholeness. How much we have projected into this description of Jesus receiving little children, without ever finding the reality behind the symbol! Psychologically, the child as new Life, as a symbol of the vitality of the Self, has long been expressed in dreams, myth, and ritual.

A dialogue then ensued between Jesus and a young

1. Mk. 10:2-12; §115.
2. Mk. 10:13-16; §116.

man who approached him with the question "Good Master, what shall I do that I may inherit eternal life?" This question is similar to the one asked earlier by the lawyer. Could these be two reports of the same incident, or are there probably two incidents? The question being as central as it is, it could easily be repeated. The question needs to be heard. It is fascinating that before Jesus answered the question itself, he asked, "Why callest thou me good? None is good save one, even God." Luke has the same words, but Matthew leaves out "even God," thereby suggesting the possibility of the reference being to Jesus himself. In Jesus' reply his self-estimate again becomes apparent. He knows he is not the Source but the channel.

In a most strategic way Jesus continued to state the Commandments, which the man said he had observed from his youth. Mark interpolates, "Jesus looking upon him loved him." He told the young man to go sell all his worldly goods and then invited the man to follow him. But the man left in sorrow. He could not or would not follow this command because he was rich and had great possessions.[1]

What is Jesus doing here? Does he state that the way to eternal life is to renounce all earthly possessions? This interpretation is familiar but not consistent with other statements Jesus made on the way. Did Jesus touch the vulnerable places in the man by asking him if he was willing to sell all? The question makes the man realize how attached he is to his possessions. Jesus is clearly testing the man's fundamental attitude toward "all." The man fails the examination and leaves.

Jesus, alone with his disciples, continued the theme of the difficulty for those who trust in riches to enter the Kingdom of God. He said it was easier for a camel to go through a needle's eye.[2] Is Jesus referring only to material riches, or does this category include all things we might be attached to: achievements, glory, egocentric goals, and power? The disciples asked, "Then who can be saved?" and Jesus answered, "With men it is impossible, but not

1. Mk. 10:17-31; §117.
2. Mk. 10:25; §117I.

with God: for all things are possible with God."[1] Translated, does this not mean that by pulling at our own bootstraps, by our own efforts alone, we are not saved? But when the effort is made by the ego with the help of the healing Source of God, it is possible to become willing, to open oneself to accept God, to become detached.

As Jesus and his disciples approached Jerusalem after the long journey from Galilee, the disciples argued about who would sit on his right and left hand. James and John approached Jesus and rather boldly said, "Master, we would that you should do for us whatsoever we shall ask of thee." "What would you that I should do for you?" asked Jesus, and they replied, "Grant to us that we may sit, one on thy right hand, and one on thy left hand, in thy glory." Jesus responded, "You know not what you ask. Are you able to drink the cup that I drink? or to be baptized with the baptism that I am baptized with?"[2]

What is the nature of the request made by James and John? They ask Jesus to do whatever they want him to do, court favors, and assume privileges to be their right. Under what kind of circumstances do we make this kind of request? What desire, what longing, and what images are behind such a request? Jesus did not refuse the request; he asked for content: "What would you that I should do for you?" Does he grant that theirs might be a legitimate request? It seems a completely self-centered, self-serving, and ambitious request that is based on the assumption that Jesus will in the future prove to be some kind of Messiah. "In thy glory"—what glory? Political? Here and now, or future? Apocalyptic? Whatever, their Messianic hope and expectation engendered their request.

Feel the poignancy in "Are you able to drink the cup that I drink, or to be baptized with the baptism I am baptized with?" In that question, Jesus alluded to the past and future of his destiny. "Baptism" refers to his pivotal experience and echoes the time, in the early stages of the journey to Jerusalem, when he spoke of the baptism still to come

---

1. Mk. 10:26-27; §117J.
2. Mk. 10:35-40; §120A-G.

and of his agonizing difficulty. The "cup" refers to his future sufferings and prefigures the agony he takes into his being in the Garden of Gethsemane. He asked, in effect, "Can you do this, too?" James and John confidently replied they could. How deep is the source of their answer, and how much insight into the full implications of the future does it contain? Jesus affirmed that they would, indeed, drink the cup and experience the baptism, but said he had no control over who would sit on his right and left hand, for that was in the hands of God. Again, he underscores the clear distinction between his human activity and the realm of the divine, which has its own laws. It is interesting that when the ten other disciples heard what James and John had done, they were indignant. When someone else does something or asks for something we want, envy and jealousy arise. That which we have left unexpressed in ourselves flares up if someone else grabs it.

Jesus dealt with the indignation of the disciples by drawing a stunning contrast between service in the secular arena, where the great ones exercise authority over their subjects, and his kind of service. Most institutions, including the church, thrive on people's need for approval, which leads to serving to that end. Jesus said, "If you want to be great in the eyes of the world, serve and minister to all." He continued, however, that he, Jesus, was not great in the sense of being an authority, nor did he serve in order to be considered great. In Luke's account of this incident, Jesus said, "I am in the midst of you as he that serves."[1] Is being a servant the way to become great or is it an outcome of having found Life? If one does follow Jesus' way to Life by losing life, then surely one of the outcomes or expressions of Life is to serve. The Self is by its very nature interrelated. Thus, service becomes a fruit, a flowing, unstrained expression of inwardness in the outer world.[2]

If we compare Mark's treatment of Jesus' criteria for greatness, we see how much his gospel was influenced by the early church:

1. Lk. 22:27; §138M.
2. Mk. 10:43-45; Mt. 20:26-28; §120J-K.

> Whosoever would become great among you, shall be your minister: and whosoever would be first among you, shall be servant of all. For verily the Son of man came not to be ministered unto, but to minister, and to give his life a ransom for many.[1]

Here, Mark identifies Jesus with the Son of man aspect in Jesus and formulates the doctrine of the atonement by having Jesus giving his life as "a ransom for many." This is the first and only time in the gospels where the doctrine of vicarious atonement is found.[2] What a far cry from the Luke statement! Jesus served as an outcome of Life, and when he later became the center of the religion of the early Christian church this service became part of the process of losing one's life; instead of an expression or fruit of the gaining of Life, it became the means to the end.

As the journey neared its end, Jesus passed through Jericho, where a rich publican named Zaccheus was anxious to see him. Zaccheus was a tax collector, which meant he was a sinner in the eyes of the orthodox Jews and a traitor for serving Rome in the eyes of the other Jews. Because he was short and there were crowds, Zaccheus climbed a sycamore tree to see Jesus. But Jesus looked up and told him to come down from the tree so that he could stay at his house. Zaccheus was surprised and joyful, but bystanders were outraged that Jesus should lodge with such a sinner. Zaccheus attempted to justify himself by telling Jesus how much he gave to the poor and how scrupulously honest he was in his profession. Jesus, acknowledging that any tax collector was in jeopardy, said, "The Son of man came to seek and to save that which was lost."[3] Again, as on many former occasions, the critics objected that Jesus associated with one considered a sinner. Jesus asserted that Zaccheus was saved because he had responded to what was Son of man in Jesus. It is clear that Zaccheus was unusual. He was rich and a publican, but he responded to the value that he sensed or had heard was in Jesus, to the point that he was willing to make a fool

---

1. Mk. 10:43-45; §120J-K.
2. See Appendix I.
3. Lk. 19:1-10; §122.

of himself by climbing the sycamore tree. To be willing to be a fool or to act for a time from the fool archetype is to open oneself to vulnerability, defenselessness, and the absurd. How much of a fool can we risk being by climbing a tree to see Jesus? What will it profit us to see Jesus if we stop only to see him as Christianity has done—namely, following him, not asking how he came to be as he was? So we follow him and not his way. Here the Son of man has the quality of redemptive functioning.

This is the next-to-last place where the phrase "Son of man" is used by Jesus, and what have we seen as to its meaning for him? The functioning of the Son of man seems to include forgiveness, creative decision making, the ability to be flexible and mobile, the confrontation with rejection and pain and death (physical or psychic), and the quality of redemptiveness. Also it is fallible and capable of being criticized, or different from the Source of the Holy Spirit.

Where in the psyche does this place the reality of the Son of man?

Surely it is not to be identified with the ego, the conscious side, nor with the deepest aspect of the Self. Yet it has a connection with both. It seems to be a dynamic element within, between human and divine. Carrying the thrust of the transcendent God, this comes into the immanent Self and moves toward the conscious. It carries the purposiveness of the Other into concrete existence.

IX

"Thou Knewest Not the Time of Thy Visitation"

How is Jesus acclaimed as he enters Jerusalem?

What is his reaction and why?

What does this statement reveal about him and his message?

What blocked his people and us from knowing such times?

The long journey now over, Jesus approached Jerusalem, the city of the opposites of light and dark, the Hebrew City of God in its all-inclusiveness, where the encounter with the authorities would hold his fate. What went on in his heart and mind as he prepared to enter? From the beginning of his ministry there had been opposition to him because of his challenge to laws and customs. The Pharisees and Herodians had very early plotted how to destroy him. He was carrying a new message of the Kingdom and some of his people could not be open to it, at least not the authorities. (For different reasons, many religious groups today might be just as opposed were Jesus to come.) The possibility of execution faced him because he chose not to resist evil. Because of his commitment to

178

totality he could not have stayed in safe territory on the fringe of darkness; he had to encompass total darkness, to take his own inner sonship to the vortex of darkness.

Throughout his short life we have seen this man always courageous and also wise. His strategy was to bring the fullest awareness of possible values out of situations of complexity; it was never manipulative. We see him using such strategy in the discourses on the Kingdom of God, where he employed parables to reveal his wisdom. We see his wise and courageous strategy as he prepared to enter Jerusalem. There were many people following him, and of this fact the authorities were, of course, aware.

The account states that he sent some of his disciples into the village of Bethany to fetch a colt, which they were to loose and to bring to him to ride on into Jerusalem. Here we are confronted by the question of myth or history. The fact that Matthew incorporates a quotation from Zechariah, "Behold, your King cometh unto thee, meek, and riding upon an ass, and upon a colt, the foal of an ass"[1] raises the question whether this was inserted into Matthew and then put into the form it is in Mark. The ass is Saturn's animal and would symbolize the *nigredo* or darkness he was to face. Or did Jesus, as some have assumed, strategically assume a role from the prophetic tradition of Isaiah, or was he doing this to transform the traditional image?

The crowds that followed Jesus stood by and shouted and called out. What did they call Jesus? A comparison of Mark, Matthew, and Luke[2] is necessary to glean a basic and minimum possibility. Mark and Matthew have, "Blessed is he that cometh in the name of the Lord," which would be prophetic; while Luke has, "Blessed is the King that cometh in the name of the Lord," which would be more Messianic. Mark and Matthew, but not Luke, have references to "Son of David," which would also be more Messianic. They all have, "Hosanna in the highest," or "glory in the highest," a familiar refrain of praise from the Hebrew Scripture with no Messianic reference.

1. Mt. 21:5; §124C; Zech. 9:9 similar to Isa. 62:11.
2. Mk. 11:9-10; Mt. 21:9; Lk. 19:37-38; §124 G.

The Pharisees reacted to the crowds' acclaiming Jesus by saying, "Master, rebuke thy disciples." Jesus answered, "I tell you that, if these shall hold their peace, the stones will cry out."[1] This answer does not mean that Jesus agreed with everything that he was being called, but that he chose not to silence the crowd. It was as if he were leaving open even Messianic acclaim as expressing something of the truth for, not about, him. They had missed his real message—to change from the hope for a person who would be the Messiah to a process within—but perhaps he still hoped something could break through. Can we conclude that in his refusal to quiet the people, Jesus was acknowledging the crowd's acclamation of him as prophet, with perhaps some Messianic flavor? Was he fully conscious that his followers did, in fact, understand something of his message, so that they must not be silenced? Matthew has a paragraph which says, "Who is this?" and the multitude answered, "This is the prophet, Jesus, from Nazareth of Galilee."[2] This is a strange thing to find in Matthew who has been constantly concerned to prove the Messiahship of Jesus.

Jesus approached Jerusalem and made, as once before, a poignant statement about the city, his people, and himself. He envisioned the future destruction of the city and country by the Roman rulers. Because the reign of God for the Jewish people could only be fulfilled through achievement of political freedom, there were bound to be clashes with the Romans. For this city which he loved, Jesus wept and said, "If thou hadst known in this day, even thou, the things which belong to peace! but now they are hid from thine eyes. . . . because thou knewest not the time of thy visitation."[3] This "visitation" had not been recognized by his people. The Christians later misinterpreted it, and Jesus stands clearly at a third and different point. Jesus was speaking here with strengthened conviction, and with amazingly self-revealing statements. He knew with certainty what could and would be a redirection of historical development, what could have saved all the

1. Lk. 19:39-40; §124H.
2. Mt. 21:10-11; §124J.
3. Lk. 19:42-44; §124I.

values that belonged to Jerusalem and the Jews if they would follow the message which he was bringing to them. This was a crucial moment of clarity about his function and vocation, pondered ever since the baptism and wilderness, but it was an agonizing moment because he also knew that his words fell on deaf ears. It was this burden that Jesus later brought to the Garden of Gethsemane in the decision to choose death. As a human, to be the carrier of this kind of insight would be harder than to identify with and be carried by the archetype of the Messiah. Jerusalem, loved and wept over, now received at its center a human whose relation to it was more than prophetic, yet was not amenable to any categorization.

Jesus left Jerusalem in the evening, went to Bethany for the night, and returned to the city with his disciples the next day. Entering the Temple, Jesus cast out the money changers and overthrew their tables and the seats of those who sold the doves. He defied the priests and the Mosaic Law, and said, "Is it not written, My house shall be called a house of prayer for all the nations? but you have made it a den of robbers." The reference to "all nations," not found in Matthew and Luke, may be a later addition, or it could reflect a universal outlook that may have been in Jesus' heart. "And the chief priests . . . sought how they might destroy him; for they feared him, for all the multitude was astonished at his teaching."[1]

The meaning of Jesus' clearing the Temple of commercial transactions is suggested in several questions. Was his a premeditated or spontaneous act of rebellion, courage, or anger—righteous or uncreative? Did it spring from some inner compulsive force over which he had no control, or from a contained, creative, strong reaction to a situation he perceived as wrong? Was Jesus here away from the will of God or directly at the heart of it? Was God's presence absent from him here, or was it the motivating force? We have already had indications of how Jesus dealt with the problem of darkness and evil in their multitudinous forms and with regard to the mystery of their origins. Here and in the discourse that follows are two occasions when Jesus

1. Mk. 11:17-18; §126C, E.

was clearly reacting to situations that in his eyes were wrong.

Commerce in the Temple was definitely irreligious, a betrayal of the Covenant with God, a desecration of the holy place of worship, and a profanation of the Sacred. Seeing this, Jesus reacted with an intensity that can be trusted only in one who is as certain of the Source out of which he acts as was Jesus. For most people the act would have been no more than an explosion of anger, but in Jesus it became a human-centered protest against the evil in his people and the authorities who had let this situation come to pass. The act seems deliberate. Perhaps only the day before, in the entrance to Jerusalem, did Jesus feel the reality of the situation which intensified his own dynamic religious commitment. The religious authorities had permitted the negative, regressive pull to deteriorate the Temple to this state of unrighteousness. Because he had come to Jerusalem with the almost sure knowledge that his way of understanding and relating to God would lead to his death, Jesus responded freely to a situation that was human but that reflected the darkness in the divine as well as in the human.

Fritz Kunkel distinguished three kinds of people: white-blooded, red-blooded, and gold-blooded. The pale-blooded are weak, spineless. The red-blooded are strong but egocentric. The gold-blooded are strong, sensitive, nonegocentric, related to the Self. Jesus' response was as a gold-blooded person. Jesus had taught that evil should be faced, not resisted. Many of his people, as is true of all people, had not dealt with evil and so were possessed by it. Seeing, in the evil perpetrated by the money changers in the Temple, to what state one can fall if unaware of inner darkness, Jesus did not act as he did merely to set an example. He reacted with passion to a situation that disturbed him deeply. Only a person very rooted in a reality beyond himself, free from personal and subjective factors, could trust such a response. Further, such a response could only be rooted in a passionate commitment to fulfill the will and need of God and not his own will and needs.

Jesus understood the two sides of possibility in persons and in God, and knew that God desired consciousness of these opposites. Here Jesus moved against the dark side, not by choosing its opposite, but by facing it and transforming it. Did the struggle for consciousness emerge as a function of the Son of man in history? This scene expresses Jesus' deepest masculine Self, discovered out of the transformation of his own evil and mingled with the quality of eros. If we are to be effective in meeting historical realities that need change, we have to move from our own limited sense of values to those rooted in the God moving purposively in historical moments.

Each night Jesus left Jerusalem and each day he returned, a rhythm that illustrates the necessity of withdrawing from a situation in order to return to it more creatively. This is the true heartbeat of creative living. When Jesus returned after dealing with the money changers, the authorities confronted him and asked him by what right had he acted as he did in the Temple and who granted him that right. Jesus had continually acted outside the context of Pharisaical interpretation of the law and religious canons. In his reply, Jesus again exhibited great strategy and wisdom. It was not only his devotion, but his lucidity on how to deal with complexity that so impressively challenged the scribes and elders. He turned and said that he would ask them one question and if they answered it, he would answer their question. His question: "The baptism of John, was it from heaven, or from men?" This question focused on the point of origin of Jesus' whole religious life, the baptism experience. It was a question to catch the authorities and it did just that. They were dumbfounded, figuring that if they replied "from heaven," Jesus would ask why they did not believe John, but if they said "from men," they would incur the anger of the people, who "all verily held John to be a prophet." Consequently, the Pharisees answered that they did not know and Jesus replied, "Neither do I tell you by what authority I do these things."[1] The issue had been strategically avoided.

Why did he not answer? Because any answer given would have been misinterpreted. Still a question remains.

---

1. Mk. 11:27-33; §128A-D.

What would have been his response if he had given one? His own unspoken answer stands at the core of his whole religious conviction and genius. When the authorities asked Jesus the source of his authority, they assumed his answer would be one of two obvious alternatives, God or human. They were asked to choose between the same two alternatives in Jesus' question to them. To their question Jesus could never have answered "human." The unredeemed human was not his norm or point of reference. It is more difficult but even more essential to see why Jesus would not have answered "God," as I feel he would not have. He might have answered, "My authority lies in my *relationship* with God. From that all my actions follow based on my perception and knowledge of His/Her will, always subject to change and alteration. My authority rests on the way I have tried to know God's will by being open to it out of the opposites, and out of this openness to judge the dynamic, evolving best."

Putting it in psychological language, at the baptism Jesus related to the new Self, the Son born within from the ego-Self axis. That, combined with including Satan in the wilderness, enabled Jesus to judge the will of God in the total situation. Jesus' authority, which emerged from the dialogic relationship of God and human and was established at the baptism, was rooted in a process to be followed and tested. This process authenticates it in a different way from the direct statement that it comes from God. Many heinous crimes are committed by, and many mental hospitals are filled with, people who think they hear the voice of God directly and are possessed by it. To discover the will of God out of an open, flexible attitude of wholehearted devotion to its content, regardless of what that is, is very different from being taken over by inflation and presumptuousness. This is one of the many great scenes of Jesus' "silence." To be sure, he speaks a few words, but essentially what the Holy Spirit informs him of in the midst of conflict is to *be* something rather than to explain. The authority of his being, his methodology, is his answer. There is nothing they can do with that.

Presumably still in Jerusalem, Jesus gives two parables which are relevant to the historical situation which he is facing and which also contain universal truths. The first is one from Matthew and is inserted in the text here. In the parable, a father has two sons and wants work done in the vineyard. One son says no, but afterwards he repents and goes; the second son says yes but does not go. Which one does the Will? The first.[1]

God wants work done in the vineyard, wants and needs human cooperation. What is the spiritual-religious reality of work in the vineyard? The vineyard produces grapes which produce wine, one of the great symbols of the spirit of transformation. The vineyard, symbolically and in reality, does not develop and grow of itself; it needs human help. Therein lies the significance of the cooperative effort required between the divine and the human. Two answers are possible and are given, affirming ambivalence and human freedom of choice. The answer to the question why the first son initially said "no" and finally said "yes" lies in the nature of the "no" that leads to repentance versus the "no" that remains a "no." They are miles apart but what makes the difference? The unrepentant "no" comes from a rebellious, negative refusal to hear and go with the father's will. The repentant "no" comes from a positively centered choice which has been honestly and courageously faced. Here disobedience is creative because it expresses the human prerogative of freedom as a first response, but also includes the integrity of knowing what is not the deepest, right response. What seems the uncreative "no" leads to the creative "yes" because the "yes" is far more inclusive.

The son who says "yes" and does not go to work in the vineyard is one who is not consciously inclusive enough of his "no" and therefore becomes possessed by it. Both sons had a "no" against the father, and the father (God) accepts this. There is freedom to fulfill or betray God even after a central commitment. Each son deals with the "no" differently, thus producing very different outcomes. At the historical level, here is a condemnation of the authorities who are not, in Jesus' estimation, doing the Will. Coming as it does, if it follows after the incident in the Temple and the confrontation with the authorities, and before the next

1. Mt. 21:28-31; §129A.

parable, it was a weighty challenge to the leaders of the day, as it is a challenge to each one of us.

In the second parable, the lord of the household gives a vineyard to be worked in to a husbandman and then goes away to another country. And he sends servant after servant to inquire how things are going, but each one is killed, even his beloved son and heir. "What therefore will the lord of the vineyard do? He will come and destroy the husbandman, and will give the vineyard unto others."[1] At the historical level where Jesus placed this parable, there was a warning to his people: they were not tending their vineyard correctly or adequately. And the parable states that the wrath of God is there if the human condition is not met. At a contemporary level, this is a stunningly challenging truth on the destruction and wrath that show in our world and ourselves when central values are not attended to.

The parable stresses, in effect, that failure of response to God's command or invitation leads to withdrawal of God's gifts. The power of resistance is freedom of choice to go the way of destruction rather than cooperation, but the price is higher. For humans, it means the fruits are not available; for God, it means the work of the vineyard is not done. Because of these parables the authorities sought to lay hold of him, but knowing he spoke the parables against them, they feared the multitudes, left him, and went away. The conflict intensified, and while the authorities were more determined than ever to silence Jesus, their hands were stayed by the crowds who followed him.

At the conclusion of this parable it is reported that Jesus said, "Have you not read even this Scripture:

> The stone which the builders rejected,
> The same was made the head of the corner:
> This was from the Lord,
> And it is marvelous in our eyes?"[2]

Whether this was from Jesus or not, it is a profound truth that the rejected part or person in us becomes the corner-

1. Mk. 12:1-9; §129C-G.
2. Mk. 12:10-11; §129H.

stone in history and in us. In any split lies the healing potential. The wound and the healing are part of the whole
saving element. What has been hurt and rejected, repressed, hidden away, holds the jewel of potential
wholeness. This is the meaning of the wounded-healer
archetype.

There was continual plotting about how to get this
man. A group of Pharisees and Herodians came "that they
might catch him in talk," and asked Jesus a tricky question: "Is it lawful to give tribute to Caesar, or not? Shall we
give, or shall we not?" Jesus answered, "Render unto
Caesar the things that are Caesar's and unto God the
things that are God's." This left them astonished.[1] What
was behind this question? If Jesus answered, "Don't pay,"
that would be treason and Rome would arrest him, and the
Pharisees would be rid of him; if he answered, "Pay," that
would be violating the theocratic ideal. His answer,
brilliant and sharp, said to pay to Caesar what belonged to
him and to God what belonged to God. What are the full
implications of his answer and what did it come out of?

For his people, paying Caesar denied their theocratic
ideal that the Kingdom of God and religious freedom could
only be attained through political freedom. Jesus stood in
sharp disagreement with this. Freedom from Rome would
be desirable, yes, but not a genuine prerequisite to establishment of the Kingdom of God. Jesus saw that the course
of rebellion against Rome which they were pursuing would
lead, as it actually did, to the downfall of the nation and the
destruction of the Temple.

He pleaded in many places that his people mend their
ways, but the message fell on deaf ears. So his answer gave
no basis to Rome for action and only frustrated and made
more potent the power of his enemies. His dictum in no
sense eliminated active interest or participation in social-
economic-political issues. The distinction to be made is
between social change being the same as the Kingdom of
God, and social change being the inevitable outcome or
manifestation of the will of God but not to be identified
with the Kingdom. At every instance the meeting of social

1.   Mk. 12:13-17; §130A-D.

situations needing change underlay Jesus' seeing the will of God in situations that were wrong or evil, and that needed human intervention.

The Sadducees, who said there was no resurrection, came to him now with a question concerning a woman who died after she had been wife successively to seven brothers. In the resurrection, they asked, whose wife should she be, for the seven had her to wife? And what is Jesus' answer? He continued with the profound comment "Have you not read in the book of Moses, in the place concerning the Bush, how God spoke unto him, saying, I am the God of Abraham, and the God of Isaac, and the God of Jacob? He is not the God of the dead, but of the living; you do greatly err." [1] He answered them, as so often, first on their ground, that there would be no resurrection, but went on to state the whole issue was irrelevant because the problem resided not in the other world but in seeing that God is the God of the living. To know the "I AM" of the Hebrew Scripture relationship, this "I AM" who is the God of Abraham, Isaac, and Jacob, is to experience the resurrected life as more important than the physical resurrection. "You do greatly err if that is what you are concerned with."

A scribe, having heard his answer to the Sadducees, then came to ask him, "What commandment is first of all?" Jesus answered with the two commandments of love of God and love of neighbor as self, as before. The scribe then repeated what had been said by Jesus and said, "This is much more than all whole burnt offerings and sacrifices." Jesus then evaluated this response with, "Thou art not far from the kingdom of God." [2] What does he mean here by this response? Jesus perceived that the man's understanding was correct, but there was no assurance that he had yet acted on it. This evaluation by Jesus shows that while he put great weight on understanding and on having the right concept as to the way to the Kingdom, that is not sufficient unless actualized. To understand the process of the death-rebirth movement indicates the vision

1. Mk. 12:18-27; §130E-H.
2. Mk. 12:28-34; §130L-P.

is there and is honored as of ultimate value, but action must implement the vision into manifestation.

In an interesting short episode in the Temple, Jesus asked, "How say the scribes that the Christ is the son of David?" and then quoted Psalm 110:

> David himself said in the Holy Spirit,
> The Lord said unto my Lord,
> Sit thou on my right hand,
> Till I make thine enemies the footstool of thy feet.

"David himself calleth him Lord; and whence is he his son?"[1] The logic seems to refute the idea that he, Jesus, could be the Messiah.

Matthew now includes another long discourse. The discourse in Mark, added to by material from Documents M and Q, is a simple, direct condemnation of most of the scribes, and a warning not to be influenced by their ostentation and hypocrisy. The other documents have extended statements always beginning with the phrase "Woe unto you, scribes and Pharisees."[2] There is a parallel account earlier[3] but this setting in Matthew is taken as more authentic and also it seems appropriate that Jesus would only let such creative and deep anger and judgment come out at this point, not earlier.

In essence, he said, "Woe unto you, scribes and Pharisees, because you shut out the Kingdom for others, you leave undone the real matters of mercy and faith, you are involved in only small matters, you clean up what shows and ignore that which does not, you are arrogant and self-righteous and full of pride." Out of what in Jesus did such imagery arise, such intensity of reaction against what he considered pure evil in persons? Were his words a negative, spontaneous bursting forth that was uncreative and harmful and self-centered, or were his words spontaneous but very creative because they came from a deep-centered place where God reigned? The second possibility seems right. It shows the man Jesus facing with conviction

1. Mk. 12:35-37; §131.
2. Mt. 23:13-31; §132I-O.
3. Lk. 11:42-52; §90.

and integrity the religious authorities of the day who had defiled and desecrated the basic religious life of the people. It takes greatness to be able to take such a stand. Courage to speak thus can only happen when one has worked on one's own evil; otherwise, one is not free from involvement. This attitude, and the source of the spirit from which it comes, witnesses to a spirit that will go on, that will not die. Jesus could trust he was not speaking from a shadow place because he had continually dealt with his own evil. It was audacious and challenging, but it came from a true center. In fact the more objective one becomes, the more angry and audacious one can become. The truths of this discourse, which Fritz Kunkel described as the first great statement on depth-psychology, are also profound truths in our own lives. They so aptly describe the split in ourselves between what we profess and how we actually behave.

A tender scene follows. People were casting money into the treasury and Jesus commented on the deep significance of the poor widow who gave all the small amount she had versus those who gave from their superfluity![1] The "all" is more important than the amount; the attitude of the poor widow more moving than the riches of the wealthy. What in us could this mean? It seems creative to relate it to the man who hid his one talent. There, the most inferior was buried out of fear; here it is courageously offered.

The final discourse in Matthew is extensive and raises many questions as to what may or may not be historical. Only the minimum possibility of historicity will be included here. It is probable that this discourse contains a great amount of Christian overlay because it deals with statements about the future, but also gives basis for projection of later events surrounding the person of Jesus as predictions from him. It shows Jesus talking with his disciples on the Mount of Olives after leaving the Temple. As he left the Temple, he spoke of the destruction that would come to the building, referring to the destruction of Jerusalem of which he had already spoken.[2]

1. Mk. 12:41-44; §133.
2. Mk. 13:1-37; §134-136.

X

"Howbeit Not What I Will but What Thou Wilt"

What is the significant action Jesus takes at the Passover meal?

What is Jesus truly praying in Gethsemane?

What does he answer at the trial to the question "Art thou the Christ?"

Out of what consciousness do all these events come?

Jesus entered Jerusalem the day of the Passover to celebrate with his disciples this Feast of the Exodus from Egypt. As he entered he instructed two disciples where to go to find the room where their gathering would take place. "Go into the city, and there shall you meet a man bearing a pitcher of water: follow him. . . .And he will himself show you a large upper room furnished and ready; and there make ready for us."[1] This instruction is enigmatic, challenging, and exciting. At that time of history no man

1. Mk. 14:13-15; §138B.

would be carrying a water pitcher; it would have been carried by a woman. This is strange in itself. What is stranger
is that the man carrying the water pitcher has been for centuries a symbol of the Aquarian Age.[1] These words could
have been said by Jesus, or by early Christianity. My feeling is that they may be from Jesus. They may be another
clue to this intensely conscious man helping evolution forward. In either case it is amazing to have them there.

At evening time they came to the place for the celebration and made ready for the Passover. We now approach a
scene that has great numinosity as a central Christian
ritual, the Eucharist. The primary concern here is to explore what did actually happen at this supper. What are
the historical Jewish roots of this ritual? What did Jesus do
or not do, say and not say? What is the significance of the
Christian ritual, especially as it developed from the original
event?

In the account in Mark, and in those in Matthew and
Luke, which closely follow Mark,[2] we see that the element
in common to these three accounts is Jesus' reported
reference to the bread and wine as his body and blood:

> And as they were eating, he took bread, and when he had blessed,
> he brake it, and gave to them, and said, Take ye: this is my body.
> And he took a cup, and when he had given thanks, he gave to them:
> and they all drank of it. And he said unto them, This is my blood of
> the covenant, which is shed for many. Verily I say unto you, I will
> no more drink of the fruit of the vine, until that day when I drink it
> new in the kingdom of God.[3]

In Matthew there is added "for many unto the remission of
sin,"[4] and in Luke is added "which is poured out for you."[5]
In Luke also is added "this do in remembrance of me."[6]
Compare this with the Pauline letter to the Corinthians:

1. For an excellent, full discussion of the astrological symbols, see
Luella Sibbald, *The One with the Water Jar* (San Francisco: Guild for
Psychological Studies, 1978).
2. Mk. 14:22-25; Mt. 26:26-29; Lk. 22:19-20; §138I-J.
3. Mk. 14:22-25; §138I
4. Mt. 26:28; §138J.
5. Lk. 22:20; §138J.
6. Lk. 22:19-20; §138I-J.

> The Lord Jesus in the night in which he was betrayed took bread; and when he had given thanks, he brake it, and said, This is my body, which is broken for you: this do in remembrance of me. In like manner also he took the cup, after supper, saying, This cup is the new covenant in my blood: this do, as oft as ye drink it, in remembrance of me.[1]

In Matthew there is also added, "until that day when I drink it new with you in my Father's kingdom."[2]

Here lies the whole basis for the dogma of Eucharist. Is it what Jesus proclaimed? Or is it probably a later Christian development? In any event, we must understand its development and the potency of its symbolism—its mythological substrate of meaning.

Besides this account, there is an account in Luke, in Document J, which reads:

> With desire I have desired to eat this passover with you before I suffer: for I say unto you, I will not eat it until it be fulfilled in the kingdom of God. And he received a cup, and when he had given thanks, he said, Take this, and divide it among yourselves: for I say unto you, I will not drink from henceforth of the fruit of the vine, until the kingdom of God shall come.[3]

This account seems the most authentic and needs deep explanation.

Jesus as a Jew approached the Passover meal with its meaning and significance deeply rooted in him. In *this* account he did *not* refer to himself in relation to bread and wine. He *did* pass the wine to his disciples and say, "Take this and divide it among yourselves." The omission of the symbol of bread and wine as body and blood, and his not participating, present a crucial and vital position, upsetting to some and formative and challenging to others. Why might he have said, "With desire I have desired to eat this passover with you before I suffer [but] I will not eat it until . . ."?

This person Jesus stood, as a Jew, in the midst of the most sacred of his people's rituals and said that he would

1. 1 Cor. 11:23-25.
2. Mt. 26:29; §138J.
3. Lk. 22:15-18; §138G-H.

not participate. Why? This ritual symbolized freedom from bondage for his people. It celebrated that the firstborn of the Jews in Egypt under Pharoah were saved from the Angel of Death by the blood mark on the door. But now Jesus, the individual, was confronted by the ritual, aware that he, as the firstborn, as the newborn, was probably not to be passed over by the Angel of Death. To share the ritual as a symbol of a collective movement of salvation, which it was, would be to deny what the Self in him knew. Inward transformation took precedence over outward ritual. This was a great moment when Jesus the individual stood free from collective meanings. He as person individualized the meaning of the Passover; thus, for him the bread and the wine, symbols of the celebration, were to be rejected at this supreme moment.

What does this say about him? What does it do to the symbols of bread and wine? The suffering and agony of this man at this time almost overwhelm the ability to recognize the enormity of his consciousness. He stood alone, not in arrogance or superiority, but in the utmost humility and with the pain of the reality going on in him. Here is one of the bitter fruits of the original baptism experience in which he and God had reached a new covenant of individual relationship and incarnation. From this he lived and taught, manifesting a transcendence in the choice of his life and within his psyche because of the descent of the Holy Spirit. Now he stood where the consciousness of his journey and destiny was the central reality above that of the journey and destiny of his people. Here he is an individual in the fullest sense, standing in a profound expression of God and God's will as above ritual because that is where he and God are. This kind of consciousness is so impressive that one can stand in awe of it as perhaps more significant than the familiar, later ritual developed from Mark. A towering figure participates in the evolution of consciousness.

What does this do to bread and wine as symbols of transformation, each requiring the slow, patient work of the Creator and the human? The bread and the wine were symbols of the Passover, a celebration of life out of bondage, but here they are freed from all specific forms of sym-

bolic, collective meaning and related to by an individual
taking upon himself the task of transformation through
death to fulfillment. The choice available to each person
leaves open the possibility of new depths of meaning of
bread and wine. It may even be that the actuality of Jesus
not taking the bread and wine (and thereby doing something to it) is a provocative and numinous image to evoke.
In both of the statements in the Luke account, Jesus spoke
of not eating or drinking "until the kingdom of God shall
come," in some sense referring to his own fulfillment. This
was a new level of covenant. Earlier he had spoken of his
ever-threatened death as the act of being "perfected" or
becoming "all-inclusive." For him, paradoxically, this was
a final act of helping the Kingdom of God come alive as
much in himself as in his teaching. In some almost
mystical way he was saying that he must continue to
fulfillment in the final act, the cross. Was the cross for him
the symbol of the inclusion of the two sides of God finding
reconciliation through his act of not resisting?

Following the Passover supper, Jesus and the disciples
departed to the Mount of Olives. It was on this occasion,
after Jesus had said what was to happen, that Peter affirmed that he would never deny Jesus. Here was Peter
again caught between terrible opposites, affirming that he
would never deny, and so soon thereafter denying.

They came to a place named Gethsemane. Jesus and
his disciples entered a garden, not the blissful unconsciousness of the Garden of Eden, but perhaps symbolically this garden in its transformed state. Paradoxically, it is here in this garden of ancient olive trees that the
final choice to eat of the Tree of the Knowledge of Good and
Evil led him to his fulfillment. Here he faced his death on
the cross as his eating from the Tree of Life. Jesus entered
with all the disciples, and he took three of them—Peter,
James, and John—with him, and said to them, "Abide ye
here, and watch," and he moved beyond them. Jesus is
alone, separate from all the disciples, three of them near
and the rest a short distance away. "And he fell on the
ground, and prayed that, if it were possible, the hour might
pass away from him." And he said, "Abba, Father, all

things are possible unto Thee; remove this cup from me: howbeit not what I will, but what thou wilt."[1]

What might Jesus have meant by this prayer? What new and perhaps fresh understanding can be seen from all that has gone before to make it consistent with him and his outlook? Here is a dialogue addressed to God as father— *Abba* in Aramaic. This is an intimate form of address that speaks of the nearness of God to him; not distant, as God in His/Her total transcendence, but God manifest in a moment of history. What does Jesus express of the utmost depth, and why? What does it come out of? "All things are possible unto Thee; remove this cup from me." This feels like an affirmation of his hope that death might not be the will of God for him, but with no swerving from it if it was. Jesus dared to convey his own most human longing to the Thou whom he loved, without deviating from seeing the Will. Why *should* he want to die? Everything in him, except the ultimate point of Being, longed to live, to continue to serve with his message. He was alive and had an incredible sense of vitality and vibrancy. He yearned to live. It is the essence of mature, deep prayer that, if one is totally committed, personal desires can and must be expressed as part of the whole, but not in expectation of fulfillment. The fulfillment comes from the desires being channeled and offered to God.

Also, in addition to bringing his full human reality, he may be once again searching to know that this was actually the will of the Thou. Ever since he started to Jerusalem, it had seemed a fairly certain possibility that the Will would be that he must meet his death as an ultimate expression of acknowledging darkness as part of the whole. It was not the darkness that killed him, but his thrust to include both sides and find the third point, the creative response.

After this complete giving over to God, the arrest comes. Only here at this precise moment, at the beginning of his prayer, could he still have exercised the freedom of choice to leave. He did not leave, but in staying, having faced the question of whether this was the will of God or

---

1. Mk. 14:32-36; §140B-C.

not, he was raising himself and God to a new level of consciousness. The remarkable fact is not his ability to face his own death, but rather that in facing his death he faced the fact that God's communication through him to people would be cut off. As a vessel for the reality of the God-Process, his death would be the end. What Jesus thought could or would be carried on by his disciples must have been minimal in his mind, considering their response throughout.

By voicing his yearning to live and having the courage to open the question of what was the Will, he saved himself from the death of a martyr or from a passive resignation to the will of God as his death has so often been interpreted. Rather, he expressed in fullest terms that in very truth it is a co-creation that God wants. It was a full human being who had opened himself to be transformed in the structure and dynamic process of his whole being by the power of God as Source. Facing his fulfillment as person was more important than his message being continued. This constant interaction between God and Jesus is a quantum leap that had been brought about by his life and activity at this time of history. Out of this interaction, Jesus is giving his answer to God by saying, "Howbeit not what I will, but what thou wilt."

How impressive it is that Jesus did not say, "Thy Will be done." The "howbeit" changes the whole dynamic. Out of all the issues just faced, he did not just say, "what thou wilt," but he prefaced it with "however, not what I will." He had thoroughly brought to God what he would like to have had as his will without, I repeat, having it be determinative. From that search he now knew the will of God must be for him to stay and face the crucifixion. This prayer of Jesus can be seen as a paradigm of prayer for any Western person. It expresses an "I" in full commitment and acknowledgment of its own reality, facing the Thou whose Will will be supreme in an ultimate situation (or all situations). It is an "I" subject to a Higher Authority. As Martin Buber writes:

> How powerful, even to being overpowering, and how legitimate, even to being self-evident, is the saying of I by Jesus! For it is the I of

unconditional relation in which man calls his Thou Father in such a way that he himself is simply Son, and nothing else but Son.[1]

Then Jesus returned to the disciples and found them asleep, and we have the poignant question to Peter, "Simon, sleepest thou? Couldest thou not watch one hour? Watch and pray, that ye enter not into temptation: the spirit indeed is willing, but the flesh is weak." Three times he came and found the disciples sleeping. The third time he said, "Sleep on . . . the hour is come."[2] What was behind his first appeal to them? What went on in him when he found the central figures in his life asleep at this most crucial of all moments? Was perhaps the reaction of Jesus to feel a terrible blow that they were in fact asleep at the moment of his greatest struggle? "Couldn't you have stayed awake to help me in my consciousness of searching for the will of God and facing possible death?" These first two questions seem to be his first inner reaction of disappointment and amazement.

Then he continued, "Watch and pray, that ye enter not into temptation."[3] What could have been the temptation? The facts of choice and of ambivalence in all situations are present. He obviously assumed they could stay awake. It is always possible to go the regressive way, and it is just that which the disciples were doing here. Instead of facing and overcoming their regressiveness—the "no" and then the "yes"—they gave in to the "no" of sleep. And Jesus continued, "The spirit indeed is willing but the flesh is weak." What is the particular aspect of the flesh being referred to here? Sleep represents rest, yes, but also a return to unconsciousness. Here Jesus is the awakener; it is different from the storm at sea incident, when he is the awakened. At this moment the temptation for the disciples was to give in to the flesh, the natural substance, without being related enough to the indwelling spirit that can transform the substance. In short, theirs was an act of profound unconsciousness because they could not face the con-

1. Martin Buber, *I and Thou* (New York: Charles Scribner's Sons, 1937), p. 66.
2. Mk. 14:37-41; §140E-G.
3. Mk. 14:38; Mt. 26:41; Lk. 22:46; §140E.

sciousness in Jesus at this point nor the demand that it would make on them. It was easier to sleep.

At the end, Jesus said, "Take your rest . . . the Son of man is betrayed. . . . He that betrayeth me is at hand."[1] What does it mean that Jesus is able to say, "Go on, rest ye"? This garden scene is a series of three "no's" and one overwhelming "yes." There was the "no" of the sleeping disciples, the "no" of letting preferences be obstacles, and the "no" of an untotal "yes." And the fourth element was the "yes" beyond it all.

Immediately Judas, with a multitude of chief priests, elders, and scribes, came and said, " 'Rabbi,' and kissed him. And they laid hands on him, and took him."[2] It was by his kiss that Judas was to signify the right person to arrest. Why did the final act of the evil principle have to come from those closest to Jesus, from his own circle? Logically, the answer is that only such a one would be able to identify him, but psychologically a deeper truth lies hidden here. Jesus chose the probability of death as the way of embracing the totality of God in His/Her evil and good aspects. Death would come because of the enemies he had made among the authorities and the impersonal forces of evil. Here is the most personal expression of evil possible, a member of his closest circle betraying with a symbol of love.

Judas represents self-destruction in the psyche. He identified with his own dark side, in exact opposition to Jesus, who focused on his totality in a responsible way. Jesus' whole life encompassed darkness at inner and outer levels; therefore, he had to meet it at this most intimate level. In the anguished painting of Jesus and Judas confronting one another by Giotto, it is as if Jesus stands at the heart of a whirlpool or of a great moving wheel and, accepting the enormous "no" of the moment, helps God to Become. And as they laid hands on him to take him, Jesus said, in essence, "You could have taken me in the Temple. Why didn't you, instead of coming out and taking me as a robber?"[3]

1. Mk. 14:41-42; §140G.
2. Mk. 14:45-46; §141B.
3. Mk. 14:48-49; §141G.

Jesus' original disciples were twelve. After Judas' betrayal as part of Jesus' active transformation of darkness, the twelve are now Jesus and eleven disciples. At this point, the disciples all left him. Luke adds, "He said to them, This is your hour and the power of darkness."[1] He stood acknowledging the power, the forces seemingly triumphant. He brought incredible consciousness about darkness. The real triumph lay in the power of the man they had seized.

"And they led Jesus away to the high priest: and there came together with him all the chief priests and the elders and the scribes."[2] "And . . . the chief priests with the elders and scribes, and the whole council, held a consultation, and bound Jesus, and carried him away and delivered him up to Pilate."[3] So begin the accounts of the two trials of Jesus before the Jewish and the Roman authorities, at the end of which they led him out to crucify him. In the midst of all the details of these two trials, several questions of ultimate significance emerge. What did the trials reveal of Jesus' own consciousness of the Messianic or Christ image within himself as the question was posed to him? How did his answers lead to his crucifixion? Behind all this, what can be said about the cause of his death and his own attitude toward it? Who immediately and ultimately was responsible for the death of Jesus? Why the answer that he gave to the question confronting him?

The overall impression of this man at this moment of his life, facing his destiny, is of his magnificent and eloquent silence. One can only stand in awe of it and try with all one's being to enter into his consciousness.

In the trial before the Jewish authorities,[4] the chief priests, who wanted to be rid of Jesus because of his deep radical teaching, found no sure basis for accusation. First, they tried to accuse Jesus of saying that the Temple would be destroyed and in three days he would build it up again. The only possible basis for this is the distortion of his statement in Mark 13:1-2, where he looked on the Temple and

1. Lk. 22:53; §141H.
2. Mk. 14:53; §142A.
3. Mk. 15:1; §143A.
4. Mk. 14:53-64; §142A-G.

predicted its downfall—in my opinion a political observation. But "he held his peace, and answered nothing."[1]

The high priest tried again with a more direct question: "Art thou the Christ, the Son of the Blessed?" (in Mark) or "Tell us whether thou be the Christ, the Son of God" (in Matthew).[2] This was the first time Jesus had been asked a direct Messianic question by the authorities. The question had come before from the demoniacs, from John the Baptist, and from Peter. The authorities had challenged him, had asked him for signs, had accused him of being in league with the devil, but had never asked him this direct question. There are four accounts of this question before the Jewish authorities: one in Mark copied by Matthew, and two in Luke from Document J.[3]

What does the asking of the question mean to the authorities? If the Jewish authorities could prove to Rome that Jesus was indeed the Messiah, then he was a threat to Rome and their political power, and on no other grounds could he have been done away with by them. To these questions there are four reported answers. Mark reports that Jesus said, "I am," and then went on to talk about the Coming of the Son of man.[4] Matthew, following Mark, reports the answer as, "Thou sayest," or in the RSV, "You have said so," and includes a reference to the Coming of the Son of man.[5] How to account for Matthew, whose whole bias has been to prove the Messiahship of Jesus, not having "I am" as in Mark? It would seem impossible that he would not use it. It is much more probable that the original answer in Mark was "Thou sayest," which was copied by Matthew and later changed in Mark. In Luke, Jesus first answers, "If I tell you, you will not believe: and if I ask you, you will not answer." And then, "You say that I am."[6] The chief priests interpreted his answer as yes, accused him of blasphemy, and prepared to lead him to Pilate.

---

1. Mk. 14:61; §142D.
2. Mk. 14:61; Mt. 26:63; §142E.
3. Mk. 14:61; Mt. 26:63; §142E; Lk. 22:67, 70; §142N, O.
4. Mk. 14:62; §142E.
5. Mt. 26:64; §142E.
6. Lk. 22:67-68, 70; §142N, O.

Why did Jesus answer as he did, and what was his real answer to himself? Whatever his answer, he knew he could not explain it to them. Though in essence he said, "You say so," he was not answering; he was throwing the question back to them and leaving them in the dark as to his true answer. This was creative strategy, not because of an end to be achieved but because of the integrity of the man at that moment. It would have been futile and foolish to attempt to explain. Their eyes and hearts were hardened. And to explain what?

What was his real answer to himself and to God in these closing days of his life? Not what happened later in development, but now, standing here, what did he know? He knew that what was behind the Messianic longing for a savior to redeem the people had been manifested inside him, and knew that the same reality could happen to others. He knew it was a genuine longing, issuing from the heart and depths of humankind, but *not* to be fulfilled by any redeemer figure. He knew that God's longing was behind or intrinsic to this. This archetype in the psyche as an archetype of the Self had its origin in God Transcendent.

Jesus knew that the content of this longing of the Jews included transformation of people into community and justice and peace. He hoped as a Jew that this would be manifest in history but not through one person. He knew that all the dynamic energy behind the Messianic image needed not to be projected into one person but to be unfolded into a process that was available to all. He knew this reality between God-human lay there to be manifested in new ways, and not to be projected into a looked-for Messiah. He knew this had to happen because of what had happened at his baptism and in the wilderness, in his choice, and because of the action from the Other side. A new step of evolution was ready and he was a vehicle for it, and yet he knew he could not be heard by the authorities, for there had been no evidence during his lifetime of open-mindedness or flexibility on their part. Was there despair in his silence? I do not feel it was despair. Discouragement and wondering, yes, but never a failure to trust the meaning of God's will. It is an eloquent silence filled with meaning. And how crucial it is to separate the authorities of his day from the people. To say the Jews killed him is totally erroneous. More accurate it is to say that the religious authorities had become rigidified and codified, were too threatened by his newness. All they could do was to get rid of him. Compare what some of our own ecclesiastical authorities could do to a figure such as Jesus today. But this is not to criticize all Christianity.

Jesus knew all these things but he chose only to say, "You say so," to the accusatory questions. Out of all that he knew, he could not say "yes" because it was not true, and he could not say "no" because it also was not true for a different reason. "Yes" would have made the issue clear cut; "no" would have cut off the energy of the image which had become a new source of God's activity inside him. A clear yes or no, that is, would have cut off the content of that process within him.

Before the Roman trial, there is a poignant scene with Peter which occurred after the authorities and their officers had begun to spit on Jesus and give him blows. Three times Peter, sitting in the courtyard warming himself, was approached by one who said to him, "You were with Jesus the Nazarene." The first time the maid said it directly to him; the second time she said it to those standing by; and the third time those who stood by accused him of being a Galilean. Peter's response became more and more violent. First, he said he just simply did not know what was being said. The second time he denied it; and the third time he began to curse and swear, "I know not this man of whom you speak."[1] This incident ends with Peter remembering that Jesus had predicted that he, Peter, would deny him three times before the cock crowed. This is historically questionable, but symbolically rich. As the cock crowed the second time, Peter remembered and wept.[2]

What most essentially lies behind Peter's response, and how do we see this in ourselves? The first approach to Peter was through the feminine. The maid asked the question of relationship which Peter could not face. In Peter's

1. Mk. 14:71; §142J.
2. Mk. 14:66-72; Mt. 26:69-75; Lk. 22:56-62; §142H-K.

responses, what do we see? At this moment we see Peter completely undone by the scene he had just witnessed. Is he frightened to acknowledge the relationship because of his fear for his own life? No, much more is involved. This is a moment of the most crucial, agonizing confrontation. His leader, his beloved friend, the hoped-for Messiah, is being rejected and he stands with him. Is he secure before God or do his legs fail him wherever he stands?

Returning to the Roman trial, Pilate directly asked, "Art thou the King of the Jews?"[1] If Jesus were a political Messiah he could be done away with, because he would be a threat to Roman power. In the Luke account three charges against Jesus are brought by the high priests to Pilate, before the question of Messiahship. He is charged with "perverting our nation," "forbidding to give tribute to Caesar," and "saying that he himself is Christ a King."[2] Of these three accusations, clearly the second and third are completely without basis. In fact, Jesus had said they could give tribute to Caesar. The other charge, "perverting our nation," might be considered to be true depending on one's point of view.

Jesus' answer in all three accounts of the Roman trial is like the one at the Jewish trial: "You say so." A simple, eloquently sound answer. As before, nothing could be said. And to this, in the Luke account, Pilate answered, "I find no fault in this man."[3] Pilate was not convinced of any danger from Jesus. In Mark and Matthew it says, "Pilate marvelled."[4] Was this true or put in by the editors? The Mark account continues by referring to the custom at the time of a feast of one prisoner being released. Barabbas was one of the prisoners and Pilate asked the crowd whether he or Jesus should be released. Pilate offered to release Jesus because he perceived that the chief priests had delivered Jesus up from envy. But the chief priests urged the crowd to demand the release of Barabbas and cry out for Jesus to be crucified. (I myself find this account quite plausible, but

1. Mk. 15:2; Mt. 27:11; Lk. 23:3; §143D.
2. Lk. 23:2; §143C.
3. Lk. 23:4; §143F.
4. Mk. 15:5; Mt. 27:14; §143E.

am sure this opinion differs strongly from that of most scholars.) Pilate asked what evil Jesus had done. The crowd continued, "Crucify him." Pilate, wishing to content the multitude, followed their wish, and Jesus was delivered over to be crucified.[1]

What, then, is the essence of these scenes if we take them simply? The Jewish authorities wanted to be rid of Jesus and the only acceptable excuse would be if he threatened to be a political Messiah. However, Jesus did not call himself the Messiah. When he was led to the Roman trials from the Jewish authorities, he again did not affirm Messiahship, and Pilate found no reason to do away with him, yet Pilate capitulated because he was influenced by the crowd. Though Pilate was definitely a weak man, he was a tool in the story, and would have been recalled to Rome if rioting had developed into insurrection. Weak or not weak, Pilate's actions were not the ultimate decisive issue. Judas betrayed, Peter denied, Pilate was weak, and Jesus encompassed, by what he had seen in Gethsemane, his own answer to God.

---

1.   Mk. 15:6-15; §143I-M.

XI

"How Am I Straitened Till it Be Accomplished!"

What did going to the cross mean to Jesus?

Why this choice?

Who and what was present at the cross?

Why the words "My God, my God, why hast Thou forsaken me?"

Jesus, on his way to Jerusalem, said the words that are the title for this chapter: "I have a baptism to be baptized with, and how am I straitened till it be accomplished!"[1] Now that baptism is taking place. What is being accomplished by Jesus? What does his dying mean for him, his people, and his God? From the standpoint of God, why is it necessary? Many questions flood us as we begin. Let us first look at the scene. Who is present at this decisive moment of history? Jesus, the two robbers, the soldiers, the chief priests, Simon of Cyrene, the centurion, women—particularly Mary Magdalene, Mary the mother of James,

1. Lk. 12:49-50; §95A.

Joseph and Salome, and in the gospel of John, Jesus' mother. And perhaps most of all, God and the Holy Spirit. The absence of the disciples is conspicuous and one may wonder where they were hiding. Jesus was taken directly from the Roman trial to be crucified, which was the Roman form of execution.

At the beginning of the journey, Simon of Cyrene was ordered to help Jesus carry the cross. Mark then describes how Jesus was brought to Golgotha and refused the wine and myrrh, and how lots were cast for his garments. The mocking by the crowd continued as the inscription "The King of the Jews" was written. Jesus was taunted with the challenge to save himself because he had saved others, then with, "Let the Christ, the King of Israel, now come down from the cross, that we may see and believe."[1] Did the chief priests and scribes say this because something in them really wanted a supernatural sign to prove that Jesus was the Messiah? Was it a taunt from them, or is this a later addition? In the hour of suffering on the cross do we dare to imagine what was moving in the thought and spirit-matter of Jesus? This was the Will, and he was fully going with it in order to express the totality and all-inclusiveness of that Will in actual flesh and substance.

Here Spirit and Substance assumed new depth of dimension. There was assent between Jesus and his Creator, especially since the Garden of Gethsemane; this was absolutely right and necessary in order to complete what had been begun at the baptism. What agony of spirit must have been his along with the physical agony! But would there not have been at the center of his being a strange, deep joy of fulfillment? Here begins the ultimate paradox of the scene. Here is a divine absurdity. Here the concrete meaning of losing one's life to save it is manifested. The physical life is going, but the deeper life of God's will in him was being lived, and what would the ongoingness from it be? Jesus on the cross—is this an expanding of the Son of man, including opposites and forgiving and completing God? Here, perhaps, the deepest meaning of "Son" is fulfilled as radical obedience to the truth.

1 Mk. 15:22-32; §144C-E.

In the Gospel of Luke, in Document J, there is a significant conversation between Jesus and the women of Jerusalem who were following him. Here again is poignant
revelation by Jesus concerning the future downfall of
Jerusalem:

> Daughters of Jerusalem, weep not for me, but weep for yourselves,
> and for your children. For behold, the days are coming, in which
> they shall say, Blessed are the barren, and the wombs that never
> bore, and the breasts that never gave suck. Then shall they begin to
> say to the mountains, Fall on us; and to the hills, Cover us. For if
> they do these things in the green tree, what shall be done in the
> dry?[1]

It is for that doomed city to weep but not for him. His con-
centraton at this moment is not subjective; it is on the
reality of the suffering of his people if they do not change
their theocratic ideal.

In Luke also is recorded the presence of the two
thieves.[2] What does their presence add? It adds the stark
presence of evil, which has already been expressed by the
authorities who engineered the killing of Jesus, and by
Judas, the betrayer in his own circle. This presence of the
thieves at the horizontal level brings darkness into concrete finiteness.

Two greatly contrasting reports are given of the words
of Jesus on the cross. Which would Jesus have said and
what did the words mean? In Mark, the words are from the
beginning of the twenty-second Psalm: "*Eloi, Eloi, lama
sabachthani*—My God, my God, why hast thou forsaken
me?"[3] In Luke, the words are, "Father, forgive them; for
they know not what they do" and "Father, into thy hands I
commend my spirit."[4] How many words and books have
been written on this choice! In most of the musical settings
of Jesus' last words both accounts are included, but in the
approach of this whole book it seems imperative to choose

---

1. Lk. 23:28-31; §144B.
2. Lk. 23:39-43; §144E. See Appendix I for a comment on the historicity
of this passage.
3. Mk. 15:34; §144G.
4. Lk. 23:34, 46; §144C, H.

between the accounts, and the choice is for the Mark account. One criterion for this choice is based on which is more likely to have come in later as more consistent with the Christian attitude. Surely, on this basis the Luke account more easily fits. In fact, it seems impossible to imagine the Mark account as being added, though it would be possible to imagine it being said by Jesus.

In the Luke account the forgiveness is there if the referent is the unconsciousness of the soldiers. If Jesus is referring to those responsible for his death, the Luke account would be an impossible statement, for throughout Jesus assumed their knowledge of what they were doing. The statement of commending his spirit to God feels similar to what he has been doing all his life, and this could be the final *affirmation*.

In Mark, what could this cry be and what might be behind it? It is certainly the cry of a dying man in terrible physical agony, hard even to imagine. Why does Jesus cry, "My God, my God, why hast Thou forsaken me?"—words from the victory Psalm 22? That seems too rational and logical for this moment. No, rather it is the cry of this human who has always stayed related to the ultimate transcendent being of God and has now known this God incarnated within himself, immanent, powerful, almost overwhelming. In a previous book, I wrote, "This may be the utterance of a man in utter agony, a man who knows that, at this moment, God can do nothing because man has channelled His/Her, God's, power into consciousness and therefore reduced God's omnipotence."[1] This seems more valid than ever. Jesus cries out not because God is not present but because His/Her presence is a new manifestation in substance producing an agonizing suffering. The Spirit of God on which Jesus has always relied is not absent to him, but is silent. God is more present than ever, is suffering incarnation in Jesus, but God in substance does not lend the same kind of support. Jesus' sense of aloneness comes because he cannot be helped by God. He is helping God in His/Her transformation by himself overcoming the split of the opposites in God. A seminar member has said this is the "apex and zenith of con-

1. Howes, *Intersection*, p. 166.

sciousness." It is possible that both Jesus and God are crucified and redeemed at this existential moment. This is his final answer to God.

After these words, which those around interpreted as a calling for Elijah, "Jesus uttered a loud voice, and gave up the ghost." When a centurion saw this he said, "Truly this man was the Son of God," or in Luke, "Certainly this was a righteous man."[1] The Luke words are to me most moving and a central evaluation of Jesus by someone not of his own people. Surrounding the Marcan words on the cross is this: "And when the sixth hour was come, there was darkness over the whole land until the ninth hour. . . . And the veil of the temple was rent in twain from the top to the bottom."[2] Matthew enlarges this to earthquake, tombs being opened, and the emergence of saints.

For whom was the event darkness? What is being described symbolically? It was darkness, surely, for the disciples and his followers—an unutterable loss. It was darkness for the women who followed him so faithfully, especially Mary Magdalene. It was darkness for his people even if they were not conscious of it. Their refusal to respond (on the whole) was a terrible dark wound and yet perhaps a necessary one. Only history can judge this. Was it darkness for Jesus? Yes, again if we understand the paradox. Darkness, not because of his attitude, but because he had included the dark part of God, bringing it into his flesh in manifestation. The phrase "the veil of the temple was rent in twain" is reminiscent of "the heavens rent asunder" at the baptism. The veil of the temple is over the Holy of Holies for the Jews, and now that is torn apart and God is revealed in a new way.

Most of all, was the death of Jesus darkness for God and for history? At the moment of its happening its meaning for history still lay completely in the unknown future, but for God are we again with paradox? On the one hand, God was losing His/Her best servant, a human vehicle, a transmitter of the way. Death was taking the living instrument, playing His/Her melody. On the other hand, at this precise moment something was happening to and for God

1. Mk. 15:39; Lk. 23:47; §144J.
2. Mk. 15:33, 38; §144F, H.

that had never happened before. God's two sides of light and dark, Spirit and Substance, were being brought together, united not by unconscious identification but by a living, throbbing human being who united both aspects through his relating to each and moving beyond them to the third point of integration. It is as if the two hands of God, the right and left, are united by a third element: a human who has taken on the burden of freedom.

More precisely, what was happening to and with the Holy Spirit? In the baptism and wilderness, the Spirit descended from God into new manifestation. This journey of the Spirit into and through substance took a new step with the crucifixion and now, being changed in the substance of this one person with intense clarity, became available to all. At the death of Jesus, the Spirit of God did not die but could move out into the world in a new way. Likewise, the Messianic image and longing which had been changed in the person of Jesus into a more personal and eternal reality and process now became free and unattached. The person in the physical body died. Yet the realities in him, the central archetypes on which his life was based, did not die. They were alive. The reality Jesus had lived and made accessible to others was there in the air, so to speak, needing a new home. His descent into the waters of the baptism led to his ascent of consciousness in the wilderness. The descent-ascent, life-death motif was the dominant one of his life. The ascent to the cross had led to the deepest descent and death, from which the Spirit—as the Substance aspect of God—emerged newly. This is a description of the resurrected life. Love became possible in a new way because of the way the "enemy," the dark, had been overcome.

In this moment what has been the sacrifice for God and for Jesus? Or has it been sacrifice, a thought so commonly expressed in Christianity? Yes, Jesus sacrificed his life, his physical life, for what he knew was necessary for the will of God. Because his integrity demanded it, the inner war must have been overwhelmingly great. And he sacrificed the one-sided aspect of God, the Spirit, by bringing it into substance and thereby uniting the opposites. Jesus sacrificed public approval and acceptance for his individual way. He sacrificed being the natural man to become a supranatural man—or to live the Son of man stretched between divine and human.

And God, what did God sacrifice? A new quantum leap had to have a human like Jesus willing to be killed and willing to have his message perish in order to make possible His/Her wholeness. The dominance of the spirit side was renounced for more totality. Entrance into the flesh always means diminution of infinite power. Limitation of the Spirit by being held in the consciousness of a human fulfilled the longing of God but also deprived God of omnipotence. The image of the cross as dialogue between God and Jesus is intensely gripping if one sees God's suffering in the loss of this human vehicle and yet His/Her sense of triumph that one person, Jesus, had taken on the problem of freedom and met Evil with Love and could be this loyal. In the book of Job, Job stayed loyal "though he slay me." Here God became something new because of what a human did. The entirety of God becomes available to humankind through this new enfleshment. Redemption is present and available through this mutual sacrifice of Jesus and God.

The question cannot be ignored as to what and who killed Jesus. He had emphasized the individual versus the collective in old established patterns, the new dimension of God's activity being in the psyche, the concept of the Kingdom as a slow, evolutionary growth, the shift from the hoped-for Messiah to a Messianic process available to all, and much more. This had certainly exacerbated the hatred of the authorities to the point that they found a way to have Jesus killed.

Who was responsible? Some of the Pharisees and scribes; religious authorities bound to old traditions; Judas; the mob; Pilate and Rome; and finally, Jesus himself, because of his choices, especially to eat so fully of the Tree of the Knowledge of Good and Evil, and because of his teaching.

What does it add to our understanding in depth that the women were there "beholding from afar"?[1] It is important that the Feminine was present, as it had been

---

1. Mk. 15:40; §144L.

throughout his life, and its presence symbolically emphasizes the substantial reality of this event. It confronts us even more to look at the whole event both from Jesus' and from God's standpoint. The person of Mary Magdalene is especially crucial because she has followed Jesus with absolute loyalty and she is the one who will go to the tomb. The presence of the mother of Jesus is not found in the Synoptics, but only in the Gospel of John. She is a moving figure historically, and symbolically she is the Feminine bearing the birth of the New Son.[1]

After his death, a man named Joseph of Arimathaea, "who was also looking for the Kingdom of God," went and asked Pilate for the body of Jesus. Clearly he, Joseph, did not want the body desecrated, and Pilate granted his request. Joseph took the body, wrapped it in linen, and laid it in a tomb against which he placed a huge gravestone. "And Mary Magdalene and Mary the mother of Joses beheld where it was laid."[2]

When the Sabbath was passed, the two Marys brought spices to the tomb to anoint the body. They were concerned about how they would roll away the stone from the door to the tomb. When they arrived, the stone had already been removed. They entered the tomb, and according to the Marcan account, met a young man dressed in white who told them that Jesus had risen and instructed them to go tell the disciples, especially Peter, that he would meet them in Galilee as he had promised. The women saw the empty tomb, were afraid and said nothing.[3] In Luke's account, there are two men who stood in "dazzling apparel." In Matthew, the young man becomes an angel whose "appearance was as lightning, and his raiment white as snow."[4]

What could be the possible explanation for the empty tomb and the vision of the masculine figure, human or angelic? The body could have been stolen by friends so it would not be desecrated. It could have been stolen by the

1. See Virgin Birth account, Appendix I.
2. Mk. 15:42-47; §145A-F.
3. Mk. 16:1-8; §147.
4. Lk. 24:4; Mt. 28:3; §147D.

Jewish enemies who were responsible for his death so that there was no possibility of his tomb becoming a shrine. The same could be said of the Romans. Another possibility is that the whole story is part of the mythic telling of what was behind the resurrection experience. All kinds of other ideas have been set forth, e.g., that Jesus was never put in the tomb in the first place and, in fact, had not died; or that it was the wrong tomb. It could be that the women, because of their own inner state, saw an empty tomb with the man, men, or angel in it, but that what they saw was not true in physical fact. Or it could be that Jesus had really risen bodily. This has, of course, been the orthodox traditional answer, that he overcame death by this physical transmutation. So, either the tomb was physically empty with the body having been stolen, or the tomb was not empty and the dynamics of the inner process made the change.

The most challenging explanation for the empty tomb is the possibility the body was stolen. But I want to consider another possibility—that the body had not been stolen and was there but was not seen as a corpse because of a transformation in the women who had a vision of a new figure. Could it have been something like this? These two women were close followers of Jesus and were present at the crucifixion; they beheld where his body was laid and they cared and came back to anoint him. What happened to them at this time? At his death their world was shattered. All the values the man carried for them as women were gone. Their inner world was, in one sense, empty. But not really empty, because what had been the carrier of the Value could have come into them as a spiritual reality, symbolized by a figure of a man or angel. And this figure could have seemed to speak to one or both of them—not unusual as an aspect of creative logos* of a woman. Their spiritual side, which had first responded to Jesus and was carried by him, could now have become conscious to them and have moved their remembering into new inner meaning.

The meeting of his death as fulfillment of his obedience to the totality of God led to a new sense of resurrection. Something happened which must now be explored. It could have started with the experience of Mary Magdalene. The resurrected life of which Jesus continually spoke and that he lived assumed a new garb. The Spirit, from baptism through crucifixion, lived on.

Symbolically, because the tomb was cared for and nurtured by the Feminine, a new birth could come from it. The tomb is essential as cradling and tending things. This step is essential after the terrible womb of the crucifixion and the possibility of a new birth. The tomb became the "manger" for this birth in the disciples. And subsequently the very prevalent myth of the divine Child grew from this experience and became attached to Jesus. The last chapter will include an exploration of these realities.

XII

The Resurrected Life

What was the experience of the disciples after the death of Jesus?

How did they interpret it?

What could be the meaning of a resurrected life as Jesus taught it?

What most lies in mystery?

The history of the life of Jesus ended. New life began out of that which he manifested. The life of Jesus the man was finished, but the life of what he lived was not. The death-rebirth archetype, the Messianic image, the Son of man image, the possibility of new life ever being born out of the virginal, all are there as Source, not lost with his death. What Jesus was devoted to, what he expressly manifested and incarnated, *is*. The message he taught exists as words spoken, as Word manifest and available.

What happened to this richness after his death? Whatever it was that happened led to a new historical development, Christianity. Out of the loss of his life and the despair it must have caused, a new vitality and a message of the risen Christ erupted and changed the Mediterranean world.

If one takes literally—as physical reality—the appearance of Jesus resurrected from death, then there remains no central question. For two thousand years belief in the physical resurrection of Jesus has been and is held by millions of people. But if the reaction is one of non-acceptance of the physical resurrection, then the mystery becomes even greater. How, then, does one really account for the story as we now have it? Whatever happened, it must have been strong and convincing enough to account for the *extraordinary* development out of it. This then is our task—to find a meaning for resurrection far more adequate than the physical explanation.

In the account we have, the book of Mark ends with the story of the empty tomb. Matthew and Luke have accounts differing from one another greatly in detail as to where, to whom, and under what circumstances Jesus is reported to have appeared. The content of what he is reported to have said varies in different accounts and none of it conforms to what Jesus taught during his life. The constants include: the establishment of himself as the Christ, his statement that supreme authority is his, the formation of the Trinity, his affirmation of his eternal presence.[1]

We are confronted then with what may have really happened to the disciples, what was the cause of it, and the outcome of it. And how did the accounts get into the form we have?

Something came alive in the disciples. What? Was it the presence of Jesus himself as reported? That could hardly have accounted for the result, for many persons experience powerfully the presence of dead persons, their spirit or essence, but one does not expect a new religious movement to be formed from that. Was it the Messianic-Christ image and the Self behind it that came alive and invigorated them? Or was it an experience of God in His/Her totality such as Jesus was always talking of? Was it the inner aspect, the God within, the *imago dei*, which the disciples now grasped and experienced? Or was it also the Holy Spirit, or was it both? This interrelationship has been dealt with in Chapter I, but it remains a crucial question.

1. See Appendix I.

Out of all Jesus' teaching-living and their close contact with him, what most now came alive that they could experience?

I believe it was something of the whole message of Jesus and his new experience of God. Although there is much evidence that the disciples did not understand Jesus during his lifetime and projected much onto him, surely some of the depth-reality must have reached them. Possibly they were experiencing the paradox of "losing life" which led to life being saved; they now had to "sell all" at his death and so the Kingdom of God becomes more urgent. As Jews they knew the numinous *Tremendum* of God but had learned that this Reality also dwelt within the psyche. They had witnessed a person who had "died to himself" to become reborn in God. The immensity of the influence of his teaching and living was changing religious hopes and ideals into a throbbing existential Life here and now. The Feast was now, could be had if they could embrace it.

The disciples' overwhelming experience of a new presence of God was felt by them to be the presence of Jesus. Perhaps this was inevitable. Jesus had so been the carrier of the new that they had no other category to use. Jesus did not have Jesus to contend with! The disciples had the strength and potency of his personality as carrier. Jesus was able to carry his relation to God without an intermediary, except in the sense that John the Baptist had been one.

So the disciples speak of the sense of the presence of Jesus, not God. The new reality of God or the image of God in them was felt as Jesus. What we find described in the accounts is the presence of Jesus. Perhaps the steps in the evolution were like this. First, there was the experience of God or God-in-the-Self; the very reality they had experienced in Jesus they now experienced within themselves. But because they had always identified this divine Presence as being in Jesus, they called what they experienced in themselves "Jesus" *as if* he were alive. But if he was alive, then he must have been resurrected. At this point the "as if" got dropped and they identified God in the Self as the risen Jesus in a literal sense.

What was the *cause* of this experience? What became alive and available to the disciples?

At the moment of Jesus' death, his disciples and followers must have been in total and complete despair. Their beloved leader, guide, friend, hoped-for Messiah, was dead. The abyss must have gaped before them. All was lost. All for which they had given up everything was destroyed.

Where were the disciples during the crucifixion? There is no report of their being at the scene. Were they looking from afar, afraid to come closer? Were they hiding for self-protection? Had they fled? Perhaps it is more likely that they were close by, overcome and horrified at the reality they were facing. The values Jesus had taught were in part inside them, but very many were still projected onto him. Now he, the carrier of them, was gone. This was the moment of their "death" and their baptism, but it was not something they consciously sought. They were hurled into it by events over which they had no control. All they had was "lost."

They were in despair and darkness. Then Something happened. Something came alive in them in this crisis. It is not hard to imagine them in despair, in small groups of two or three talking together, or perhaps all together, and out of the darkness Something came alive in them, a rebirth happened.

What was available to them at his death? What had occurred in his life that was present when he died physically? The God whom he served and helped integrate into a larger wholeness was available in a new way. God now had moved from Spirit and Transcendence into potential Immanence in every psyche. That which Jesus incarnated included the light and dark in the Transcendent. A whole new aspect of the dialogic relation of God and human emerged, including outer and inner. The Holy Spirit—first expressed in the Hebrew Scripture as part of God's Transcendence—had now descended into the inner world of persons, and although this first happened to and in Jesus, the statement of the Holy Spirit being available as guide and teacher in difficult conflict situations confirms its immediate availability.

Essentially, the Messianic-Christ image moved from hope in a person to participation in an archetypal process. Jesus was no longer concerned only with the people Israel as a community, but with redemptive possibility for all individuals. The archetype was not projected by Jesus into a collective hope for his people but was focused inwardly and individually as expression of the Self in him and in others.

What does this mean? All this archetypal newness was in Jesus. But when he died, the newness did not die. Rather, the essence of it became alive in the disciples but was understood by them as Jesus' presence as Messiah-Christ and as God incarnate.

If this happened to the disciples, what was the outcome for them and their image of the Messiah? Jesus, now perceived as alive, could be the Messiah, and the whole Messanic image was enlivened again. It was now both something "without," projected onto Jesus, but also something "within," for the central archetypal reality behind the Messianic image was now alive in them. However, the Christ image of Christianity did not include the feminine and the dark aspects.

And so what happened to God and the image of God and the Holy Spirit? All became centered and fixated in the person of Jesus, incarnated in a new way, perhaps; transformed into Spirit-Substance. But the belief in the literal incarnation led to seeing a one-time event in Jesus, and this belief had a limiting as well as a beneficent effect. The manifoldness of God became defined and limited. It cut off the full dynamic possibility of the resurrected life.

Death, dying to self-will, all that Jesus had taught and lived in the paradox of losing life to save it, could produce abundance, vitality, and perceptiveness.

A new meaning of resurrection—behind the physical events—emerges. The resurrection becomes something that happened during Jesus' lifetime, as part of the fundamental death-rebirth process he lived and taught. His archetypal pattern—his own inner myth, not the myth about him—has been crystal clear. When Jesus the human vehicle died, these deep changes in the structure of religious and archetypal reality remained without a vehicle for a suspended moment in time. Then they lodged in the disciples and, carried further by Paul, became Christianity.

Resurrection, then, for Jesus, was living the reborn life here and now, not in another world. And the condition for it is not belief in Jesus as Christ but a total action of a turning on the part of the individual. The resurrected life could move us from the narrow confines of a life whose central focus is subjective, ego-centered, limited by personal desire, dominated by power and lust in all its forms, to a life of objectivity, concern for the total value in situations, passionate and urgent to fulfill the Will that makes for integration and wholeness. The living of this Way of Life does not split love from hostility and hate, leaving them deeply buried in the unconscious. Rather, it unites all opposites into a new Yes, a Love that transcends them and pushes life forward, in spite of all obstacles. This life requires a courage to encompass possibilities that seem impossible. It demands a taking hold of the core of our being, surrounded by defenses, and placing it at the service of the Great I AM, transcendent and shining as potential in situations and in the psyche.

That history has gone as it has, *psychologically*, must have been purposive. But the purpose has been served and larger dimensions and horizons are now needed. The experience of the disciples conditioning the whole development of the last two thousand years, focusing on the inner God expressed in the face of Jesus as Christ, has yielded great value in opening up the inner world, as a step beyond Judaism. But it has been done at a sacrifice of the value of the Jewish concept of God in His/Her dual aspect of Love and Wrath.

The shift that is demanded for bringing the resurrected life into being is one then of moving the central point of reference from Jesus as Christ or authority, to God understood as that which works, longs for, yearns for human cooperation to bring about fulfillment of the Kingdom on earth. This shift is one inherent in the archetypal development where Jesus has carried the symbol together with the meaning behind it.

Somehow, the new age must and can be one where the reality behind the symbol of the Christ, the deep Self, *imago dei*, can be experienced as the expression of the transcendent God of Judaism with all its *tremendum*. And what must be added is Jesus' emphasis on the Son of man as the expression of the Self (reflecting God) in action, but not the ego. It is this Son of man in each of us which may truly live the resurrected life in us.

The fruits of this emergent thrust to consciousness are urgently needed now to save our and God's world. Whether we choose this new step of moving with the numinous gift in the teaching and life of Jesus or remain content with our present-day symbols may tip the balance not only for our own lives but for the ongoing of the planet.

Everything seems to be pointing to destruction in the world. Yet much is moving to newness and life through the need to let go of old forms and images and the discovery or rediscovery of new ones. It is perhaps an irony that the Synoptic gospels, the only ones purporting to speak of the historical life and teachings of Jesus, should have been the most neglected, as compared to the more Christian books of John, Revelation, and the Epistles of Paul, and now offer, with the help of depth-psychology, a source for living through dying—the life of relatedness and fullness.

The issue today is no longer Christianity or the church or Jesus, but the God-human process of dying and rebirth carried into every phase of personal and social living. This is the resurrection needed in the human soul, and in society. It involves the kind of commitment and transformation described throughout this book, where the deep, rich, personal meanings behind the Christ image, the Son of man, and the Holy Spirit have been explored.

Evolution has brought us where we are in our natural development, continuous with but beyond all other living creatures. But within the natural is implanted that which makes for a life beyond the natural. This has been called the supranatural in this book. And it is the potential which moves the natural (with all its aggressiveness, defensiveness, hostilities, and beauties) into an emergent which constitutes the resurrected life.

The answer of Jesus to God throughout this book is a Yes of attitude and action; it is a graspable transformative reality within the human that can be helped by the human to move in the direction of God's will, understood as the uniting, reconciling, healing of opposites and ambivalences into a Life that is fully desired by the human and the divine.

APPENDIX I

The Critical Basis
for the Selection and Study of Passages

The principles of biblical criticism used in this book are as follows. The basic understanding of most scholars is that Matthew and Luke use two documentary sources in common. They each copy virtually all of Mark, and they have a common source, Q (Quelle), not used in Mark. In addition to these common documents, Luke had available Document J (Jerusalem, for the last weeks of the life of Jesus). Document Q was divided by Dr. Sharman and his predecessor, Dr. Burton,[1] into Document G for Galilee and Document P for Perea. This was based on the fact that Matthew and Luke use the first part of Q in the same order (Mt. 3:7-11:30; see Sections 17-43). They use the later part of Q in a different order. Luke has it as one continuous source (Lk. 3:7-8:30; §78-115), and Matthew scatters it throughout his gospel. Therefore the Document P material is used in its Lucan order.

In addition to this material from the source documents, there is also material in Matthew and Luke which both preceeds and follows that attributed to Mark. This includes the birth stories, the genealogies, and the postcrucifixion appearances—and the latter do not conform in their description of these events. The Virgin Birth account and the Resurrection account have their origin in profound and universal psychological-religious experiences and mythic descriptions.

In addition to these sources there is one gospel material that is found only in Matthew or in Luke. Matthew

1. Ernest Dewitt Burton, *Some Principles of Literary Criticism and Their Application in the Synoptic Problem* (Chicago: University of Chicago Press, 1904).

especially has much editiorial addition or even later Christian interpolation—e.g, Matthew's references to the church, which presupposed the establishment of the church in Jesus' time.

The distinction of the source of this material in Matthew is one of the critical problems of the gospels, i.e., it is from Document M, which could put it in the historical category, from the editor Matthew, or early Christian accretion.

In the study of the gospels done by the Guild for Psychological Studies, there are also redaction criticism and form criticism done along with the above source criticism.

The choice of passages to include as historical is based on my own decisions out of the objective work of over forty years. This includes continuous individual and seminar work with many persons in analysis, criticism and discussion of meaning. The chief criteria of historicity are, as I have said earlier, the principles used by many many biblical scholars, especially Perrin,[1] of dissimilarity, consistency, similarity, and multiple attestation with Jewish and Christian tradition. The basis for it all cannot be included in this brief Appendix.

The sequence of this book follows, on the whole, the sequence of the book of Mark. It has been impossible to indicate all the places where Matthew and Luke copied Mark, or exactly how they each weave their material together. This would have turned the book into a book on the critical analysis of the gospels, which it is not.

Also, the basis of inclusion of passages in Matthew and Luke from other sources is made where the events described come in sequence of Mark. For a thorough following of that sequence see Henry Burton Sharman's *Records of the Life of Jesus*. There, the display of material makes it abundantly clear how Matthew and Luke weave their material from other documents into the Marcan order.

The cohesion and consistency of Jesus' work and teachings which emerges from this approach to selection convinces me that we have come very close to an authentic recovery of the events of this man's life.

1.   Perrin, *Rediscovering*, p. 53.

APPENDIX II

Psychological and Religious
Techniques of Transformation

For a detailed description of ways of dealing with the process of personal and social transformation, a previous book, *Man The Choicemaker*[1] contains much relevant material. However, I am adding some suggestions of other ways, tried by many people for many years.

There are certain ways to work with material from the unconscious parts of us. (This does not include work with dream material, which requires specialized knowledge and assistance.) The first requirement is a serious attitude about all that can—and will—emerge from the unknown in the inner being, the psyche. Self-knowledge must be taken as a real and deep work. To dally with the inner unconscious work, not to treat it with respect, is to do great harm to the religious process desiring our wholeness. The deepest realities want to be known. They must be listened to, actualized, and then transformed consciously.

(1) Working with art forms, especially graphic arts, music, body movements (dance or mime), and dialogue:

    (a) Use paints, crayons, finger paints, clay. Let things (not preconceived) emerge from an inner

1. Elizabeth B. Howes and Sheila Moon, *Man the Choicemaker.* (Philadelphia: Westminster Press, 1973); *The Choicemaker* (Wheaton, Illinois: Theosophical Press, 1977).

depth place. Let them take what form they will. Or take some specific image—one which is meaningful to you—and follow what it wants to be.

(b) Use improvisations on an available piano—letting hands and fingers find meaningful sound (with eyes closed).

(c) Use mime and gesture to express feelings.

(d) A most vivid and central way to work with this inner world is by way of written dialogue between the I—your ego—and some aspects of the inner unconscious which need to be related to. The ego converses with another aspect of us. It responds (on paper) to the "I." It begins an I-Thou dialogue.

(2) Working with anger, darkness, shadow, evil—clearly dealt with by Jesus, as is clear from the accounts:

The old ways of dealing with denials and repressions are not adequate, and whatever truths are behind these things must be faced and transformed. This can be done by all the means described—dialogue, art, body movements, and so on. By acknowledging and working with them, they are not added to the world's evils.

(3) Meditation and Prayer:

There are so many ways of meditation and prayer, and they have been dealt with in *Man the Choicemaker*. It seems inappropriate to try to make a statement succinct enough for an appendix. Suffice it to say that both affirmative prayer of relatedness to the "Thou" and exploration of the inner world of the psyche are imperative to live the Way of Jesus.

(4) Projection:

In projection, some unknown aspect of oneself is seen in another, and responded to with excessive positive or negative emotion. Such an aspect may be involved in shadow, evil, or anger, or it may be a masculine or feminine component of oneself. The components may themselves be, positive or negative. And projection itself is positive as a way of coming to know oneself. It is negative only when the components are left unclaimed. It is urgent to deal with projection and claim the aspect for oneself, both for the sake of one's own wholeness, and also for the sake of the reality of others, that they not carry more than their own identity. Violence and wars result from leaving out on others the negatives in us—as does persecution and discrimination. Once such a projection is recognized —via a response to another disproportionate to either fact, length of knowledge, or intensity of feelings, then one may begin to reclaim (really a claiming for the first time) that aspect for oneself. One may dialogue with that person, hoping to reach that in oneself behind the projection. One may paint, asking that in oneself behind the projection how it wishes to express itself. If positive and creative, this aspect can add richness to one's being. If negative and destructive, this aspect will have to be contained as one's own reality. In either case, the outer world is left freer to carry its own weight.

GLOSSARY

Apocalyptic: Pertains to a revelation by means of a heavenly vision concerning the final period of world history. The revelations were contained in apocalyptic literature current in Judaism from 200 B.C.E. to 200 C.E. The end of this age is marked by a catastrophic struggle in which the forces of good, sometimes led by a Messianic leader, triumph over the powers of evil which dominate the present world.

Archetype: A collective (human) patterning of images, as observed in dreams and in mythic motifs found in folktales, legends, and myths. Jung discusses such motifs as Hero Journey, Dragon Slaying, Descent into Cave (Nekyia), Death-Rebirth, Virgin Birth, Savior, Trinity, and Quaternity. The archetypes are universal—with different clothes from person to person and culture to culture. They are products of the human psyche, the inner realm of being, the "collective unconscious," and are common to all humans.

Ego: The focal point of human consciousness; that aspect of the individual usually stated as "I"; the point of reference for all conscious actions.

Eros: The psychic principle of relatedness; the feeling-toned half of the feeling-thinking opposites in the human psyche.

Eschatalogy: That branch of theology dealing with last or final things, i.e., death, judgment, immortality.

Imago dei: The self in the human psyche is seen by Jung as a God image. Heroes and heroines in myth and legend often carry this image.

Immanent: Inherent to; inborn; indwelling; that which is present throughout the universe (said of God); living within.

Logos: The psychic principle of ideation; the thinking-toned half of the feeling-thinking: opposites in the human psyche.

Mutation: The process of changing. More specifically, a sudden variation in some inheritable characteristic of an individual animal or plant.

Myth: Myth is not an untrue tale or story. A myth describes the inner, meaningful world of the psyche.

Numinous: R. Otto, in *The Idea of the Holy*, (London: Oxford University Press, 1923) coined this word to describe something that is evoked, awakened, of "creature-feeling" in the presence of the supreme power; a connection between Self and Other and the Mystery (*mysterium tremendum*). The numinous has awesomeness (*tremendum*), majesty (*majestas*), and urgency or energy.

Projection: Seeing traits and behaviors in others rather than recognizing them in oneself. (See pp. 228-29).

Psyche: (Greek, soul.) That which is other than just body; the inner psychological aspects of a human being.

Quantum leap: Any sudden and extensive change or advance; a sudden alteration in the energy levels of atoms, molecules, and so forth.

Self: An archetype which functions as the ruler of the collective unconscious realm of the psyche. It contains both light and darkness in its symbolization of wholeness. It is the Center within, which is the integrative function, bringing meaning.

Shadow: The dark, hidden, unknown, inferior, but not necessarily negative, side of personality.

Spirit-Substance: A pair of complementary opposites, both of which are related to human beings—spirit as the pneuma, the animating principle; substance as the matter, the stuff which is animated.

Symbol: Something—word, person, animal, or action— which stands for a particular meaning or cluster of meanings otherwise unknown or mysterious. An outside something stands for something inner.

Synchronicity: A meaningful coincidence, but with no causal relationship, between a psychic state or event and a physical state or event. The term was coined and used widely by C.G. Jung.

Synoptic: Seeing the whole together; presenting a general view of the same series of events—as in the Gospels of Matthew, Mark, Luke.

Transcendent: Supereminent; supreme; impalpable; in theology that which exists apart from and superior to the material universe (i.e., God, spirit).

Unus Mundus: The unitary world, seen not as fragmented but as unified, all of a piece.

INDEX BY SUBJECT

I

J

K

INDEX OF RECORDS SECTION

SCRIPTURAL INDEX

Mark

1 Corinthians